# Through the Eyes of Eyes of a Child

EMDR with Children

A Norton Professional Book

# Through the Eyes of a Child

## EMDR with Children

ROBERT H. TINKER, PH.D.

SANDRA A. WILSON, PH.D.

W. W. NORTON & COMPANY    NEW YORK · LONDON

For information about permission to reproduce selections
from this book, write to Permissions,
W. W. Norton & Company, Inc., 500 Fifth Avenue, New York, NY 10110.

The text of this book is composed in Berkeley Book
with the display set in Diotima and Ruzicka Freehand
Manufacturing by the Haddon Craftsmen
Book design and composition by Justine Burkat Trubey

Library of Congress Cataloging-in-Publication Data

Tinker, Robert H.
Through the eyes of a child : EMDR with children /
Robert H. Tinker, Sandra A. Wilson.
p.   cm.
"A Norton professional book."
Includes bibliographical references and index.
**ISBN 0-393-70287-1**
1. Eye movement desensitization and reprocessing for children.
2. Psychic trauma in children—Treatment.  I. Wilson, Sandra A.  II. Title.
RJ505.E9T56   1999
618.92'8914—dc21      98-31997  CIP

W. W. Norton & Company, Inc., 500 Fifth Avenue, New York, N.Y.  10110
http://www.wwnorton.com
W. W. Norton & Company Ltd., 10 Coptic Street, London WC1A 1PU

1 2 3 4 5 6 7 8 9 0

Dedicated
in loving memory
to
Mother Edith Duncan Tinker
(1910–1998)

# Foreword

THE FIRST TIME I MET DR. ROBERT TINKER, he was a participant in a workshop I was presenting on the "Application of EMDR to Children with Learning Difficulties and Inappropriate Behavior in School" at the first international EMDR conference sponsored by the EMDR Institute in 1990. I was eager to share my experiences and wanted to let people know how beneficial this new treatment modality is to children and adolescents. Dr. Tinker, who was one of the few people in the audience who had used EMDR extensively with traumatized children, shared my enthusiasm. Since that first meeting, he and coauthor Sandra Wilson, Ph.D., well known for her EMDR research projects, have made significant contributions to the development of EMDR. Their collaborative efforts have produced the first large-scale EMDR research study, the Oklahoma City project, and now this extraordinary book, which will pave the way for future exploration of the many possibilities available with EMDR as it applies to the healing of children.

As the Coordinator of the EMDR Institute in Pacific Grove, California, I receive numerous inquiries from parents, educators, and health care professionals about the efficacy and appropriateness of applying EMDR to children. The authors answer a multitude of these questions, including how to select targets, when to initiate EMDR with children, and how to predict treatment outcomes and the success rate with a variety of diagnoses. The eight phases of the EMDR method (Shapiro, 1995) are outlined with particular attention to children of various ages and with a broad spectrum of presenting issues. Case examples are used creatively to illustrate how the standard EMDR protocol is modified to engage children in the process. Unlike adult clients, who come to therapy of their own volition and have the cognitive ability to follow the therapeutic process, children quite often are resistant to therapy and unable to describe and express their discomfort. To address these issues, the authors emphasize throughout the book the importance of consideration for childhood developmental stages and offer specific strategies to achieve a therapeutic alliance with children and to incorporate the cooperation of parents. For example, in chapter 1, the concept of "theme development" is introduced as a means to stimulate associative chaining in young children and to motivate them to stay in the process. In subsequent chapters the detailed descriptions of sessions with clients as young as 2–3 years of age and children with highly complex traumas provide effective protocols and guidelines for adapting EMDR to children.

The authors artfully blend humor with poignant narratives from actual cases and in-session transcripts to demonstrate how accelerated information processing (Shapiro, 1995) can be applied to most of the major diagnoses of children. They stress that EMDR with children can seem simplistic, often eliciting unbelievably quick responses, while emphasizing that the method is an integrative process to be used judiciously and by skilled clinicians.

*Through the Eyes of A Child* is a valuable resource for EMDR clinicians and especially for the many mental health practitioners who work with children and adolescents. The innovative suggestions and well-designed protocols will enhance therapists' ability to help children become empowered to make choices, to overcome self-defeating belief structures, and, most importantly, to reclaim the joy of childhood innocence. The number of clinicians using the EMDR methodology with children has increased substantially over the last 10 years; however, there are currently few publications documenting its efficacy and application to children. Not only is this auspicious book a welcome and essential addition to the EMDR literature, it is also imperative reading for anyone who intends to employ the tenets of EMDR with young clients.

—Robbie Dunton

# Contents

# Acknowledgments

WE WOULD LIKE TO THANK Francine Shapiro for inspiring and supporting this book. If not for her, the world would be a different place. Robbie Dunton also deserves a special thanks for inspiring EMDR work with children from the very start, and for supporting us in our work with children.

Many personal and professional friends and colleagues have contributed their wisdom and insights, which have nurtured us and the book itself. We would like to thank a few of them: Lee Becker, Donna Becker, Karin Kleiner, Richard Kleiner, Howard Lipke, Atle Dyregrov, Arne Hofmann, Jac Carlson, Bessel van der Kolk, Andrew Leeds, and Bruce Perry. Those who have been readers for the book deserve a special thanks; their comments and suggestions have been invaluable.

Our editor, Susan Barrows Munro at Norton Professional Books, has known how to mastermind this project through to completion, striking the right balance between encouragement and more encouragement. Regina Dahlgren Ardini did a terrific job as associate editor, winnowing out the wheat from the chaff and arranging it correctly.

Those who have contributed the most, both in terms of their pain and their generosity, are the children and their families whose presence illuminates this book. They have informed us so that we can go on and inform others. We thank them for sharing their pain so that others may benefit.

A final thanks goes to the most important people of all: those in our families. They are the ones who not only admired and supported, but also dealt with lessened time from us; they all get our deepest thanks and love: Tonya, Marie, Michael, Deborah, Joni, Doug, and Craig, our children; and Amber, Courtney, Matt, Allen, Jordan, Jay, Sophia, Spencer, and Curtis, our grandchildren.

# Preface

I FIRST HEARD ABOUT EMDR from a Denver colleague (Len Loudis), late in 1990, within a year of the publication of Francine Shapiro's original research on EMDR. Like most, I remember distinctly when I first heard about EMDR. I had to ask Len several times, "What are those letters again? What do they stand for?" I was interested in what he was saying about EMDR, as he described psychotherapeutic changes that seemed to go beyond most therapy experiences. Len was also well versed in theory, and discussed how changes occurring in EMDR seemed to fit with recent knowledge about brain functioning, neuropsychology, and psychotraumatology. If such psychotherapeutic changes were being described by a lay person or a neophyte therapist, I would have tended to discount them, but Len was a psychologist with over 20 years of experience, and his basis of comparison was from extensive application of many other psychotherapeutic modalities. He was incredulous about the rapidity of the changes he saw in his clients and I was affected by his excitement. I signed up for the next training in 1991, within a few months of my talking with Len.

Four years later, when Lee Becker was being presented with an award for his work in Sandra Wilson's research in EMDR (Lee was the statistical expert), he stood at the podium and said, "Do you remember your first time? (long pause) Do you remember your first time hearing about EMDR?" When the laughter died down, he went on to say how he had heard about it from a colleague as he was riding up a ski lift a few short years ago. It seems everyone remembers their first time hearing about EMDR. We all started as skeptics. "You do what? And what happens? *Sure.*" When I went to my first training, I felt a rather intense mixture of skepticism and curiosity. I thought that if EMDR worked, it didn't work for the reasons that were touted or it didn't work as often or as well as was claimed. After all, I had seen a number of new approaches to therapy come along every few years, each with its proponents, each claiming to be better than the last, and I was not going to be taken in by yet another. However, each new approach had seemed to have some merit, and generally it seemed worthwhile to stay open-minded and be willing to "see" the elephant from a different perspective, rather than insisting that it "really" looked just one way. Besides, I was impressed with Dr. Shapiro's insistence that EMDR only be taught to licensed mental health professionals. She also encouraged research on EMDR in every training presentation she gave. It was not going to be another therapy to be marketed to businessmen to increase sales. This approach appealed to my scientific conservatism. While I had learned about every approach to therapy that I could and had taught a "Theories of Psychotherapy" course for a number of years at a local university, I fully adhered to no single school or approach to therapy. I found credible the research analyses that indicated change occurred in therapy partly as a result of therapist variables (such as experience, technique, ability to establish a relationship) 25% of the time; partly as a result of client variables (such as motivation, degree of disturbance, ego strength) 25% of the time; and half the time we didn't know exactly why the changes occurred. I regarded myself as eclectic, pragmatic, skeptical, and conservative—interested, but not ready to be taken in by any strange new therapy.

In the training practicum itself, I was struck by the number of mental health professionals around me who were having intense emotional reactions. While I did not have an immediate intense reaction myself, I experienced an insight that seemed profound, which had never occurred to me before in any of my previous therapy. It had to do with my mother's death from cancer when I was 6, and how subsequently I had felt unlovable, even into adulthood. I wept as I told my wife about it later. Like many other clinicians, I was impressed by what had happened in EMDR on a personal basis. In fact, I think one of the main reasons for the rapid spread of EMDR is clinicians' personal experience with it during practica in the trainings. When therapists experience personal changes of a profound nature in training, such experiences greatly impact their willingness to accept the uncertainty and stress of applying a new approach that violates many long-held and cherished assumptions. As a facilitator (one who assists the experiential learning of trainees during the practice sessions at the trainings), I have experienced the emotional high of seeing several groups of trainees become excited about the changes they are producing and experiencing in the practica. When there is such a high rate of positive experiences in training sessions, it solidifies the sense that EMDR is unusually effective, even with the "difficult" cases of mental health professionals.

When I first used EMDR with one of my clients, a woman I had been working with for two years who had a longstanding history of emotional, physical, and sexual abuse, I didn't know what to expect. Through many years of therapy, with a number of therapists, she had gotten to a level of resolution where she was able to say that she had a great deal of intellectual understanding (all that she needed, in her words), but the memories of abuse continued to trouble her intensely on an emotional basis. All the prior therapy she had undergone with me and with others had not changed the emotional distress she still felt about the abuse. After several EMDR sessions, which focused on her traumatic past and in which she abreacted deeply and intensely, she announced, "I'm where I need to be emotionally. It wasn't my fault. I was just a child. I did the best I could." The change seemed miraculous to her (and to me). Nothing else we had tried had worked like this. Rarely had anything else I had ever done in therapy worked like that. Encouraged by this initial result, I began using EMDR with other clients, including children. I continued to obtain results of a very positive nature. I frequently videotaped sessions (with the knowledge and consent of parents or adult clients) to document the results of this new approach. It seemed to me that if I did not document the changes I saw, I wouldn't quite believe them myself. At other times it seemed that if I did not observe the EMDR changes almost daily, I would be an EMDR skeptic myself.

At the time I was beginning to apply EMDR, I had frequent contact with a number of licensed psychologists, as I was also working as a feedback specialist with the Center for Creative Leadership, at the Colorado Springs branch. As others heard me discuss EMDR experiences, they too got EMDR training, and in turn would discuss their excitement about EMDR. One of those persons was John Hartung, who convinced Sandra Wilson (now my wife and coauthor), to conduct the first large-scale study of EMDR efficacy with adults. Sandra undertook the study without funding, and did a brilliant job of designing a state-of-the-art research project. The thorough administrative oversight she provided allowed the study to be completed in minimal time. As one of the research therapists, I remember the excitement when we started getting the results of the statistical analyses from the computer. Whereas I had perceived positive outcomes with the participants I had worked with, I did not have a good sense of how successful the other four therapists had been. The initial analyses confirmed that the results were highly positive for all the therapists (even the one who had not taken the second weekend of training in EMDR).

Thus, in Colorado Springs, word of mouth played a major role in the spread of interest in EMDR, and in the generation of research. At this point, a follow-up study to Sandra's study has been published (Wilson, Becker, & Tinker, 1997), another Colorado Springs study on EMDR has been published (Scheck, Schaeffer, & Gillette, 1997), and other studies conducted by us are in progress in Colorado Springs. One of the studies is on the use of EMDR with children, another is on the use of EMDR as a method of job-related stress reduction for police officers, and a third is on the use of EMDR with phantom limb pain.

Furthermore, when the Oklahoma City bombing of the Alfred P. Murrah

Building occurred in 1995, the early research data, which had been submitted for publication (Wilson, Becker, & Tinker, 1995), along with 15-month follow-up data that we had just analyzed, inspired the decision to provide EMDR treatment to rescue workers and persons traumatized by the blast. With the support of Francine Shapiro and Robbie Dunton of the EMDR Institute, Inc., Sandra spent five months in Oklahoma City as director of the EMDR Project, cosponsored by the EMDR Humanitarian Assistance Program (EMDR-HAP) and the Spencer Curtis Foundation. The project provided 700 sessions of free EMDR treatment to over 200 traumatized survivors and rescue workers. The pro bono undertaking also trained close to 300 licensed Oklahoma mental health professionals without charge. As part of that project, I traveled to Oklahoma City seven times to provide EMDR treatment and to assist in training other therapists in EMDR with children and adults.

In that effort, I learned a lot about EMDR, and came to see it in a somewhat different light. The intensity of the abreactions there and the rapidity with which they moved toward positive resolution suggested to me that a striking aspect of EMDR treatment is its emotional resolution, which often seems to occur prior to changes in cognition and behavior. Once the emotions changed, it seemed that the desired (but not believable) cognitions (e.g., "I did the best I could.") realigned to be compatible with the emotions (i.e., became emotionally believable), and then the behavior could also change (e.g., the person could function at work again). We also learned that in an emergency situation, EMDR could help the individual move from not being able to function at home or at work to the level of being able to function in those areas. However, in the long run, more work needs to be completed with many of these persons at deeper levels, as they feel that many aspects of safety and basic trust have been violated.

I began using EMDR with children shortly after my first training. I had little idea of what to expect, except for the basics I had heard in the training. I was quite excited by the results that occurred with these children. I had applied EMDR only to children who had undergone simple traumas (traumas which are singular, over, and in the past), and who had supportive families. While I knew I was being cautious about which children I chose, over time I have come to appreciate how important that caution was. Had I applied EMDR to children without those characteristics, I would likely have become much less sanguine about the efficacy of EMDR with children.

In recent years, I have traveled to Africa, Hawaii, Norway, and Scotland to train therapists in the use of EMDR with children. In Africa, I trained therapists from Rwanda to work with Rwandan children who had been traumatized in the genocide that had occurred in their country. In Hawaii, I trained therapists to work with children traumatized by Hurricane Iniki in 1993. About 40 children were diagnosed with posttraumatic stress disorder (PTSD), despite having participated in earlier psychoeducational treatment of four sessions. In a field study of those treatment-resistant children, conducted by Claude Chemtob and Joanne Nakashima, both EMDR and the training the therapists received were validated with excellent outcomes. That field study was presented at the 1996 International Society for Trauma Stress Studies Convention, and has been submitted for publication. In Norway, therapists from seven countries (England, Scotland, Norway, Sweden, Denmark, Finland, and Germany) were trained in using EMDR with children. In Scotland, therapists working with children traumatized in the 1996 Dunblane shooting received training in using EMDR with children by Sandra and myself, again with excellent results.

Through these trainings, as well as trainings conducted in the continental United States, through my clinical practice, work in Oklahoma City, and participation in research projects, I have come to know EMDR as a powerful tool that has changed much of my outlook on the world. I feel more effective as a therapist, and can often state with some confidence that I can help an individual with a particular trauma, whereas prior to EMDR I would have been much more hesitant in what I could say. When I hear television or radio reports of persons traumatized by events, I often think that they could be readily helped through EMDR, and in a short period of time (unless they had experienced many previous traumas, which then would take longer). One of the goals that Sandra and I have established as a priority is to develop (through the Spencer Curtis Foundation) an EMDR free clinic, which would provide three to five free sessions of EMDR to persons who had been traumatized and could not afford treatment. Persons requiring additional therapy would later be referred to other community resources. The free clinic would be staffed by EMDR therapists who would donate half of the cost of each session. Because EMDR lends itself to such short-term effectiveness, such a clinic is highly feasible, and in addition to donation of time by EMDR therapists, it would be supported by other sources of community funding.

My personal experiences with EMDR forced me to look at my own life and make life-enhancing changes in many areas. As a result, I am recently remarried and experience life as exciting and rewarding in the context of a loving, supportive, and growing relationship.

I have noticed another change as well. I am less inclined to deny the emotional pain of my clients. For example, if I had a client who was in intense pain and I couldn't do anything about that pain, I was more likely to distance myself from that distress. I noticed a parallel situation when we worked with phantom limb pain participants in our pilot study. They reported that after they told their physicians about their phantom limb pain, and efforts were made to alleviate the pain to no avail, the physicians became reluctant to discuss the pain with the patient or referred to the patient in some deprecating fashion, which indicated that the pain was somehow the patient's fault. This also happens to some degree in psychotherapy. If the client doesn't improve, we find a way to blame the patient or discount their experience. It has been suggested that the "borderline" term is not really a diagnosis, but rather an epithet reserved for those persons who don't improve from our ministrations. With EMDR, however, I find that I actively look for the pain, because I have confidence that EMDR will be able to reduce or eliminate it fairly quickly. I spend less time avoiding or diminishing it.

Recently, a colleague (Howard Lipke) mentioned to me that for him, EMDR had accomplished something he never thought would happen: It helped him understand human craziness. Not the craziness of schizophrenia or brain injury, but the ordinary craziness of people who have been traumatized and act strangely and idiosyncratically from then on. He never thought he would achieve that understanding, for no approach or theory that he had ever learned in graduate school seemed to provide the level of understanding he sought. The understanding he reached is rather simple and direct: When someone is traumatized, the resulting symptoms, which otherwise seem so inexplicable and irrational, are fully understandable as related to trauma. Then the rapidity of changes that occur in EMDR and the cause-and-effect relationships that are laid bare in the course of EMDR treatment provide an understanding of human nature and human suffering that goes beyond anything he had previously conceived. The understanding allows for a theory to be developed about how trauma makes people crazy and how EMDR can dismantle that craziness.

Working with EMDR has certainly been an exciting journey for all of us in many different ways. Its promise continues to be exciting.

# Through the Eyes of a Child

## EMDR with Children

# one

# Children and EMDR:
# The View from the Mountaintop

"I turned my feelings into a Ping-Pong ball and smashed them
out the window."
—JUDY, AGE 11

IN THE DECADE SINCE Francine Shapiro (1989a, 1989b) formulated and introduced eye movement desensitization and reprocessing (EMDR) to the mental health community and the world, thousands of clinicians have been trained internationally. What has caused this explosion of interest and training in EMDR? I would suggest that the adoption of EMDR by many practitioners is due to a number of factors, including the emotional immediacy of the experientially-oriented trainings; the results that clinicians observe in their clients; the spiritual understandings that occur in some clients; the desire and need for an effective form of brief therapy; the increasing realization that psychological trauma underlies many of the *DSM-IV* diagnoses (American Psychiatric Association, 1994); the desire to use a nonpharmacological intervention despite the hegemony of the pharmacological establishment; the need to deal with the encroachment of managed care on psychotherapy practices; frustration with the lack of effectiveness of traditional approaches with many clients; the knowledge that the use of EMDR is supported by positive and solid results in controlled research; and finally the great delight and wonder that clinicians experience as they witness adult clients suddenly working through lifelong emotional impairments, or child clients who won't have lifelong emotional impairments because of early resolution accomplished in EMDR.

Even though research always lags behind practice in the field of psychotherapy, a substantial amount of EMDR research has been generated in the years since Dr. Shapiro's original study was published in 1989. For example, a recent meta-analysis of the efficacy of treatments for posttraumatic stress disorder (PTSD) (Van Etten & Taylor, in press) concluded that psychological treatments, including EMDR, were as effective as medication (although medication trials had higher drop-out rates, averaging 36% versus 15% for psychotherapy studies). Additionally, there was no follow-up information for medications after they were discontinued as opposed to the psychotherapy trials.* Of the psychological treatments, EMDR and behavior therapy were found to be the most effective. Further, the authors noted that EMDR was more efficient, requiring fewer sessions than the behavior therapies, making it unlikely that exposure is a sufficient explanation for the effectiveness of EMDR. In contrast, a less objective review (which was not a meta-analysis), written by some of the harshest critics of EMDR (Lohr, Tolin, & Lilienfeld, 1998), ignored the efficiency issue and concluded that EMDR did not live up to the claims made for it. However, the review by Lohr and colleagues contains so many omissions and inaccuracies that the authors' conclusions are questionable. Such biases and inaccuracies continue to contribute to the perception that EMDR remains unproved and controversial.

## THE LAG IN THE APPLICATION
## OF EMDR TO CHILDREN

While it is clear that many mental health professionals have become interested, intrigued, excited by, and involved in this new approach, there has been a relative lack of information about how to apply EMDR to children. Guidelines for using EMDR with children in clinical practice have been sketchy. Definitive, controlled research on applying EMDR to children has not yet been published. Only a few case studies about EMDR with children exist in the literature.

It is not surprising that the application of EMDR to children lags behind that of adults. First, more clinicians work with adults than with children. Second, EMDR was originally formulated for use with adults. As it is a major departure from how therapists typically work with clients, it takes a fair amount of resolve on the part of the therapist, and sometimes a leap of faith, to apply it to adults. Often, the emotional response of adults is intense. What if children were to react with similarly intense emotional reactions? Would the therapist be able to pro-

---

*Our study (Wilson, Becker, & Tinker, 1995), included in that meta-analysis, actually had a 0% dropout rate, and a three-month follow-up (also with a 0% dropout rate). Later, we conducted a 15-month follow-up, showing that treatment gains were maintained at 15 months (Wilson, Becker, & Tinker, 1997).

vide the appropriate nurturing, support, and control? What is a bit intimidating with adults thus seems even more intimidating with children, and might be seen as requiring even more skill, sensitivity, and perhaps an even greater leap of faith. Children are viewed as fragile; they do not have the coping skills of adults. Traumatized children are regarded as especially vulnerable (Briere, 1992; James, 1989; Schwarz & Perry, 1994). No therapist wants to take the chance of retraumatizing such a child.

Clearly, there is a need for a more extensive knowledge base for applying EMDR to children. Only about 25% of those trained in EMDR obtain specific training in applying it to children. Francine Shapiro's textbook (1995) devotes only five pages to working with children. A few clinicians (myself included) present workshops on applying EMDR to children, but many therapists cannot attend such workshops, which are held in only a few locations each year. Yet, even therapists who work only with adults can benefit from learning how to apply EMDR to children, in order to better understand and treat adults who have been traumatized as children. Such adults often respond with child-like representations (thoughts, feelings, and actions) to new crises and in EMDR, requiring the therapist to adapt the therapy in that direction.

I have written *Through the Eyes of a Child: EMDR for Children* for the practicing clinician who has been trained in EMDR (Level 1 or Level 2) and who works with children. It is also directed to clinicians who are skilled in working with children, but have not yet taken the EMDR training; I hope this book will provide enough information that they can decide whether to pursue the basic training in EMDR. Even if this book is used in conjunction with Shapiro's text (1995), it is not likely to provide enough experiential information to use EMDR skillfully with children. For the safety of clients, especially children, the optimal use of this book is as a supplement to the Level 1 and Level 2 trainings. The value of the experiential learning in those trainings cannot be overestimated. Finally, *Through the Eyes of a Child* is directed toward the EMDR therapist who works with adults, for the additional understanding and skill it can provide to adult clients who have been traumatized as children. Many of the protocols for children can be used with adults, and provide an additional set of interventions that may be appropriate for adults who have been traumatized as children and with adults who have become stuck in the therapy process, regardless of the reasons.

## INTEGRATING EMDR WITH PRIOR TRAINING

Most clinicians find it reassuring to know that they do not have to give up their previously acquired skills or abandon their theories, which usually have been acquired at great personal expense and after lengthy study.

Typically, clinicians who have taken the EMDR training have felt its effects in their own lives and seen how it affects others in the EMDR training. They have then interpreted its results in terms of their own theoretical orientation. For example, if the therapist is cognitive-behavioral in her* orientation, she can see the procedure as a form of imaginal exposure, where the client accepts mental exposure to the upsetting elements of the traumatic event. The desensitization that occurs then allows the client to change his behavior (e.g., ride in a car again without panic). If the therapist is psychodynamically trained, he will see elements in EMDR that fit psychoanalytic concepts: The associative chaining that occurs can be seen as a form of free association, and the importance of early traumas, revealed in EMDR processing, fits well with psychodynamic conceptualizations.

The person-centered therapist will experience EMDR as the ultimate person-centered therapy, as the therapist always follows the client in the process, and intervenes only when the client gets stuck (i.e., doesn't make progress). Further, the clinician is nondirective with respect to content that is elicited. The therapist sees emotions bubbling to the surface, much as Carl Rogers envisioned that as the highest level of emotional functioning. Gestalt therapists will note how EMDR promotes more complete awareness of different aspects of conscious functioning, including thoughts, feelings, physical sensations, and images. The body memories that are evoked in EMDR also fit Gestalt concepts. Body-oriented therapists will find their central concepts supported. Those who use systematic desensitization will see EMDR as a form of desensitization that works more quickly. Also, as EMDR promotes relaxation in the face of the imaginally evoked trauma (Wilson, Silver, Covi, & Foster, 1996), it can be seen as a form of reciprocal inhibition.

Those who have been trained in hypnosis will be tempted to see EMDR as a form of hypnosis, especially those who have been trained in naturalistic and Ericksonian methods of trance induction. However, there is no evidence that a client needs to be in an altered state to benefit from EMDR, and EMDR works more quickly than hypnosis (in my experience), just as it works more quickly than systematic desensitization. Further, two studies (Goldstein & Feske, 1994; Renfrey & Spates, 1994) included scales of hypnotic susceptibility and found no correlation between those scores and EMDR outcome.

Existential therapists will note how often existential issues come up in EMDR

---

*Throughout the text, in order to avoid the cumbersome construction "he/she," the use of male and female pronouns will be alternated, so that half the time the clinician is referred to as "she" and half the time as "he," with the same procedure followed for clients not otherwise identified. Identifying details about specific clients have been changed so that, although written permission has been obtained to include the client in the present book, the privacy of such clients and their generous parents will be protected.

processing, and how the client often creates new meaning in life. The Jungian therapist can be comfortable with the use of dream imagery in EMDR and the use of dreams as targets (starting points) for EMDR processing—as can the psychoanalytically trained therapist. The Jungian will also frequently see archetypal themes emerge in EMDR and may notice more dimensions of persona and shadow being elucidated as the process unfolds.

The clinician trained in family therapy will note that changes made by an individual in EMDR can promote changes in that person's family structure and functioning. Frequently, many of the traumas processed in EMDR originate in the family. Rational-emotive therapists will be attracted to the use of cognitions as well as the elicitation of emotions as the EMDR protocol is being set up. However, in EMDR it is the client who most often generates the cognitions, not the therapist. Multimodal therapists will note how EMDR incorporates elements from a variety of therapies and identifies the elements that Arnold Lazarus abbreviates as BASIC ID (Lazarus, 1981). Narrative therapists will note how EMDR promotes the development of new, more positive narratives, as well as more coherent and complete narratives about traumatic events. As Bessel van der Kolk has pointed out, traumatic memory is not initially narrative in nature; rather it is stored as somatosensory fragments that are not formed into a coherent narrative or stored as declarative memory (van der Kolk, 1994). However, pilot research with brain imaging techniques indicates that somatosensory memories can become narrative memories after successful EMDR treatment of PTSD (van der Kolk, 1998).

## EMDR AS TRAUMA-BASED THERAPY

EMDR is often referred to as a trauma-based therapy. That is, it has primarily been applied to persons who have been psychologically traumatized. This means that it is effective with PTSD as well as the anxiety and depression related to psychological traumata. If such trauma causes many of the psychological disorders of childhood, then EMDR can be widely applied. If, however, childhood disorders most often have their origins in other causes, then EMDR becomes a less useful treatment. Interestingly, outside of EMDR, the field of psychology is coming full circle to issues of 100 years ago that emphasize the importance of psychological trauma in the genesis of psychological disorders, and reexamining the work of Charcot, Janet, Breuer and Freud, among others. Their early work focused on the causal role of childhood trauma in adult disorders, especially conversion hysteria. Freud can be seen as the cause of, and the recipient of, the first backlash (against acknowledging the pervasiveness of child abuse), when he challenged the conventional psychiatric wisdom of the day in

Germany, that hysteria was caused by heredity and/or masturbation, by suggesting that hysteria was caused by sexual attacks on the child, which were subsequently repressed in memory (dissociated?), leading to symptom formation. Although he later changed his theory, there is evidence that he did so for nonscientific reasons (Masson, 1992). It is ironic that now, 100 years later, the same issues are being debated, and those questioning whether traumatic memories can be repressed have formulated the term "false memory syndrome" to refer to a purported syndrome of persons whose memories of childhood abuse emerge in adulthood, sometimes in therapy (although most often not; Elliot, 1997). Those aware of the 100 years of investigation into the later emergence of forgotten or partially remembered earlier traumas know that it has been well documented in areas of combat, accidents, natural disasters, and child abuse. It is only in the area of child abuse that the issue has become a political issue and hotly debated. Why recovered memories are controversial only in this one area is an interesting question.

## THE ROLE OF TRAUMA IN THE GENESIS OF CHILD AND ADULT PSYCHOPATHOLOGY

As we reexamine the role of trauma in the generation of psychological syndromes of adulthood and childhood, we find that its role has been obscured or minimized over the past century. For example, it is difficult to look through the *DSM-IV* and find connections between disorders of childhood (or adulthood) and antecedent emotional events. Yet, every practicing clinician knows that she is frequently dealing with individuals who have been traumatized, often repeatedly.

Over the past 15 years, John Briere (1992) has written cogently about this connection between child abuse trauma and psychopathology of children and adults. Schwarz and Perry (1994) have documented that the developing brain is more susceptible to damage and neurochemical imbalances than the mature brain. On the basis of their review of neurophysiological research, they posit the development of "malignant memories," which exert a pervasive effect on the developing nervous system and self-system of the child. This information, taken in conjunction with high rates of child abuse and family disruption, suggest that traumatic events are not uncommon for many children in our culture.

Giaconia and colleagues (1995) found that by 18 years of age, more than two-fifths of youths in a community sample met the *DSM-III-R* criteria for at least one trauma and more than 6% met criteria for a lifetime diagnosis of PTSD. In fact, Schwarz and Perry (1994) estimate that approximately one million children in the United States develop PTSD each year, out of the three million who are directly exposed to violence. It remains to be seen whether a greater emphasis on how children are traumatized will be a more productive approach than the more traditional approach of simply naming syndromes and then attempting to treat them without explicitly considering the role of trauma in their genesis. Donovan and McIntyre (1990) argue that a developmental-contextual approach, which focuses on the developmental level of the child and the context in which the child's symptoms originated, is a more productive approach than the categorical one (DSM diagnoses), which ignore the context in which the symptoms arise.

This viewpoint has become increasingly prevalent, not only in clinical work, but also in academic circles. For example, Mash and Dozois (1996), in a review of child psychopathology research, state, "In this introductory chapter, we address several central themes and issues related to conceptualizing childhood dysfunction and its determinants. In doing so, we provide a developmental-systems framework for understanding child psychopathology that emphasizes the role of developmental processes, the importance of context, and the processes in shaping adaptive and maladaptive development" (p. 3).

In the past, biological psychiatry has focused on the diathesis-stress model, which indicates that the more organismic impairment an individual manifests, the less environmental stress it takes to produce a pathological condition. While probably not incorrect, it causes a focus on determining the amount of organismic impairment that an individual has (is this ever possible to determine?), and then undertaking approaches to minimize or eliminate the biological impairment, such as the use of medication or other medically-based treatments. However, a renewed focus on the role of trauma in psychopathology has quite different implications: It means that we seek to find out ways that children become traumatized and work to eliminate those sources of trauma.

In my clinical work, I see both children and adults, and one day I may see an adult whose adult relationships have been impaired because of abandonment traumas that occurred when he was very young. The next day I might see a child whose parents are becoming divorced, and who woke from a nap and neither parent was there; feeling abandoned, the child began having nightmares and wetting the bed. His astute parents recognized these as signals of distress and scheduled appointments for EMDR. Within a few sessions, the child stopped having nightmares and wetting the bed. However, because of the ongoing nature of the divorce, the child needs additional therapeutic assistance until after the divorce is final. So, in my practice I see what happens when these traumas are not treated—lifelong impairments result—and I see what happens when they are treated with EMDR—the symptoms are reduced or disappear. To be fair, I have seen these positive changes occur in conventional therapy, but in EMDR the work goes so quickly that the comparison is more clear-cut and striking.

John Bowlby's writing on attachment and bonding (1982, 1988) is pertinent here. He found that problems in attachment of infants with their caregivers led to impaired functioning and psychological disturbances later in childhood and in adulthood. Harry Harlow (1959) found similar effects when monkeys were raised by wire or cloth mothers instead of a living mother. Kendall Johnson (1998) found that there is a strong correlation between high-risk adolescent behavior (such as running away, suicidality, and drug and alcohol abuse) and prior traumatization. Again, these findings suggest the significance of early experience (trauma?) on the developing brain and on subsequent behavior.

Converging lines of evidence, then, suggest that trauma has great etiological importance in childhood disorders. EMDR, being a trauma-based therapy, is therefore likely to have wide applicability in treating the emotional disorders of childhood.

## ACCELERATED INFORMATION PROCESSING

Besides being a trauma-based therapy, EMDR is also described as a method involving "accelerated information processing" (Shapiro, 1995). This means that clients seem to reprocess their traumas more quickly in EMDR than in other therapies and become desensitized to the painful memories and images. The meta-analysis mentioned previously by Van Etten and Taylor (in press) confirms the greater efficiency of EMDR across a number of studies. As one of my adult clients put it, "In EMDR, linear time has no meaning." She was referring both to how her memories of a sexual abuse incident were as vivid 30 years later as on the day the incident happened, and how EMDR caused those memories to lose their painful aspects in a single session. Something in the EMDR procedure causes changes to occur quite rapidly, and it doesn't seem to matter how long the memories have been stored and exerting a negative effect on the client. Describing this aspect of EMDR as "accelerated information processing" seems warranted, in order to distinguish its rapidity of effects from other therapies. The accelerated effects can be even more dramatic in children. Prior to EMDR, I frequently worked with children having nightmares or night terrors. While therapy was often effective in diminishing or eliminating these problems, it took a number of sessions, and a number of different approaches: drawing the nightmare, changing the child's imagery, working with parents to change upsetting events related to the dreams, using metaphors, stories, hypnosis, and play therapy. It strains credulity to see a child go from fearful to joyful with just a few sets of eye movements in EMDR while targeting the nightmare images. For some reason, children respond very quickly to EMDR. Initially, I was quite skeptical that anything of lasting significance could happen in so short a period of time, and so I was quite surprised when parents would report that the nightmares and bed-wetting had ceased. Not only did these rapid results happen with nightmares, but in other problem areas as well.

An important discrimination to make is whether the traumatization is in the past and over with or whether the situation is ongoing. If the situation is ongoing, EMDR can help, but the resolution is likely to be incomplete until the external situation is corrected. Improving the ongoing situation may require a variety of interventions of a psychological, sociological, and/or legal nature. However, if the traumatization is in the past and without ongoing aspects, more rapid and complete resolution can be expected with EMDR.

## CATEGORIES OF TRAUMA

In this book I will present a typology of trauma to assist in predicting treatment outcome in EMDR. Traumas will be referred to as simple or complex, acute or chronic, and singular or multiple, as these are useful categories for predicting the effects of EMDR. Simple traumas (which are over, in the past, and without current referents) are quickly treated by EMDR, whether they are acute or chronic. An example would be a child who was molested a single time by a baby-sitter who is no longer a part of the child's life. If there were multiple occurrences of molestation by the baby-sitter, EMDR is still likely to be highly effective, although a few more sessions might be required than if there were a singular episode of molestation. On the other hand, complex traumas (which are not over and in the past, but rather have current, ongoing elements) are more difficult to treat and likely to require a number of therapeutic interventions other than EMDR. For example, a child who was molested by her father (and he remains in the home) may respond well to EMDR in terms of symptom reduction, but the child and the family may require a host of other interventions, such as family therapy, marital therapy, legal interventions by a guardian ad litem, supervised visitation if the father is removed from the home, or regular visits to the home by a caseworker. Previous multiple incidents of molestation by the father would further complicate the picture. In these cases of complex trauma, EMDR becomes a part of an overall, integrated treatment plan, designed to keep the child safe and provide for treatment.

Overall, EMDR could be predicted to be most effective with singular, simple traumas of an acute nature, diminishing only marginally in effectiveness as the trauma becomes chronic. EMDR would be posited to be less rapidly effective with multiple and complex traumas especially as they became more chronic.

## ELEMENTS OF EMDR

Francine Shapiro (1995) describes EMDR as having eight phases: (1) client history and treatment planning, (2) preparation, (3) assessment, (4) desensitization, (5) installation, (6) body scan, (7) closure, (8) reevaluation. All of these phases apply to children, but in a simplified or modified fashion. For now, a brief discussion of each phase will illustrate how they can be applied to children. In later chapters, more detailed modifications will be discussed, calibrated to the developmental level of the child.

## Client History and Treatment Planning

A thorough history of the child's problem is generally obtained from the parents (or custodial parent or primary caregiver) in the first session, without the child being present (unless the child is older and expresses an interest in attending). In this way, the parents can be candid and the child can avoid a boring or upsetting interview. In this session, the clinician can also obtain a thorough developmental history, starting with family history and information from pregnancy and birth. In some cases, information prior to pregnancy and birth becomes important in order to ascertain where the child fits into the family constellation. For example, if the child is anxiety-ridden, it may be important to know that the mother had similar problems as a child and so did the maternal grandmother, or that an older sibling had died, with the result that the client child was being treated very protectively. With a child who has attention-deficit/hyperactivity disorder (ADHD), it is often important to know who else in the extended family has had similar difficulties, and how they were handled by their caregivers. Thoroughness often needs to be balanced with clinical judgment, as some families have multiple problems and require much history-taking, while others require relatively brief family and developmental histories. Generally, the more knowledgeable the clinician is about child development and child psychopathology, the better. There are a number of very good developmental history forms on the market that can be of help to the clinician during this phase. These forms can also be mailed to the parents for completion prior to the first appointment, thus allowing more time in the session for discussion and a greater focus on developmental issues.

Legal issues may need to be assessed in this phase. If the child has been physically or sexually abused or in an accident, and needs to testify in court, consultation with involved attorneys may be necessary before beginning EMDR.

Once the history-taking is complete, significant events or problem behaviors can be targeted for EMDR, along with specification of future desired behaviors, feelings, or attitudes.

## Preparation

When working with children, the parents or caretakers need a complete explanation of EMDR. The discussion with the parents about using EMDR with children can be accomplished in the first session. The clinician can describe the "nuts and bolts" of the EMDR procedure, so the parents can visualize how EMDR is conducted. The clinician should also explain why she is considering using EMDR with their child. Usually this involves discussing the problems for which the child was referred and why the therapist thinks EMDR would be a good therapeutic approach for those specific problems. The clinician could indicate how their child is similar to others whom the clinician has treated, and how that suggests that EMDR could be effective with their child. For example, if the child was having nightmares for several months after an automobile accident, the clinician could indicate that nightmares with other children have been excellent targets for EMDR because of the problem resolution obtained from them, and go on to inform the parents that the accident itself, as well as the nightmares, could be targeted in EMDR.

Advantages and disadvantages of using EMDR can also be part of this discussion. An advantage is that the effectiveness of EMDR can be ascertained within a few sessions. Efficiency is a hallmark of EMDR. In addition, EMDR is a very simple task for a child, certainly much simpler than most forms of child therapy. Since changes seem to occur for children (and adults) in an automatic, non-volitional fashion, the child doesn't really have to do anything, except follow the EMDR procedure. Parents can participate in the session if necessary, and such participation is generally of a nonthreatening nature to the parent(s) and the child. Overall, parents can be informed that EMDR is effective, efficient, and comfortable for both parent and child. The clinician can also state that clinical information seems to indicate that EMDR works with a wider range of childhood problems, and more consistently, than other approaches the therapist has used (if that's true; it is for me!).

Reasons for not using EMDR would relate to some children not being capable of handling the intense emotions that are sometimes brought up in EMDR, with the result that they refuse to continue with EMDR. The child is consequently left in a state of heightened emotionality with no resolution of the trauma. However, it is not possible to know that this is going to happen ahead of time. In these cases, the clinician can discuss with the parents what steps she would take in this eventuality. Those steps generally consist of using soothing and self-soothing approaches such as the safe place, reassurance, and returning to other therapeutic modalities, for example, drawing, use of sand tray, free play, and therapeutic games. Most parents will understand that such emotional reactions cannot be predicted ahead of time, and will be satisfied to know that the clinician knows what to do to help the child if he refuses to continue.

Some parents might consider it a disadvantage that EMDR does not have validation at the scientific level of proof (but most parents are not interested in that distinction). If the parents are concerned about this issue, the clinician can explain that most (if not all) therapies for children are only validated at the clinical level unless they are conducted in a laboratory setting—which is considerably different from the typical outpatient setting. Unfortunately, the psychotherapy literature indicates that while psychotherapies for children work well in laboratory settings (about as well as psychotherapies for adults), there is little controlled research that shows they are effective in the outpatient settings where they are most practiced (Weisz, Weiss, & Donenberg, 1992). Further, what has been found effective in the laboratory setting (e.g., behavioral and cognitive-behavioral approaches strictly applied for a specified number of sessions), is typically not standard practice in an outpatient setting. Therefore, parents who opt for a more traditional therapy are most likely not opting for greater effectiveness, but rather for a traditional therapy that is better known than EMDR.

## Informed Consent

With children, informed consent about intense emotional reactions is generally not necessary, as children tend not to react with the abreactions (intense emotional outpourings associated with the original event) that are more typical of adults. If an adult becomes abreactive in an EMDR session, and the abreaction is not fully processed, then the self-quieting and relaxation techniques detailed in Dr. Shapiro's (1995) textbook can be used. If the adult continues to feel overly vulnerable during the time between the sessions, and he has been given supportive instructions to call if additional intervention or help is needed, he is likely to do so. However, if a child becomes frightened by the intensity of her emotions during an EMDR session, such fear is not likely to show overtly; the child is more likely to refuse to continue with EMDR, either in that session or in the next one. Between sessions, the troublesome behaviors that were the reason for the referral are likely to remain the same or intensify (rare). The therapist should inform the parents that these are the most negative reactions that can be anticipated with a child. While informed consent statements can be used, they tend to have drawbacks, in that no matter how detailed they are, they cannot cover every eventuality. Also, the more detailed the form, the more intimidating or anxiety-arousing it can be to parents. It is preferable to conduct a thorough discussion of EMDR pros and cons with the parents and then document the discussion in the chart in a detailed fashion.

## Preparing the Child

EMDR can often be introduced to the child as simply as, "Let's try something." It is generally safest to start by setting up a "safe place," and installing it with a set of eye movements or hand taps. This gives the child a sense of the procedural steps involved, as well as a sense of the positive effects that can be obtained in EMDR. A "safe place" is a place in which the child feels safe, happy, and comfortable. "Installing" the safe place means pairing imagined images, sounds, smells, feelings, and physical sensations of the safe place with a set of eye movements or hand taps. Such a procedure seems to augment the effectiveness of the safe place if it needs to be used later in the EMDR session or between sessions. A great deal of explanation is generally not necessary for younger children (ages 2–7). For older children (ages 8–12), a short explanation that EMDR is helpful in getting rid of bad feelings about events or alleviating the problem areas for which they were referred is generally sufficient.

## Assessment

With children, the assessment phase is similar to that with adults, but certain aspects may have to be left out, due to children's cognitive abilities. Children aged 9 and above can generally provide an image, a negative cognition (NC), a positive condition (PC), and a rating of the believability or truth of the positive cognition (validity of cognition or VOC). With children aged 5–8, the NC, PC, and VOC are likely to be unobtainable, although it's useful to attempt to elicit these in case the child does have the cognitive ability. I've worked with children as young as 6 who have been able to give good negative and positive cognitions and the resulting VOCs.

If I'm working with a child who is younger than age 5, I don't attempt to elicit the cognitions; I simply ask about emotions after the child provides a target image. Children have an easier time identifying emotions than cognitions, so many 3- and 4-year-olds can tell you what they feel when thinking about an upsetting event. Or they can point to a facial image (EMDR-HAP provides a laminated set of emotional faces for use with children in identifying emotions). Older children (9–12 years old) generally can use the 0–10 SUDS (subjective units of disturbance scale) ratings, as can many 5–8-year-olds. Children who are 5 and younger are usually capable of showing with their hands and arms how big the feeling is, or they can indicate it by marking on a line drawn on a piece of paper:

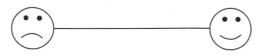

Children as young as 4 usually indicate the location of feelings in their bodies. Of course, these are general guidelines for most children; the experienced clinician can adjust according to the developmental level of the child.

## Desensitization

With adults, this phase usually consists of eye movements, but can involve hand taps or auditory stimulation. With children, the alternating left-right stimulation may be in the form of eye movements, hand taps (or variations of hand taps, such as drumming), or auditory stimulation, but the younger the child (especially under age 6), the more likely it is to involve hand taps. As with adults, ratings of negative and positive cognitions (VOC), emotions (SUDS), and physical sensations can be elicited from the image of the upsetting event. However, with younger children, it may not be possible to obtain them all. Very young children (ages 2–5) may only be able to think about the event or just get an image of it, without being able to give measures.

## Installation

With adults, the installation consists of pairing the positive cognition with the target memory, so that the traumatic memory in the future can be recalled in an adaptive framework that emphasizes self-efficacy. With children, installation can be completed if, during the assessment phase, the child has been able to formulate a negative cognition, a positive cognition, and a rating of how true the positive cognition (i.e., self-belief) feels on an emotional level (VOC). Thus, when the SUDS has decreased to 0 or 1, the installation can be completed. However, younger children (under age 8) may not be able to formulate negative and positive cognitions, so no VOC can be obtained. In this case, no installation is possible, unless the clinician can help the child formulate an appropriate positive cognition from material that has emerged during the processing. If a positive cognition has emerged during the desensitization phase, or is developed with help from the clinician (e.g., "Good boy!"), then that can be installed during this phase.

## Body Scan

The rather complex body scan, which requires the adult to hold the installation elements (target memory and positive cognition) in mind while scanning the body for disturbance, is usually too complex for most children. However, a simplified version can be used, where the child is asked to scan his body for feelings while holding the target memory in mind. Generally, children seem to have the most trouble understanding this part of the EMDR procedure; if the body scan is not productive or informative, the therapist can move on to the next phase.

## Closure

This phase is especially important, as the child needs to feel safe and protected at the close of the session, whether the processing has been completed or not.

If the child does not feel safe, it is unlikely that she will wish to be involved in EMDR in the next session. The safe place, installed at the beginning of the EMDR, can be used to close down the session. If necessary, it can be combined with other approaches, such as relaxation and self-quieting methods. Stories, games, drawings, and visualization exercises can also be part of the closure phase. The therapist can inform the child that changes of a positive nature may continue to occur after the session, and ask the child to notice those. The child can document any changes by writing them down or drawing pictures of them for the next session. The sense of shared participation that can arise from such between-session activities can be exciting and heartwarming. The therapist also can inform the parents about the EMDR targets and other pertinent information so they can report any behavioral and emotional changes they observe between sessions.

## Reevaluation

This phase consists of checking on the work of the previous session and is implemented at the beginning of the following session. This phase is of particular importance in working with children, as in-session changes are often more difficult to perceive with children than with adults. The therapist should consult with the parent about changes in behavior, emotions, or cognitions. Thus, it is important to keep the parent abreast of the work with the child, so that the parent can be an informed observer. I recall working on bed-wetting with a 10-year-old boy as part of an EMDR session, but failing to inform the parents of that. Both the parents and I were surprised when in the next session the boy proudly announced that he had stopped wetting the bed (apparently they had given up on monitoring his bed-wetting, possibly because they were discouraged or because they were more concerned about his other problems). Subsequent tracking of the enuresis confirmed that what he said was true, but it would have been better if the parents had been informed from the start.

Reevaluation with children also consists of bringing up the target memory from the previous session. If the processing is incomplete, that becomes the starting point for the next EMDR work. If the processing is complete (SUDS = 0; VOC = 7), then the therapist can address new targets.

## THE IMPORTANCE OF THE ELEMENTS OF EMDR

In the years since 1991 that I have been using EMDR with children, I have given considerable thought to what seems to be important in the EMDR protocol that makes it so effective. Dismantling (component analysis) studies with adults have not shed much light on the issue. They have either used such small numbers of participants that statistical power is weak, preventing accurate conclusions, questionable procedures (e.g., used an analog procedure, which is not an accurate representation of EMDR), or atypical participants (i.e., who are not representative of most traumatized individuals). Further, if it is postulated that eye movement is an effective ingredient, then a control condition with the eyes not moving is necessary. If it is not eye movement that is important, but rather patterned, repetitive stimulation or alternate left-right stimulation, then the control has to be very different. For example, a poor control would be to have the therapist moving fingers across the participant's range of vision (Pitman et al., 1996), flashing a light at midline (Renfrey & Spates, 1994), thumb tapping (D. Wilson et al., 1996), or using left-right auditory stimulation, because these are all EMDR variants. Rather, the control would have to omit any form of patterned, repetitive stimulation or alternate left-right stimulation and employ an entirely different form of stimulation instead.

If it is postulated that dual attention is an active ingredient, then a control condition eliminating dual attention is needed. If distraction is a necessary part of EMDR, then a control condition for that is required. If lack of distraction is important (i.e., the therapist helps the client stay in the process), then a control condition is needed for that. If all four are active ingredients, then four separate control conditions would be important. This kind of research is immensely complicated. At this point, good dismantling studies have yet to be conducted, although Van Etten and Taylor's meta-analysis (in press) indicates that when all studies comparing eyes fixed with eyes moving are combined, eyes moving is more effective. A possible interpretation from Van Etten and Taylor's meta-analysis is that EMDR with eye movement is more effective than EMDR without eye movement, and EMDR without eye movement is more effective than no treatment. It will be interesting to see if this hierarchy of effectiveness will be supported as more studies are completed.

However, it seems more important to delineate the effective ranges of EMDR applicability in order to answer such questions as, What does controlled research show about how well EMDR works with children with PTSD, with phobias, with other anxiety disorders, with ADHD, with attachment disorders? How persistent are the treatment effects of EMDR with children? These practical questions are more important to the child clinician than the more theoretical issue of which elements of the EMDR treatment package are more important.

In the meantime, I have a some ideas about what seems important in the EMDR protocol, based on my clinical observations and knowledge of associated research.

Clinically, I have noticed that having the child (or adult) call up images, thoughts, feelings, and physical sensations in order to recall the impact of a traumatic event is a very powerful approach. Often, a child (or an adult) who thinks she is not very bothered by an upsetting event will begin to feel strong emotions and be surprised by their intensity. Or a child who has been in prior therapy will say, "I've already dealt with that," but then when asked to bring up those four elements (images, thoughts, feelings, and bodily sensations) will be surprised by the intense emotions that well up. And this occurs before the eye movements begin. It is notable that different schools of therapy place heavier or lesser amounts of emphasis on some of these elements than others. Probably only the multimodal therapy of Arnold Lazarus emphasizes all of these elements in a balanced or integrated fashion. What may also be significant about these foci in EMDR is that taken together they may activate processing in both hemispheres or many parts of the brain at the same time, thus facilitating a more complete resolution of the traumatic event than most therapies allow. As Bruce Perry (1998) indicates, no part of the brain can change if it is not activated. Perhaps EMDR activates more parts of the brain than other therapies, and this simultaneous activation is an important part of EMDR.

And what about the eye movements? How important are they? In addition to my clinical impressions that they are very important, and the most powerful form of left-right alternating stimulation, I am aware of three pieces of research that relate to this issue. Risse and Gazzaniga (1979), colleagues of Roger Sperry (noted for his split-brain research and for his Nobel Prize in the neurosciences), extended Sperry's split-brain methodology to normal individuals who were not epileptic. In this research, they anesthetized the left hemisphere of their participants, and then showed them a series of objects and pictures. The memory of those items registered only in the right hemisphere, as the left was anesthetized. When the anesthesia wore off, they were asked to point with their right hand (left hemisphere) to the objects and pictures they had been shown. The subjects were unable to do so because the information was not in the left hemisphere. However, when they were asked to point with their left hand (activating the right hemisphere where the information was stored but was not consciously or verbally accessible), they began to do so intuitively, and then began to "remember" the objects as they pointed. Something in the motor act facilitated the right hemisphere memory transfer to the left hemisphere, where it became consciously processed and verbalized. It would be interesting to see if eye movements would similarly facilitate the transfer of information from the right hemisphere to the left.

In a study of anosognosia, the neuroscientist Vilanour Ramachandran (1995) found that eye movements did indeed assist in the transfer of information from right hemisphere to left. Ramachandran studied individuals who had a left-sided paralysis as a result of a right-hemisphere stroke, and were oblivious to their hemiparesis (anosognosia). As part of that research, he irrigated the left ear canal of one of the patients with cold water, which caused a series of vestibular changes and involuntary rapid, left-right eye movements. Following those eye movements the patient was aware of and able to discuss her paralysis, until the effects of the cold water wore off, and she returned to her previous state of unawareness. Ramachandran hypothesizes that the eye movements generated by the cold water are similar to the eye movements in REM sleep, which help process the day's events. He speculates that the eye movements "arouse" the damaged right hemisphere, allowing it to become more functional, so that the anosognosic patient becomes aware of information previously inaccessible, or unconsciously stored. He notes that other researchers have noted the same phenomenon (Bisiach, Rusconi, & Vallar, 1992). In a footnote, Ramachandran noted that after writing his article on anosognosia, it was pointed out to him that there was a new psychotherapy that made use of eye movements to enhance patient insight. Given the results of his research, he stated, "it makes perfect sense from the point of view of my theory!" (p. 49).

Finally, Bessel van der Kolk has obtained preliminary evidence from SPECT brain imaging that traumatic memories seem to be localized in the right hemisphere prior to EMDR, but do not show such localization following successful EMDR treatment (van der Kolk, 1998; van der Kolk, Burbridge, & Suzuki, 1997). To be fair, he states that he thinks that successful non-EMDR therapy would show the same effects. The irony here is that the preliminary evidence is there for EMDR, but not other, more established therapies.

Taken together, these three studies suggest that eye movements may facilitate the transfer of traumatic memories from the right hemisphere, where they are stored, to the left hemisphere, where they become accessible to conscious processing.

Thus, eye movements may be an important form of stimulation, helping to explain some of the unique effects of EMDR treatment. In fact, Ramachandran (1995) postulates an "anomaly detector" in the right hemisphere, which may be activated by the eye movements. Eye movements, and other forms of left-right stimulation that activate both hemispheres at the same time, may facilitate the transfer of information back and forth between hemispheres, leading to greater integration of awareness. Some of this information may be "unconscious" right-hemisphere information, that is, nonverbal, outside of awareness, or stored as somatosensory fragments.

Bruce Perry (1998) has somewhat different ideas about what makes EMDR effective. He says that as a child moves from a mental state of calm to arousal to alarm, fear, and terror, the respective areas of the child's brain that are activated are cortical, cortical and limbic, limbic and midbrain, midbrain and brainstem, and finally brainstem. Thus, if a child thinks of an event that brings up immediate terror, that child is not capable of abstract thought at that point. Rather, his brainstem is activated. Patterned, repetitive stimulation, which provides input to the brainstem, may "trick" the brainstem and allow for new learning. Perry also points out that healing rituals across societies typically involve four elements:

1. using an interactional process, which may involve the community, part of the community, or just a dyad
2. activating belief systems
3. establishing a narrative
4. providing patterned, repetitive stimulation

Thus, a rain dance, drumming, praying, meditation, and chanting may contain most or all of these four elements and can be seen as different types of healing rituals. EMDR also can fit into this paradigm, but would have to be regarded as a special case where healing occurs unusually quickly and consistently. The efficiency of EMDR then might be considered in terms of how well it employs each of the four elements.

## Associative Chaining

Another aspect of EMDR that appears to have major importance is that of associative chaining (i.e., following the client's thoughts as he moves from one item to another, regardless of where that leads), which has an important role in the history of psychotherapy. It is well known that Freud abandoned hypnosis in favor of free association in his treatment of adult patients. However, free association appears to be very difficult for most adults and impossible for most children. Unstructured play therapy is probably the closest analog for children, where the effects of traumatization can be seen in repetitive play.

In a symposium paper, Donald Levis (1990), who, along with Stampfl (1967), had pioneered the use of implosive therapy,* reported on a modification of the implosive technique, which he began using in 1984. Instead of ignoring extraneous images and associations, which sometimes arose in implosive therapy, he decided to pursue them, and discovered that they often led to early traumatic memories, which were recalled with great emotional intensity and associated physical symptoms related to the original trauma (body memories). He reported that full recovery of the memories led to reductions of the symptoms and positive changes in the personality structure of the individual. There are striking similarities here with EMDR, as well as some major differences.

---

*Implosive therapy is a form of behavior therapy in which the client's anxiety is aroused by images of situations that are fear-producing. In contrast to systematic desensitization, where the anxiety is minimized, in implosive therapy the therapist seeks to maximize the client's anxiety. When the anxiety is evoked in an intense form and nothing "bad" happens, the client's anxiety gradually diminishes, according to Stampfl and Levis.

EMDR makes use of associative chaining, using eye movements or other forms of patterned, repetitive stimulation each step of the way (i.e., between each set of associations). In EMDR the material evoked is similar to that reported by Freud and Levis, but in EMDR the focus is on conscious rather than repressed memories, and abreaction is not seen as being necessary. In fact, with children, abreactions are uncommon. Another difference is that pairing the associative chaining with eye movements seems to accelerate the process, so that it does not seem to be as drawn out and difficult as Freud and Levis report. The pairing also seems to make it a gentler and easier process, so that even traumatized children are not likely to be further traumatized by the procedure (as can happen with talking, even when discussion is undertaken with extreme tact and skill). And, as will be discussed later, EMDR can be employed with very young children with rudimentary language skills.

## Physical Sensations

In addition to alternate left-right stimulation and associative chaining, another important aspect of the EMDR procedure is the focus on physical sensations. Van der Kolk (1994) pointed out the importance of body memories (somatosensory representations) in people who have been psychologically traumatized. Shapiro (1995) noted that physical sensations associated with the original event (trauma) are often expressed and released in EMDR processing. In my experience, this evoking of the physical sensations occurs more often in EMDR than in any other psychotherapy (except perhaps the body-oriented therapies, which involve actual manipulation of the physical body). Many individuals in EMDR treatment report (with astonishment) feeling once again the pain in their body that they originally endured, whether it is the rape victim who experiences the pain of the rape, the accident victim who feels the pain of impact, the adult beaten in childhood who reexperiences the body pain from the beating, or the surgical patient who became conscious during surgery and reexperiences the pain and terror of the surgery in the EMDR processing. It typically comes into awareness, and then fades, not to return. What are the mental processes that underlie the brain's ability to cause the body to vividly feel the original sensations?

One possible answer comes from Candace Pert (1997), who points out that the brain, the endocrine system, and the immunological system are all interrelated through their chemical messengers. The brain produces informational molecules that are read by the other two systems, which have receptor sites for them. The immune system and the endocrine system also manufacture informational substances that are read by the brain. A person who becomes ill, but who laughs a lot or takes a proactive attitude may recover quickly. The laughter increases endorphins in the brain, which then strengthen the immune system.

Dr. Pert has conducted much of the ground-breaking research on these chemical messengers and their receptor sites. Early in her career, she discovered the receptor sites in the brain for endogenous opiates, which then set off a scientific scramble to discover what those endogenous opiates were, which led to the discovery of endorphins. She also coined the term "the body-mind," reflecting this interconnectedness of the body and mind. The entire field of psychoneuroimmunology developed from her early work.

The phenomenon of phantom limb pain (in which pain is felt in the limb that is no longer there) suggests that pain is registered in the mind, but experienced as if it is in the missing body part. Perhaps the body memories that are evoked in EMDR processing are similar. The pain is "locked" in the brain, and something in the EMDR procedure allows it to be unlocked and reexperienced. Our pilot research with phantom limb pain suggests that EMDR is similarly effective in releasing the pain, whether it has been there for one, twelve, or twenty-five years (Wilson, Tinker, & Becker, 1997). It does seem that the clinical data will cause neuroscientists to explore the neural pathways and interactions that will explain how it happens, much as what happens when a drug causes a clinical benefit which cannot be explained by existing knowledge. How exciting science becomes when new information doesn't fit into existing frameworks!

However, physiological reductionism should not hold sway over clinical observations. That is the view that if the neuroscientists can't measure the phenomenon, it must not exist. Every thought is a neurochemical event; every memory is a neurobiological sequence; every emotion has a neurological substrate. With common mental events, we are unlikely to say that if we can't measure them, they don't exist. For example, if we can't localize a thought in the brain through brain imaging, we are unlikely to say the thought doesn't exist. However, if our heart aches after we think about a tragic event, some people deny the heart pain or think of it as a metaphor, until they find that there are receptor sites in the heart for brain neurochemicals. Then they can understand that the heart can feel pain brought on by emotions. "Body memories" are frequently evoked in EMDR; eventually, neuroscientists will become interested in tracing how this phenomenon occurs. But it is important to remember that neurophysiological analysis is simply another level of analysis, albeit a very interesting one, and one that fits well our current scientific paradigms.

One level of analysis is not necessarily more valid than another. Perhaps more variables can be more strictly controlled at the neurophysiological level, but psychological and sociological levels of analysis can be equally important. Although it may be much easier to fund research exploring how a new antidepressant affects brain chemicals than to fund research exploring why many people are depressed, both levels of analysis provide important information. Which levels of analysis are regarded as being more important has more to do with political realities than scientific exigencies. It often seems that descriptive research in the field of psychology obtains more funding than treatment research. For example, there is a great deal of research on the effects of sexual abuse on children, but very little on how to treat therapeutically such children. Perhaps, though, this relates as much to where our skills lie as to political realities. That is, we are much better at comparing abused children to nonabused children in a research design than we are at effectively restoring the lives of abused children. Perhaps science ignores problems it can do little about, and focuses on paradigms where there is more control, regardless of how unimportant those problems are.

I'm reminded of the story of the man who lost his car keys in the dark. When another person saw him searching for the keys under a lamppost, he asked him what he was doing. The first replied that he was looking for his keys. The other man asked if that was where he dropped them. The first man replied, "No, I dropped them over there in the dark." Of course, the other asked why he was looking for them under the lamppost. The first man replied, "Because that is where the light is."

Scientific exploration too often follows this model. With the advent of an effective trauma psychotherapy for children, perhaps that narrow focus on merely describing children with various symptoms or problems will change, and we will behave less like the person who lost his keys. That would certainly be a boon to child clinicians.

## The Importance of Early Trauma

Another important aspect of EMDR is that it highlights the importance of early childhood experience. If an adult focuses on a recent trauma, his associative chain often leads back to earlier traumas in his life, if any exist. If there have not been any, the present event is adaptively resolved, and no further treatment is needed. If prior traumas exist, each trauma is dealt with separately. At times, however, if the worst or earliest trauma is dealt with first, other traumas do not have to be individually reprocessed. Clients report that the negative affective content is so diminished that the memory of other events is no longer troublesome. EMDR is thus genetic in its orientation, typically going backward in time to the genesis of the psychological problems. EMDR with children is analogous, except that the traumas have not been exerting their negative effects for so long a period of time. The clinician who uses EMDR on a regular basis, therefore, becomes aware of the genesis of psychological problems in early trauma, and subsequently sees how a person's life changes in a positive direction when those early traumas are resolved and no longer exert an influence on the person's life.

Thus, the early work of Charcot, Janet, Breuer, and Freud in trauma is confirmed, validated, and perhaps rediscovered with the use of EMDR. The difference is that EMDR provides a method of treatment that is so simple and effective that it can even be used with children with excellent results, as opposed to the work of the pioneers, which was attempted only with adults, often many long years after the traumas occurred (with the exception of little Hans—but even there, Freud never worked with Hans directly, consulting instead with his parents [Freud, 1909]).

## THE SAFE PLACE

While it has long been recognized that children become traumatized (largely through retrospective work with adults), treating children for trauma has a less lengthy history. Fortunately, a number of books have recently appeared, informing clinicians on how to work with traumatized children. Writings by Donovan and McIntyre (1990), Herman (1992), James (1989), Johnson (1998), Monahon (1993), Putnam (1997), Shirar (1996), and Terr (1990) are excellent resources for the practicing therapist. These writers and therapists emphasize a focus on helping the traumatized child feel safe in the therapeutic relationship. In EMDR as well, the issue of safety is of primary importance, which is why, in addition to a safe relationship, the "safe place" is a starting place for using EMDR with children. My impression is that therapeutic work with children improves the therapist's skill in working with adults. For example, if a recently traumatized adult was previously traumatized in childhood, she will very likely react in some ways that are typical of a child at the original age of traumatization. Or a man originally traumatized in childhood may respond in some child-like ways in dealing with the trauma in his adult psychotherapy. A therapist who has skills in working with traumatized children will be able to apply those skills in working with and understanding the traumatized adult.

## THE ILLUMINATION OF THEORETICAL ISSUES

Using EMDR with children also provides a different perspective on theoretical issues that engender impassioned debate in trauma work with adults. For example, it has been argued that EMDR is simply a form of exposure, similar to systematic desensitization or prolonged exposure—an habituation model, which posits that the more often one is exposed to an upsetting stimulus (formerly associated with the trauma), the more likely the fearful responses will diminish. Although this does not fully account for the rapidity of EMDR treatment effects with adults, it fits even less well with children, where the treatment effects can be even more rapid. If five or ten minutes of EMDR lead to cessation of symptoms in a child, due to the "exposure" of the child to memories of a traumatic event, and this is considered exposure therapy, then all therapy would have to be considered exposure therapy. Thus, with children, it becomes very difficult to see EMDR as a form of exposure, unless the term "exposure" is broadened to become all-encompassing. However, it is unlikely that cognitive-behavioral researchers or theoreticians are willing to redefine exposure in this way, as shown in this quote from a recent study: "In vertebrate and invertebrates, exposure gradually reduces defensive responses to cues to which the subject is exposed; this habituation depends on the dose of exposure. Continuous stimulation in neurons and immune and endocrine cells tends to dampen responses, and intermittent stimulation tends to increase them" (Marks, Lovell, Noshirvani, Livanou, & Thrasher, 1998, p. 324). As EMDR employs intermittent stimulation and the results are not dose-related (van Etten & Taylor, in press; Wilson et al., 1995), it is difficult to see it as a form of exposure.

Further, when children are exposed to trauma, they respond with behaviors, thoughts, and feelings that are not easily ameliorated by additional exposure. Suppose a child has been sexually abused. How could anyone suggest that imaginal or in vivo exposure could be beneficial for the child? Similarly, with other forms of abuse, medical traumas, war traumas, family disruptions due to divorce, automobile accidents, and natural disasters, there is a recognition that children would be retraumatized by exposure approaches. Even adults have difficulties with exposure approaches, and a certain amount of ego strength is necessary for tolerating the emotional pain that is generated. Some adults deteriorate when undergoing such approaches (Pitman et al., 1996). However, most children are able to tolerate the more gentle approach of EMDR, employed in the context of a safe relationship, using a safe place, and interspersing self-esteem–enhancing EMDR procedures if necessary.

There is another theoretical issue with adults that EMDR with children seems to clarify: the importance of cognitions in trauma therapy. Other modes of therapy conceptualize change in different ways. For example, cognitive therapies suggest that it is important to change the cognitions and then the emotions will tag along (e.g., rational-emotive therapy; Aaron Beck's cognitive therapy for depression). Behavioral therapies (prolonged exposure, imaginal exposure, in vivo exposure, systematic rewards and punishments, token economies) suggest that if you change the behaviors, the emotions and cognitions will subsequently change. Insight-oriented therapies hold that if you change the client's insights and self-understandings, emotional and behavioral changes will follow. Psychoanalytic therapy indicates that if the conflicts become resolved through "making the unconscious conscious" or removing repressions, that emotions and behavior will change. All of these approaches can point to clinical successes, demonstrating that these approaches work some of the time with some clients.

Fewer therapies focus on changing the emotions first. Indeed, how does one go about changing emotions first? If someone walks into my office and says, "I'm frightened," I can't legitimately say, "Just stop being frightened," and expect to be regarded as helpful and intelligent. I have to assume that his friends and relatives have already said that, the person has told himself that, and that it hasn't worked. However, EMDR frequently seems to cause emotions to change first, with cognitions and behaviors realigning with the new, less intense affect. Because EMDR is frequently referred to as providing "accelerated information processing," I had interpreted "information processing" as being primarily cognitive in nature. However, the more I used EMDR with children and adults, the more I began to watch for the emotional shifts that "turned the corner" for the client. It often seemed like the negative emotional constellation simply washed out in a brief moment, much to the astonishment of the client and myself. Following such an experience, the adult client would often refer to a palpable sense of the negative emotions leaving, saying such things as, "I felt this 'whoosh' feeling" or "It felt like I just expelled something from my body" or "This negative feeling just lifted out of me." I have not ever witnessed anything comparable in the other forms of therapy I have employed over the past twenty-some years I have worked as a therapist. This shift phenomenon also happens with children, although they are less able to describe it well and provide fewer visual or facial cues when it happens. The child might say, "The picture is fuzzy" or "It doesn't bother me now," when, a moment before, the event was highly disturbing to the child. A 10-year-old girl, whose behavior had been problematic for three years after her mother's death, stated during her first EMDR session, just after the moment of change, "I feel like I flushed it all out of my system." So it appears the same thing happens with children as with adults, but because children provide fewer facial cues and are less articulate, it is more difficult to discern.

Because these rapid emotional shifts occur with children, and often very young children with limited verbal and cognitive skills, it appears that while cognitions may facilitate the process of EMDR, they may not be necessary for successful resolution of traumas or PTSD in children. Although PTSD is referred to as an emotional disorder (Foa, Rothbaum, Riggs, Murdock, & Walsh, 1991; American Psychiatric Association, 1994), most of the ways of dealing with it prior to EMDR have been to focus on behaviors and cognitions. The cognitive-behavioral approaches, which conceptualize PTSD as emotionally-based, attack it through behaviors and cognitions, that is, by having the client go to the place of the trauma (a behavior), the anxiety eventually subsides, allowing the client to think differently about it. Even relaxation-based approaches, such as progressive relaxation, systematic desensitization, and biofeedback-assisted relaxation, are primarily about changing behavior (increasing relaxation—a behavior—in the face of disturbing thoughts) with the idea that emotions and cognitions will follow suit. It seems possible that as we study the effects of EMDR on children, the results of such therapy and research will inform our understanding of adult psychopathology and what the ingredients of effective change are, not only with children, but also with adults.

## PRECAUTIONS

As I have already indicated, safety of the child is a predominant consideration in using EMDR with children. Two other precautions are in order.

1. *The age of the child.* Children between the ages of 8 and 12 seem to handle the procedure readily. However, the younger the child, the more the clinician needs to be cautious not to retraumatize the child. In dealing with children aged 5 to 8, more time needs to be taken to build a safe relationship, with greater reliance on the safe place and self-esteem-building targets in EMDR. Ages 2 to 4 require even more attention to helping the child feel safe in the therapeutic encounter, with activities geared to the interests of the child, such as play, artwork, and simple games. The clinician may need to conduct a number of sessions with a focus on these non-EMDR activities if the child is highly apprehensive. Then, EMDR can be interspersed among the other activities as the child's apprehension diminishes. For example, the therapist might start with having the child draw pictures with a positive theme, such as an activity he likes to do. Later, the pictures could be of his family, and still later, of something that makes him feel bad (scared, mad, sad). The last image could then be used as a target for EMDR, holding it up, so the child could look at it as hand taps are being used.

2. *Session completion.* Adults are usually able to accomplish associative chaining naturally, moving from one image, thought, feeling, or memory to another. Children often don't do this on their own, which requires the therapist to help with the process. This can be accomplished by "theme development" where the therapist helps with the associative chaining by requesting, "Think of another time when you . . ." The theme development can be along the lines of emotions, thoughts, actions, or situations. For example, if dealing with a frightening nightmare, after the nightmare is desensitized, the clinician might request, "Think of another time when you were very frightened by a nightmare," and continue with the same request until the child is unable to think of other nightmares. If there is only one nightmare, the therapist can say, "Think of another time you felt that scared," and continue as above with emotional theme development. If focusing on behavior, the therapist might ask the child, "Think of another time when you did something that bad."

The point is that it is necessary to clean out channels (associations on a single theme) with children, as with adults, before moving on to new topics. If a child has been multiply traumatized, more caution is needed. Generally, this means treating the child as if he were emotionally much younger. More attention needs to be paid to the safety of the relationship, the safety of the child in the relationship, and going more slowly with EMDR. This often means interweaving more activities around EMDR, using EMDR on small fragments of traumatic situations, and using positive targets (e.g., happy times) in the process. If the child is in an ongoing situation that is difficult and contributing to the problem, caution must be exercised in handling the whole situation. For example, if the child is upset by his parents' acrimonious divorce, and they continue to be in conflict, it may be necessary to involve the parents in changing their behavior either at the same time or before the child is engaged in EMDR. It may be necessary to suspend EMDR until the parents have changed their behaviors.

With these general precautions in mind, and the background information about EMDR provided in this chapter, we are now ready to look at much more specific information about applying EMDR.

# two

# Trauma, Diagnosis, and EMDR: Initial Considerations

"Now the tornadoes are stuck in the mountains."
—JULIE, AGE 5

GETTING STARTED WITH EMDR is not very different from getting started with other psychotherapeutic approaches with children, as it entails gathering information prior to making an intervention. Clinicians skilled in working with children and their families will have their own methods of collecting such background information, based on their training, clinical experience, and theoretical orientation. Although this book is not a primer on diagnostic interviewing, I do render a plea to obtain a rather thorough knowledge about the child, her developmental history, and her current circumstances before implementing EMDR. Developmental history forms are useful for collecting thorough developmental information, but require the clinician's knowledge to amplify certain areas, such as trauma history. Current circumstances generally include the family environment, the school or preschool situation, the nature of the day care provided, and any other aspect of the environment in which the child spends time. Only after the clinician has gathered information from all these sources does she have the requisite knowledge to make an informed decision about beginning (or not beginning) EMDR.

## TRAUMA-BASED DIAGNOSES

A trauma-based or ecological diagnosis is often more useful than a *DSM-IV* diagnosis when using EMDR. Let's say, for example, the clinician learns that the client, who is now 7, was molested at age 5 by an adolescent male baby-sitter on a single occasion. From age 5–7, the girl has had problems with anxiety and depression, difficulty falling asleep, nightmares two or three times a week, intrusive thoughts about boys hurting her, and never feels safe in the living room, where the molestation occurred. She has had no other known traumas, and has a nurturing and supportive family. The goal of diagnosis is to determine a course of treatment and a prognosis based on that course of treatment. Based on my clinical experience (and that of others) in using EMDR, the above description provides enough information to predict that the girl will likely require two or three sessions of EMDR to be symptom-free.

On the other hand, if the girl had been repeatedly molested by the sitter over a year's time period, the girl could likely be helped in less than ten sessions. Other aspects of the molestation would be pertinent in determining the length of the treatment, such as the age of the girl, whether force was used, whether fear of death was involved, the duration of the traumatic episode(s) (e.g., minutes versus hours or days), severity of injuries, if threats of violence against disclosure were made or self-esteem–damaging statements were voiced repeatedly, whether the judicial system retraumatized the girl at the very vulnerable time immediately following the traumatic incident(s), and the degree of negativity of other aspects of the girl's social and family systems. For example, if the family was not supportive of her, treatment would most likely take longer, and the family should be involved in non-EMDR treatment, such as family or couple therapy.

The point is that predictions can be made about the length of EMDR treatment based on the nature of the experience, the age of the girl, the supportiveness of her family, and her prior experience with trauma. These factors are much more predictive than symptoms that lead to DSM-IV diagnoses, which are irrelevant for predicting outcome. In the above example, the girl could be diagnosed as depressed, anxious, sleep disordered, phobic (about the living room), as having learning disabilities if her school grades went down, as a behavioral problem if she acted out in anger or aggressiveness, or as ADHD if her hyperarousal at school affected her ability to concentrate.

None of those diagnoses from the DSM-IV would have predictive utility in the sense of suggesting when she might get better or whether she might do better on antidepressant medication, antianxiety medication, medication for obsessive-compulsive disorder, stimulant medication, or whether psychotherapy might be appropriate. If her family belonged to a managed care plan, she would first be referred to a physician, who might be inclined to prescribe medication after only hearing the symptoms; all she might get would be a prescription for medication, with several medications being tried in succession, to see whether one or another might be helpful. Or, if the physician decided to refer her to a mental health professional in the managed care system, the mental health professional might use up the limited number of sessions treating family dynamics or suggesting behavioral approaches for classroom management (e.g., programs for reinforcing time in seat or time on task, among other things), perhaps referring back to the primary care physician for ADHD medication. If neuropsychological testing were undertaken, abnormalities might show up, which would be considered for remediation. For example, on the Wechsler Intelligence Scale for Children, a Verbal-Performance discrepancy, with Performance scores higher than Verbal scores is frequently taken as evidence for a "learning disability." However, Martin Teicher (1997) has shown that abused children manifest this pattern much more frequently than children who have not been abused. Also, there is evidence that when individuals have been traumatized, their left hemisphere (verbal) functions diminish in comparison to their right hemisphere functions (van der Kolk, 1997). Nonetheless, the child could be targeted for language remediation, geared to improving her learning disabilities in reading, spelling, and writing.

Unfortunately, none of these approaches or diagnoses has any predictive value for a child who has been traumatized. In medicine, the diagnosis is usually predictive of the course and outcome of the disease and determines the treatment selected. In the mental health field, however, relationships are not so clear-cut. One person can be depressed for years; another, for only months. One person may be alcoholic for five years; another, for the rest of his life. A treatment intervention that works for one child may not work at all for another. Thus, it is noteworthy that in one corner of the diagnostic field, when EMDR is used, knowledge of a person's having been traumatized, the circumstances of the trauma, and the environment can be predictive of treatment and outcome.

Interestingly, researchers in Germany have developed the Cologne Risk Index, which predcicts the likelihood that a given individual will develop PTSD based on the characteristics of the trauma (Fischer & Riedesser, 1998). Their research indicates that the characteristics of the individual have very little relevance as to whether PTSD develops; rather, the characteristics of the trauma itself provide most of the predictive power for PTSD determination. These psychologists suggest that Freud steered the fields of psychology and psychotherapy in the wrong direction when he downplayed the importance of the trauma itself, according overriding importance to the qualities or the individual (e.g., ego strength, superego weaknesses, id-superego conflicts) in his theory (G. Fisher, personal communication, September 15, 1998). Items on the Cologne Risk Index have a great deal in common with the characteristics of trauma that are predicitive of EMDR treatment course and outcome (see table 2.1). Thus, it appears that trauma characteristics can be used to predict both the development of PTSD and aspects of treatment in EMDR, and the individual qualities of the child can be regarded as much less important. Among other things, this approach (primarily diagnosing the trauma rather than the individual) helps us stay away from blaming the victim.

It makes good sense to ask about a person's history of trauma, not only because of the treatment efficacy of EMDR, but also because of the frequency of traumatic incidents in children's lives. It is well known that the leading causes of death in children and adolescents are accidents and suicides. Since these are greater with those who have been psychologically traumatized (Johnson, 1998), a strong case can be made that untreated effects of trauma have life-threatening consequences and cause the formation of psychological symptoms in children. Left untreated even longer, these childhood symptoms can develop into adult disorders.

## THE PERVASIVENESS OF TRAUMA

Listening to the evening news on television or radio or reading a newsmagazine or newspaper, we are aware of the pervasiveness of trauma in everyday life. We know that family members, friends, and acquaintances are often subjected to traumatic events. According to Sedlack and Broadhurst (1996), the National Incident Study of Child Abuse and Neglect found that between 1986 and 1993, the number of abused and neglected children doubled, increasing from 1.4 million to 2.8 million. Further, over the same period, there was a fourfold increase in the number of children seriously injured by abuse, from 143,000 to 570,000. The study identified poverty as a major risk factor, along with being in a single-parent family. For example, children in families with annual incomes of $15,000 or less were 22 times more likely to be abused than those from families with incomes in the $30,000 range. Researchers in PTSD (Breslau, Davis, Andreski, & Peterson, 1991) estimate that 9% of the population in the United States can be diagnosed as having PTSD, and if traumatized individuals, lacking the full diagnosis, are included, the percentage rises to14–15%. This means that approximately 40 million people in the United States suffer from traumatic symptoms of some sort. If only 25% of those are children, almost 10 million children have traumatic reactions of some degree that interfere with their psychological functioning. If one-third of those estimated 10 million children are fully PTSD, then over 3 million children would currently be diagnosed as PTSD. Continuing to overlook or minimize the connections between traumatic events and childhood emotional distress will continue to obscure the predictability of treatment, course, and outcome and will deny help to millions of children.

I seriously doubt that trauma can be eliminated from our lives. Tragedy is part of living. If we can do a better job of recognizing it as a cause of emotional pain that takes many forms, we can then treat its effects more humanely and effectively. We can also work to eliminate or minimize the aspects of traumatization over which we have control. It makes more sense emotionally and economically to protect children from traumatization than to attempt to treat them after traumatization has occurred.

## EFFECTIVE TREATMENT FOR TRAUMA

We have found (Wilson, Becker, & Tinker, 1997) that at 15 months post-EMDR, almost two-thirds of a large sample of traumatized adults (n = 66) showed reliable improvement from three sessions of EMDR. The majority (about 90%) of those who had reliably improved were assessed as fully recovered, as measured by standardized instruments. If over half of the 40 million children and adults exhibiting PTSD symptoms in the United States could be helped by EMDR in approximately three sessions, it would have huge implications for public health issues. We are now conducting controlled research with children to assess the effectiveness of EMDR with traumatized children between the ages of 7 and 11. Clinical experience, published case studies, and a field study (Chemtob & Nakashima, 1996) with treatment-resistant, traumatized children in Kauai, Hawaii (who still had PTSD symptoms four years after Hurricane Iniki, despite a prior psychosocial intervention) suggest that EMDR is also effective with children. The investigators provided three sessions of EMDR to 32 children who were treatment nonresponders and met clinical criteria for PTSD. Using the Children's Reaction Inventory (CRI), the Revised Children's Manifest Anxiety Scale (RCMAS), and the Children's Depression Inventory (CDI), they found substantial reductions in CRI scores in both anxiety and depression following treatment. There were also significant, though more modest, reductions in RCMAS and CDI total scores. Treatment gains were maintained at six-month follow-up. Health visits to the school nurse were significantly reduced in the school year following treatment.

As the public becomes educated about the role of trauma in generating emotional distress and learns that there is now a treatment for it that is cost-effective and available to children, it is more likely that not only will the use of EMDR will increase, but also that the public will request it directly.

## MINIMIZATION OF PTSD IN CHILDREN

Unfortunately, PTSD in children is underdiagnosed because of the criteria listed in the *DSM-IV*. PTSD is the only *DSM-IV* diagnosis that has to be defined by the event itself. Criterion A in the *DSM-IV* indicates that the traumatic event has to be life-threatening for the diagnosis to be PTSD. In other words, if a person develops all the symptoms of PTSD after an upsetting event, it is not "true" PTSD if the event was not life-threatening. Thus, many people, especially children, are not diagnosed with PTSD if the event does not appear to be life-threatening to the diagnosing professional. An example would be a child who develops PTSD symptoms after a parental divorce. Since a divorce is not literally life-threatening (from an adult point of view), the PTSD diagnosis is not likely to be applied. It is a little like saying that a broken leg is not "truly" a broken leg unless it occurred in a certain kind of event (e.g., in a life-threatening accident). Then all other broken legs are classified as something else, and when statistics are compiled on the incidence and prevalence of broken legs, the actual numbers are underestimated. Unfortunately, this is the situation that exists with the present PTSD system of diagnosis. Until the definition is changed, we will continue to underestimate the incidence and prevalence of PTSD in children. My clinical experience indicates that if an event causes the full range of intrusive, avoidance, and hyperarousal symptoms that characterize PTSD, then the event must have been traumatic.

Further, PTSD in children can result from an accumulation of traumas, none of which, or only some of which, may be life-threatening. An example of this is an 11-year-old boy who was in our study. When the boy was 4 years old, his father held his mother and him hostage, threatening to kill all three of them. When the father finally let them go, they crawled out the front door and took refuge in a car, while a SWAT team stormed the house. The father shot himself, ran out of the house, and died on the street. The boy did not develop PTSD symptoms until his grandfather died of natural causes, seven years later. He did not have a close relationship with his grandfather. It would certainly make sense to diagnose this boy's symptoms as PTSD, although the precipitating event (the grandfather's death) does not meet Criterion A of the *DSM-IV*. If he had manifested PTSD symptoms immediately after his father's death, when he was 4 years old, the diagnosis would fit. Since that did not happen, do we therefore consider him "latent" PTSD after that event until his grandfather died? I suggest dropping Criterion A from the diagnostic requirements to help avoid such conundrums.

Another example about how the impact of traumatic events tends to be minimized or overlooked with children occurred on one of seven occasions that I went to Oklahoma City after the bombing of the Federal Building there in 1995.* The adults were stunned by the terrorist act and many of the children became very quiet. Only after the adults had resolved the trauma to some extent were they able to attend to what was going on with their children. These observations are not meant critically, as it is not surprising that the adults, caught up in their efforts to assist survivors and families of victims and their own sense of violation, grief, and loss, found it hard to notice the wide-eyed quietness of their

---

*My going was part of an EMDR nationwide project headed by Sandra to provide EMDR to survivors and first responders (firefighters and police) in Oklahoma City. The project was cosponsored by the EMDR Humanitarian Assistance Program and the Spencer Curtis Foundation.

children or even to recognize that something was amiss. So the children's needs, unless they were extreme, tended to go unnoticed. Even when there was acting out, it was not necessarily connected to the event. For example, a teacher remarked that children at her school were not showing any disturbance after the bombing, although perhaps they were getting into more fights on the playground. A comment like this only partially connects the behavior with the event; at the same time, it seems to discount the importance of the connection.

Overall, the impact and importance of trauma in the lives of our children tend to be discounted. Unawareness of the effects of trauma and the pervasiveness of trauma with children, misallocation of trauma-related symptoms to other diagnostic categories not related to trauma and not predictive of outcome, coupled with problems with the PTSD diagnosis itself, all contribute to this discounting. Add to this the fact that the PTSD diagnosis has been in use for less than 20 years (it was first listed as a *DSM* diagnosis in 1980), and applied to children for less time than that, and we have a field that is wide open for additional knowledge about how to diagnose and treat the effects of trauma on children.

## TRAUMA CHARACTERISTICS AS PREDICTORS OF EMDR OUTCOME

All science is based on prediction. Freudian psychology has been criticized for being postdictive; that is, Freudian theory can "explain" an end result, but it cannot predict it. Scientifically, a theory is only as good as its predictive ability, otherwise it goes the way of the medieval theory of phlogiston, which attempted to explain which materials would burn and to what extent, but could not predict. *DSM-IV* diagnoses do not predict, as they are symptom-based. Supplanting the *DSM-IV* diagnostic system with a system that is predictively accurate would be a scientific improvement.

As I have mentioned, EMDR progress and outcome can be predicted from the characteristics of the traumas that a child endures. This predictibility is enhanced by the consistency of traumatized child-clients' response to EMDR itself. The importance of this predictibility cannot be underestimated, for it provides a framework for clinicians to let parents know what to expect from EMDR with respect to estimating the time most likely to be involved in therapy as well as the cost. In fact, it also gives clinicians a good sense of therapy prognosis and outcome. Although every case is different, the more the clinician knows about the trauma, the more accurate her estimates can be for what to expect with a given traumatized child.

The prediction of EMDR treatment outcomes has substantial scientific implications. Among other things, it suggests that diagnoses that can be linked to accurate predictions could be emphasized in diagnostic manuals. Certainly, descriptions of symptom clusters can be useful, but if it is found that a specific symptom cluster does not have predictive utility, it may eventually have to be abandoned in favor of a symptom cluster that does. For example, if "stomach ache" does not have predictive utility in conjunction with a treatment, but "ulcer" does, the diagnostic precision of "ulcer" will eventually hold sway over the more general term.

Following are the parameters of trauma that clinically have been shown to be predictive of EMDR outcome:

1. *Simple versus complex.* Simple traumas are over and in the past: the dog bite, the car accident, the sudden death of a loved one, the sexual assault by someone no longer in the child's life, the tornado that destroyed the family home. Simple traumas are where the EMDR miracles occur; the single-session "cures" that seem miraculous to both the clinician and client.

Complex traumas have ongoing elements: the incest where the father is still in the home or allowed to visit; the divorce that is not over, where the parents fight bitterly, involving the child in the altercations; the car accident that resulted in a parent's permanent disability or the child's ongoing painful medical care; the fire that burns down the family home and there is no replacement as yet. With complex traumas, EMDR can be effective and dramatically speed up the process of therapy, but it becomes a part of a therapy where many approaches may be required. For example, in the case where paternal incest has occurred, family therapy as well as marital therapy may be required. Legal interventions and social service involvement may also be necessary, with the therapist helping to coordinate these approaches for the best interest of the child. Or, if a child has been traumatized by his parents' divorce, meetings with the parents and lawyers, petitioning for a guardian ad litem, in addition to EMDR, may all be required to help the child.

2. *Acute versus chronic.* In EMDR, it doesn't seem to make much difference, in terms of the length of therapy, whether the trauma is acute or chronic, although acute traumas (with a duration of roughly three months to one year) may resolve somewhat more quickly. With respect to acute traumas of less than three months' duration, it makes sense to wait until PTSD symptoms appear, and then to use EMDR to treat them. In Oklahoma City, for example, first responders worked at the bomb site for a number of days, grimly doing what they had to do. Most then functioned reasonably well for a month or two, but after that (for those who developed PTSD), nightmares, flashbacks, and other PTSD symptoms began intruding to such an extent that they became unable to function at home and on the job. It was at this point that they were often referred for EMDR, which provided enough improvement so that they were able to function adequately at work and at home. They could sleep, because the

nightmares were gone, and they were able to think on their jobs, as they no longer had intrusive thoughts. It should be understood that not all first responders developed PTSD, and daily critical incident stress management (CISM) debriefings were conducted in groups for all first responders. EMDR became applicable for those who later developed PTSD symptoms. It would not have been useful to attempt to apply it before the symptoms developed. In one of many examples that could be given, I worked with a man who had been transporting bodies and body parts to a morgue several miles away. He functioned well in doing this work, and for a month or so afterward, but after that began having nightmares that were so real, he could no longer tell if something had really occurred or whether he had just dreamt it. He became afraid to go to sleep at night and felt unable to function in his personal life and on his job. He had an intense abreaction in his first EMDR session, felt an emotional release, and was able to sleep again after that session. Two follow-up visits promoted further gains. Phone contact a year later indicated that the gains were maintained. If he had been treated before his PTSD symptoms emerged, there would be no way to tell if EMDR had produced a benefit for him.

Analogously, if a child is in an automobile accident, he is not automatically a candidate for EMDR. Usually, it makes sense to wait to see if symptoms develop, and then apply EMDR at that time. Some parents, however, may want to use EMDR preventatively, as trauma can have a cumulative effect. These parents may want their child to have one or two EMDR sessions even though the child has manifested no symptoms. In my experience, what happens is the child is surprised at the intensity of feelings that come up in reprocessing the trauma, leading me to think that some preventative work has been accomplished because of the intensity of feelings that have emerged, and the parents have the satisfaction of inoculating their child against any additional trauma that might come up in the future. When one or two sessions are used in this way, however, it is difficult to know for sure if a real benefit has accrued. This is a question that can eventually be answered empirically through longitudinal research: Does it really make a difference later on if EMDR is used preventatively with children exposed to traumatic events (whether they have symptoms or not)?

3. *Single versus multiple trauma.* It's no surprise that children who have been multiply traumatized are likely to be in treatment longer than those who have fewer or singular traumas. In fact, a separate diagnosis has been proposed for those persons who have been subjected to extreme stress over a long period of time: complex PTSD or disorders of extreme stress, not otherwise specified (DESNOS), with symptoms that are more severe than ordinary PTSD (van der Kolk & McFarlane, 1996). Also, Briere (Briere,1992; Briere, Woo, McRae, Foltz, & Sitzman, 1997) has shown that children who have been sexually or physically abused over a longer period of time have more serious symptoms

and reactions than those who have not been subjected to repeated abuse. However, even multiply traumatized children can be treated fairly quickly with EMDR if the child is now in a safe environment and there is no threat that the abuse will recur.

4. *Age at first traumatization.* The younger a child is traumatized, the more profound the consequences (Scheflin & Brown, 1996; Williams, 1994; Williams & Banyard, 1997). Here, Bowlby's theories on attachment disorders can perhaps be fitted into a more general theory about traumatization. That is, an infant who is traumatized in the first year of life after removal from a loving caretaker or from some other kind of trauma, is likely to have emotional reactions which interfere with attachment. If this is true, attachment disorders can be integrated into trauma theory. Schwarz & Perry (1994) postulate that the developing organism is more susceptible to the harmful effects of early trauma, with trauma negatively affecting the development of the brain and nervous system in various ways. However, EMDR can be effective even with traumas occurring in the first two years of life. For example, Davy (chapter 4), who was traumatized by surgery at age 14 months, and Jackie (chapter 3), who was severely sexually abused at age 18 months, were each treated successfully with EMDR. The difficulty for the clinician seems to be getting the child to access the memory or some aspect of it while engaging in alternate left-right stimulation.

5. *No violence versus violence.* When a young child is threatened with violence (for example, is told that the perpetrator will kill him or his family), the trauma is much more difficult to treat than if no violence was involved. The same effect is true if coercion or threats are involved. I remember working with a 3-year-old girl who had been sexually abused by the husband of her baby-sitter and threatened with her life if she told. Treatment was very difficult, as she was terrified to access the memories, for fear that she and her family would be killed if she told. This was quite different from treatment of a 3-year-old who had been in a car accident where there was no intentional violence and no threats or coercion. However, if a child were in a car accident, and threatened with violence if she told, the accident trauma would be harder to treat. The issue here becomes one of helping the child feel safe and protected. Very often, the younger the child, the harder it is to do that. A 10-year-old can be reassured that he can be protected from a perpetrator (if it's true!) in ways that a 3-year-old can't be.

6. *Degree of dissociation.* A number of studies have shown that the greater the degree of dissociation at the time of the trauma, the greater the likelihood that the traumatized individual will develop PTSD (Putnam, 1997). In EMDR, we find that the more a child or adult dissociated during the traumas that were experienced, the more they are likely to dissociate in EMDR. Fortunately, there are a number of methods to minimize and control the dissociation of children

in EMDR (discussed later). However, the degree of dissociation that occurs in EMDR affects the length of treatment. If a child dissociates each time a traumatic incident is brought up in EMDR, the therapist must proceed slowly and may have to help the child develop nontraumatic targets prior to accessing the traumatic memories.

Thus, if a child was repeatedly abused by a family member, starting at a young age and continuing over several years, where violence was threatened and applied, and the perpetrator remained in the family, EMDR treatment is not likely to be rapid (i.e., the trauma is complex, repeated, started at a young age, with violent aspects, and the child will likely dissociate in EMDR). On the other hand, if a 6-year-old child is beaten up by an adolescent from out of town and has a supportive family, EMDR treatment is likely to proceed rapidly.

Table 2.1 shows each of these trauma characteristics (as well as some others) and how they affect treatment outcome in EMDR. Note that acute versus chronic is the only characteristic that doesn't have a major effect on treatment outcome. This should not be interpreted that chronic trauma doesn't affect the child more than acute trauma, rather that the efficiency of EMDR is not altered much by the acute versus chronic dimension.

It could be argued that these aspects of trauma are predictive of outcomes for other therapeutic approaches as well as EMDR. However, to my knowledge there is no research with children to support that assumption. Because EMDR shortens treatment more than other approaches with children, the direct rela-

## TABLE 2.1
### *Trauma Characteristics Predictive of EMDR Outcome*

| TRAUMA CHARACTERISTIC | DEGREE OF EFFECT |
| --- | --- |
| Simple versus complex | Major |
| Single versus multiple | Major |
| Age of first occurrence | Major |
| Impersonal versus personal (e.g., flood versus assault) | Major |
| Degree of interpersonal violence and threat | Major |
| Degree of dissociation during EMDR | Major |
| Fear of death | Major |
| Duration of traumatic situation(s) | Major |
| Retraumatization by the judicial system | Major |
| Negative experience from social and family systems | Major |
| Closeness of relationship to perpetrator | Major |
| Acute versus chronic | Minor |

tionship between trauma characteristics and treatment outcome stands out in comparatively bold relief when EMDR is applied.

## PRESENTING EMDR TO PARENTS

Educating the parents has become easier over the past few years, as more and more parents have heard about EMDR and ask for it specifically. In areas where EMDR is less well known, the clinician can provide more detailed information through explanations and readings. For example, Shapiro and Forrest (1997) provide two good case examples of working with children, and EMDRIA provides a pamphlet entitled "What is EMDR?" which provides information in a useful format.

I generally explain EMDR to parents as a therapy for trauma and for "emotional stuck points" (ESPs). As this follows the diagnostic ecology part of the initial session, both the parents and myself generally have a good idea of what issues will be the targets of EMDR. The traumas are usually clear-cut, but not always. Sometimes the parents are aware of traumas, but the child is not, as they have occurred so early in life that they are not remembered, or the child has repressed or suppressed them. For example, Jackie, who was mentioned earlier, was severely sexually abused at age 18 months. Four and one-half years later, at age 6, she apparently had no recall of the abuse, which had occurred over several months and was so severe that she required medical attention for vaginal and rectal tearing. However, despite the apparent lack of memory, she manifested the behaviors of a traumatized child. Jackie didn't laugh, play, or smile much; she was overly docile and would go willingly with any adult; she dissociated with pain (for example, at the doctor's office); she was not appropriately assertive and would allow another child to take a toy away from her without protest. It was these behaviors that caused Jackie's mother to seek treatment for her.

On other occasions the parents know something is wrong but are not aware of any traumatization. An example here is a 14-year-old boy who had an attachment disorder, despite having nurturing parents. He had been very sick and hyperactive in infancy and it was thought this perhaps was why he had not attached to his parents or other people. It turned out that he had been traumatized at age 3 or 4 when he had been left at a day care center while his family went on an excursion. At the day care center he felt alone and abandoned and feared his family wouldn't return. In EMDR, he remembered that he had chosen not to go with his family, which may have heightened his fear that he would be abandoned. Following that session, he began attaching more to his parents, as evidenced through eye contact, hugs, kisses, compliance, and appreciation. Accurate diagnosis prior to treatment in a case like this is almost impossible. In fact, this case is a good example of how PTSD can be underdiagnosed in children, because the event was not life-threatening.

What is more typical, however, is the situation where the trauma is fully recognized by all parties. A case in point here is that of a 6-year-old boy who was in our children's study. His uncle had committed suicide in the living room of the boy's house. Later, the boy's father threatened suicide. The boy began soiling himself at school and dissociating to such an extent that he would remain seated, staring straight ahead when the class was dismissed for recess. Of course, his schoolwork was suffering as well. Nightmares were also a problem. These symptoms were alleviated within the five sessions provided in our study.

Emotional stuck points (ESPs) tend to be less clear-cut than specific traumas. For example, a child doing poorly in school and experiencing poor self-esteem might be seen as needing tutoring, group therapy, karate lessons, or the chance to develop a set of special skills (music, art, computers, sports) that would help him feel good about himself—but not necessarily EMDR. Of course, developing skills like these would be excellent and valid approaches. However, when EMDR is used with self-esteem targets, it can be determined within a few sessions whether it will be helpful. Other ESPs might be depression, anxiety, anger, noncooperation, or unethical behavior, such as lying and stealing. Self-esteem targets can be especially useful with children diagnosed as ADHD, as they are frequently and repetitively traumatized by the school systems, their peers, and their families.

## Explaining the Process of EMDR

After I explain that EMDR can be used to help with traumas and ESPs, I generally indicate that EMDR involves having the child think about the upsetting event(s), after which I have him move his eyes rapidly back and forth for about 15–30 seconds. I explain that other forms of alternate left-right stimulation (such as hand taps or drumming) might be used if the child cannot accomplish the eye movements. I go on to explain that after a few seconds of eye movements (or other left-right stimulation), I would stop, instruct the child to blank out his mind or let everything fade and then take a deep breath. Then I would ask the child what comes up next in his mind. I'd say that typically something shifts, and the child reports a new image, thought, feeling, or physical sensation. I'd then ask the child to hold that in mind and engage in another set of eye movements, hand taps, sounds, or combinations of these (as when the child is engaged in drumming). This procedure continues until the event no longer seems upsetting to the child.

At this point parents often ask, "Why does a weird-sounding procedure like that do anything at all, let alone anything positive?" I then explain that we have only educated guesses at this point, but it might have something to do with alternate left-right stimulation of the brain, or with REM sleep, going into only as much information about EMDR as the parents can stand or understand. I discuss how the procedure also involves setting up a safe place, which can be used by the child during EMDR at home, or that the parents can help the child use between sessions.

## Explaining EMDR with Examples

At this point, if I am aware of some case examples that are similar to the child's issues, I can discuss them with the parents, reminding them that each child is different, and that these are only general parameters of what can be expected. If the child's problems or problem situations are different from what I have encountered previously, that too can be discussed, with the EMDR being undertaken as a short trial. The benefit of EMDR in those cases, is that one can tell within a session or two whether it will be effective or not. If it is not effective, the EMDR can be discontinued and other approaches implemented. Most parents find it reassuring that many sessions will not be used fruitlessly on an intervention that does not produce results.

## Explaining EMDR with Research Information

Since EMDR is a relatively new therapy (within the last 10 years), some parents want to know what the status of research is with EMDR. This means staying current with the research literature—which, fortunately, is not difficult, as EMDRIA provides this information through its newsletter. There are also Internet Web sites that provide a wealth of current information about EMDR, with respect to research and practice. However, questions about research are infrequently asked. How often is the average clinician asked for research validation on the other methods he uses? But, there are increasing demands to justify clinical effectiveness. EMDR has come along at the right time to assist in the response to those demands: It is highly researchable, which, along with its effectiveness, has a lot to do with how much research has been conducted within the last few years.

## Using Informed Consent Forms

Clinicians often ask whether it is necessary to use informed consent forms for EMDR. Clients need to be well informed about psychotherapy in general and the training, qualifications, and payment policies of their therapist. Much of this information can be presented in written form to the client, and many states require evidence of written informed consent on these issues. Once such information is provided, is it useful or necessary to provide another written form about EMDR for children? Part of the answer depends on how safe EMDR is for children. If EMDR is likely to retraumatize children, and is riskier than other forms of therapy for children, then there might be a greater need to inform parents that there is a risk of retraumatizing their child. If, on the other hand, EMDR is no more risky, or is less risky than, say, talking to a child, engaging in play therapy, drawing pictures, or playing a game, then there is less need for a separate written form explaining the dangers. In my experience, there is very little risk in using EMDR with children when the child is approached with clinical sensitivity and the protocol is followed to the fullest extent. A very interesting finding from the Kauai study is that no children were harmed and most reported that they enjoyed the process (Chemtob & Nakashima, 1996). This result is similar to what we found in our follow-up study with adults: No one was reliably worsened. With children, in almost all cases, the worst that happens is that EMDR does not provide a benefit. Preliminary results from our study with children confirm this impression. Further, "no benefit" happens less with EMDR than with any other form of therapy I have used with children.

Although I have never seen childhood symptoms worsen due to EMDR, I have experienced a few children not wanting to continue. When that happens, EMDR is discontinued until the child is once again ready. That can take as long as six months, but usually it takes less time than that.

In general then, I inform the parents that the least positive outcomes are related to nonimprovement and incomplete sessions. Rather than asking the parents to sign a detailed informed consent form, I prefer to have an open discussion about the pros and cons of using EMDR with children, and then to document that in a detailed form in the chart. This procedure avoids the "nocebo" (opposite of placebo) effects of a detailed informed consent form. The more detailed such a form, the more off-putting and anxiety-arousing it can be for parents, stifling discussion and usage rather than promoting it. A detailed note in the chart provides as much legal protection (according to most attorneys), and avoids the negative effects of a consent form.

It is also pertinent to note that the American Psychological Association has placed EMDR on its list of "probably efficacious" psychotherapies. As other "efficacious" and "probably efficacious" therapies do not require separate disclosure forms, such a form for EMDR would seem unnecessary.

## Parents as Collaborators in Treatment

Another important aspect of treatment has to do with informing the parents about what you have worked on and what you are going to work on with EMDR, so they can watch for and document changes. With children, EMDR often works so rapidly that at times the clinician may think that nothing has happened or that the child has merely gone from negative thoughts and feelings to positive ones in such a short period of time, without overt emotion, that the change is not likely to affect behavior outside of the session. I once consulted with a clinic where the staff had been trained in EMDR but had stopped using it with children because they thought they weren't getting positive results. When I described the rapidity of change in EMDR with children and the lack of emotional pyrotechnics within the child's session, and discussed the importance of involving the parents as observers, the therapists began using EMDR with children again, this time with good results recognized and acknowledged by staff, parents, and children.

In helping parents become good consultants (observers) to the therapy process, I encourage them to be specific, behavioral, and numerical in their descriptions of their child's behavior. I emphasize direct observation of behavior; for example they might record that their child wet the bed two times in the past week, and there was a smaller wet spot the second time. Or the mother might note that her son argued with her only two times each day, as opposed to eight times per day prior to therapy. Nightmares can be recorded in their frequency; the time it takes to fall asleep can also be documented. The therapist should be as detailed as necessary in collecting information from the parents. The important point is that with EMDR and children, changes are not always apparent within the session, or they may seem trivial or inconsequential, so that careful documentation of change between sessions is important.

## TWO CASE EXAMPLES

Two cases will help to illustrate more directly the process of getting started with EMDR, with the first case being an example of a simple trauma, and the second case illustrating a more complicated presentation.

### Simple, Acute Trauma

Julie, who was 5 years old, was referred by a psychiatrist who was seeing her parents for marital issues. He referred Julie specifically for trauma treatment. Julie's parents had been involved in three automobile accidents in the last year and a half; Julie, in two of them. After the second accident, Julie "freaked out" according to her mother, and was screaming and crying hysterically. The referring psychiatrist indicated that after the second accident Julie began having nightmares about people trying to kill her (which makes some sense, considering the two accidents). She developed a fear of riding in cars, including the family's large station wagon. She became very frightened when separated from her parents, whereas prior to the accidents she had had no such fears. Just prior to referral, she became quite fearful when she lost sight of her mother while grocery shopping. The psychiatrist noted that prior to the second accident, Julie seemed to be handling the marital discord for which her parents were seeking treatment reasonably well.

In the initial interview, Julie's parents provided more information about the accidents and the changes in Julie's behavior. They indicated that they themselves were having trouble with symptoms from the three accidents, for which they were in treatment, as well as being in treatment for marital problems, which in part were related to the accidents.

In describing Julie's nightmares, they reported that she would sometimes have more than one per night, and that she had nightmares at least four times per week. This had been continuing throughout the two and a half months since the last accident. Another change Julie's parents noticed was that "she talks to others any way she feels," implying that she had become less considerate of others' feelings. She saw the movie "Twister" and became afraid that a tornado would kill her. She would remark that other people were trying to kill her, even saying that her 3-year-old brother was trying to kill her. Because of the nightmares, she tried to avoid going to sleep at night. She also became afraid of being killed by lightning, afraid that other children didn't want to play with her, afraid that her mommy would die, and generally seemed on edge about everything.

In the first session with Julie, we set up a safe place, which was her room, in her bed. She described her room as having a lot of books, a lot of stuffed animals, and a picture of Pocahontas. Although only 5, Julie was able to use eye movements in EMDR, and the safe place was installed using one set of eye movements. Following that, we targeted the most upsetting accident, and the first thing that Julie said in EMDR was, "I thought my mommy was going to die." Within the space of a few sets of eye movements, Julie went from being sad and fearful to saying, "Everything's going to be fine" and "It's all right."

As this all transpired within 15 minutes, it would be hard to think that a lot had changed, but in the next session, the following week, Julie's mom indicated that Julie had been less whiny and had been doing better. Although we had not worked on nightmares, she had had only one since the last appointment. In this second session then, we worked on nightmares. Julie drew two pictures of nightmares, which we used as starting images (targets) in EMDR. One was of a nightmare where "thunder broke the sun," with the sun cracking as she and her brother look on; and the other was of a tornado coming to kill her. In this session, we also used EMDR on the second accident.

Following that session, Julie had two or three more nightmares, which disappointed me, but it indicated that there was more work to be done. Julie's mom indicated that a lot of anger was coming out so we targeted that as well as the nightmares we had worked on in the previous session.

After that session, Julie had no further nightmares during the next month, and seemed to be back to normal behavior again. Julie's mom stated that Julie was no longer whiny, had no nightmares, was no longer afraid of tornadoes, and was no longer afraid to let her mom out of sight when they went shopping. More importantly, she said that Julie seemed "happy with herself again" and was more "like a kid again." Overall, she reported that Julie was playful, cheerful, and no longer unduly apprehensive, even when riding in a car. In the final session, we focused on other things that were scary to her (sharks, some TV shows).

Since then, Julie has been doing well. Of particular note is the improvement in the relationship between her and her mother. While this relationship had been good prior to the accidents, it was fraught with tension and difficulty, although through no fault of mother and daughter, as they both were struggling with behavior and emotions that were difficult to understand and control. One cannot help but wonder what their relationship would have been like, had Julie continued to have nightmares, be angry, whiny, and unduly apprehensive; parents, even very good parents, can become highly frustrated with such behaviors, especially when they are attempting to deal with other serious problems with limited resources. The long-term legacy of a conflicted mother-daughter relationship can be profound on both parties. Alleviation of the conflicted interpersonal aspects of the traumas becomes an important aspect of trauma resolution, but one that is hard to document or measure. But it is what is most appreciated by parents.

## No Identifiable Trauma

The second case is more complex, because there is no identifiable trauma and there are a number of different possible sources for the problems being manifested. It is similar to many cases of children referred for outpatient therapy, where the presenting problem is behavioral, but the cause of the problem is unclear.

Buddy was 7 years old and in the second grade when he was referred for aggressive and harmful behavior at school. The school had requested that Buddy's mother and stepfather obtain a psychological evaluation in order to determine the cause of the problems and a course of action for remediation. In the initial session, Buddy was accompanied by his mother and stepfather, who provided information about the presenting problems, background information, and developmental history. They described Buddy as being good at drawing, loving and caring with friends and family, but nervous and trying hard to stay out of fights at school. Other problem areas at school were Buddy's talking too much, having difficulty paying attention, and having difficulty completing homework. At home, anger was a problem. When asked to do things, Buddy would often whine and yell, stomp around, and slam doors.

In infancy, Buddy was an easy baby to take care of, after an unremarkable pregnancy and birth. Early on, he slept through the night. His parents separated when he was a year and a half old, but Buddy apparently did not react strongly to that, as his dad had not been around a lot. However, his mother described it as being a difficult time for her, as Buddy's dad did not pay child support. Developmental milestones were achieved at age-appropriate times, if not somewhat early. His mother said he talked so fast between ages 2 and 3 that he was hard to understand. She described him as getting "too wound up." However, this was during the postdivorce period, and Buddy may have been reacting to his mother's difficulties.

On Buddy's dad's side of the family, there was a younger brother (Buddy's uncle) who had learning disabilities and barely made it through school. Another younger brother, described as "spoiled" and "irresponsible," baby-sat Buddy at times, until problems there were recognized. On one occasion, he took Buddy with him on a motorcycle ride without a helmet, and was stopped by police; on another occasion he let Buddy shoot a gun with him. The sitting ended abruptly when Buddy was between 3 and 4 and the uncle was discovered dressing Buddy like a girl, and putting eye make-up on him. On a later occasion, when Buddy was constipated and his mother put some ointment on his rectum, he remarked to his mother, "Mom, that's just like what Uncle G used to put on me." Buddy was closely questioned about that, and watched carefully to see if his behavior seemed altered in any way, but nothing seemed changed. His mother felt there was not enough information to pursue filing a complaint of possible sexual abuse and she didn't want to alienate her ex-husband's family.

Buddy's stepfather had been in his life since about age 4, and the relationship appeared to be a good one, as did his relationship with his mother. Further, at this point, Buddy visited his dad and stepmother every other weekend, and those relationships seemed reasonably good also. Buddy did say that his dad yelled at him a lot. He also said that he wished that his parents hadn't gotten divorced and that they could get back together. However, these are commonly expressed opinions of a child of divorce at his age, and seem more like a validity check for honesty than an indicator of trauma.

Because Buddy was having trouble completing work in school, was inattentive, and having difficulty completing homework, I completed some psychoeducational testing with him, using the Kaufman Assessment Battery for Children. No clear deficits showed up in either sequential or simultaneous processing, with Buddy being average to above-average in both. However, he showed a significant weakness in understanding what he read, which caused his mother to enroll him in an after-school reading program. These results, coupled with his developmental history information, were supportive of a reading difficulty, but not ADHD.

Since Buddy was referred for aggression at school (he was getting into fights almost daily), and he often seemed angry and uncooperative at home, I decided to target the anger in EMDR to see what would happen. By this time, I had had eight sessions with him, collecting information, evaluating intelligence, processing style, and building a relationship. His mom had begun reading to him 15 minutes each night. At this point, it had been noted by his teacher that he sometimes became frustrated with reading and spelling, and would get into fights shortly after. Fights also occurred after other kids teased him. Further, his mother noted that Buddy wanted to be the best at sports, and would get angry if others didn't recognize him as such.

In targeting the anger, he chose an image of others blaming something on him when the school class was preparing for Easter. He stated, with the image in mind, "He pushed over someone's basket and their egg broke. He said I did it." Buddy said that his anger level was 10 on the 0–10 SUDS scale. After two sets of eye movements, he saw himself walking off, being annoyed. He then got an image of fourth- and fifth-graders pushing him out of the way. He felt the anger in his hands at this point, but reported feeling less mad. He stated, "I can avoid them." His SUDS was now at 0. His next association was, "When I make people laugh. I hit my face in the mud and everybody laughed." The next image was his being at home and doing bunny hops on his bike. After this five-minute EMDR session, Buddy set goals to get his schoolwork completed on time, and to walk away from confrontations with other students at school.

When he and his mom returned two weeks later, the first thing his mother said was, "What did you do, give him a brain transplant?" She noted that he seemed more at ease and was much easier to talk to. If she called him, he'd say, "I'm coming, I'm coming!" instead of pretending he didn't hear. Further, during the last two weeks at school, he did not get his name written on the board for fighting or being disruptive in class. In the second EMDR session, I again targeted the angry feelings and aggressive behavior. This time, after checking to see that the previous target remained desensitized, we started with an image related to another boy not letting him play football with him any more. He stated, "They say I tripped them. They don't want me on the other team." He felt "mad," but this time rated the anger at a SUDS of 4. After a single set of eye movements, Buddy said he felt better, but was still mad. After another set of eye movements, his anger was at a SUDS of 1. Then he got another image, "I wanted to trade cards with my friends. Mom said I couldn't." Mad and sad feelings started at 2 and quickly went down to 1.

After this session, Buddy continued doing well, but his behavior was not perfect. He did get into one fight after school, sticking up for a friend. On another occasion, he was asked to leave science class, but otherwise his name was infrequently written on the board for misbehavior. He was beginning to bring his papers home from school, began reading more, and would ask his mom to read to him at night. His mother also set up a longer-term behavioral program with him, that if he didn't watch TV for a month, he would earn $20. In EMDR, again after checking SUDS on the target from the prior session, we targeted his parents' divorce. He rapidly began getting positive images, suggesting that he did not have negative chains of thought related to the divorce, which had happened when he was 2. Then we targeted what things made him unhappy. He replied, "When I don't get to play football. When everybody is playing with Jason (a classmate). When Jason doesn't let me." He reported a SUDS of 10, and felt the emotion of unhappiness everywhere in his body. After a set of eye movements, he indicated that the image had become "faded, blurry," and after another set he reported, "It's gone." We then focused on an image of another boy tackling him by the street, with a feeling of anger coming up. SUDS started at 10, which he felt in his hands. An image came up of his getting into trouble and being sent to his room. This time the feeling was of sadness, reported at 10. Repeated sets of eye movements (about four) brought the feeling down to 1, after which Buddy reported feeling happy.

In the next session, Buddy came in with both sets of parents. His birthfather reported that Buddy's behavior had improved at his home as well. He noted that Buddy was much more cooperative. Since the last session, there had been no fights. His mother observed that he was noticing the connection between what other kids do and their discipline in school. Because of behavioral changes, he was well on his way to earning $20 for not watching TV. On his report card his teacher complimented him on his improved behavior. She wrote, "Buddy has been working hard on his self-control, with success. I am proud of you!"

At this point Buddy had had twelve sessions, total; three of them, EMDR. His behavior had dramatically improved. Although EMDR seemed central in his improvement, other methods of assistance were employed: His mother read to him on a nightly basis, he was enrolled in a reading program after school, he made commitments to change his behavior, he set up a behavioral program with his mother to abstain from watching TV. However, the major changes seemed to come from increased self-control, lessened anger, and increased cooperation, which were directly related to the EMDR targets. His parents were delighted and Buddy himself was proud. I was astonished. I was used to employing family therapy, individual therapy, and behavioral methods to achieve changes, but the process usually took longer. For example, we might have had several family therapy sessions where we would have talked about Buddy's anger and what it was related to. We might have discussed the divorce and what it related to, what

Buddy's reaction to it was at the time, and what he thought about it now. I might have gone to Buddy's school, talked with his teacher, observed Buddy in class, and made suggestions for setting up behavioral programs after I had gained some insight into what the antecedents were for Buddy's aggressive behavior. I might also have helped the parents set up star charts at home to encourage increased cooperation, increased compliance around chores, and decreased angry outbursts. At the same time, in individual therapy, I would be encouraging Buddy to express his feelings, to talk about the things that upset him at home and school. But it seemed something about the EMDR had made all that less important; that something had diminished Buddy's anger, and the other changes had occurred rather effortlessly. I was intrigued that, with his anger diminished, Buddy was now willing, even eager, to make further changes. This is what a therapist would hope for, that an angry child would reduce his anger and then make other changes, but usually it is a long, slow process. Since I could identify no specific trauma, I began to think that perhaps EMDR could be used with intense feelings, even if a specific trauma had not apparently caused such feelings. Of course, it was possible a trauma was involved, but just not identified. Buddy's background could possibly be seen in that light, with the divorce of his parents and the questionable behavior of his uncle. However, we had not targeted any trauma. Could it be that EMDR might be effective against traumas that are not targeted or not known? To me, it makes some sense that if intense feelings are "stuck" and remaining unresolved, it wouldn't matter whether the intense feelings had a specific or singular cause from a trauma, or whether they had come from other, possibly multiple, sources that were not necessarily individually traumatic.

Another pertinent question is whether the changes would last. In this case, the answer is yes, they did—but only for a year. Buddy's mom contacted me about a year later; Buddy was having difficulties similar to the ones for which they had originally sought treatment. Buddy was now 8, and in the third grade. In the initial interview, with Buddy and his mom, she indicated that he had been backsliding in the past month. In class, he had lost his focus. He'd wander, talk a lot, not stay on task. The same thing was happening at home. He had become less cooperative, more defiant. His mom ended up nagging him more. Socially, he was getting in more arguments with his friends. He was reported harassing another boy on the way home. Overall, he seemed to have a loss of control. In playing computer games, he would get furious and his face would become beet-red. Prior to the last month, if he became frustrated with a computer game, he'd simply turn it off. There was now more conflict between Buddy and his mom, with Buddy saying that she yelled at him a lot. This time, Buddy was avoiding physical aggression with peers; his problematic behavior was more restricted to verbal aggression. His mother noted that Buddy seemed to be upset about fre-

quent arguing between his dad and stepmother on the weekends when he visited there. On the positive side, Buddy was now reading above grade level. He
was reading more fluently, and he would read every day. He was also doing well
in math and was at grade level there. Also on the positive side, his parents had
brought him back in for treatment as soon as the problems had been identified.

The crucial event that had precipitated a referral back to therapy was that
Buddy became angry about being excluded from a group of peers on the playground, stood up on a piece of equipment, and pulled down his pants. For that,
he received a half-day suspension in the office at school (and a referral back to
me).

This time we had a series of four sessions, using EMDR in each of them. In
the first session we targeted the kids who bothered him on the playground. At
age 8, Buddy now was able to come up with negative and positive cognitions,
which he hadn't been able to do when he was 7. His negative cognition was that
he was "unwanted" and his positive cognition was that "people like me." His feelings were "sad" at a SUDS of 10. Within the space of five minutes, he was down
to a SUDS of 0 and a VOC of 7, and we were able to then focus on the playground incident in which he had pulled down his pants. That fully resolved in
the next session. Within the next three sessions, Buddy again reduced his anger,
and became more cooperative at home and at school. We again terminated, as
there were no more issues that could be uncovered, and his behavior again was
positive and stable. Precipitating causes for his behavior were still unclear.

Now, three years later, Buddy is back in therapy again. This time it's not for
fighting, but because his grades had declined to mostly Fs. When he decides to
do his work, he does remarkably well, according to his mother. He now indicates that the worst things that have happened to him are that his parents got
divorced (when he was 2) and that his mother and stepfather moved to another town (three years ago). These issues will be targeted in future sessions.

What can we learn from this rather complicated and unusual case? From an
EMDR standpoint, it is complicated because there is no clear trauma, but,
rather, recurrent behavioral problems that rapidly resolved with EMDR. It is
unusual because, in my experience, problems tend not to recur in EMDR.
Perhaps Buddy's problems recurred because EMDR is being applied outside the
area of a specific trauma. Perhaps what I regarded as thorough interviewing with
Buddy and his parents was not thorough enough. Did I miss something about
Buddy and his emotions that was crucial? Perhaps I stopped therapy too soon
in each instance. Would it have been better to have kept him in therapy for a
longer period of time? But, that could have been difficult, as therapy is mainly
for people who want to make changes, or who have been identified as needing
to make changes. Many therapists have had the experience of scheduling additional appointments after the problems have been resolved, only to find that the

sessions seem to go nowhere. Most therapists then terminate at that point, encouraging the client to come back if problems re-emerge. That is what I did, trusting that Buddy's parents would bring him back if there were more difficulties. In fact, they were so delighted and grateful with Buddy's positive changes, that I was relatively confident that would happen.

Perhaps there should have been a focus on family therapy, or even multi-family therapy with Buddy and both sets of parents. That is a hard sell, as money, schedules, and the motivations of many people become involved. Since Buddy's behavior had improved, it would have been hard to convince family members (especially the father who at one time refused to pay child support) to have additional sessions, on the hope that it would prevent a future relapse. Actually, in the last group of sessions, the family was making a heroic effort, driving 300 miles round trip to bring Buddy to therapy, as they had moved to a distant town.

Perhaps, initially, Buddy had been too young to articulate what was wrong, and his parents didn't know him well enough to discern what was wrong. He may have been uncommunicative. He may have inherited a difficult temperament or learning difficulties, which would contribute in a general fashion. As Buddy matures, he is more able to articulate what is really upsetting to him. For example, originally it seemed that the divorce of his parents was not a major problem. Most recently he stated that the divorce and his move to another town were the worst things that had happened to him. Earlier probes about the divorce in EMDR didn't go anywhere. It may be that the divorce has bothered him more as he has gotten older or that the move to another town has made it more difficult to visit his father. He is also upset by arguments between his father and his stepmother, and by his father yelling at him "too much."

Another possibility is that as he matures, he revisits the conflicts in a new fashion, much as a traumatized child works out his trauma repetitively, at different developmental stages. In his last session, Buddy had what I consider a breakthrough. In EMDR, when we targeted the effects of the divorce, he said that it was his fault. I was surprised by this, as I had done considerable probing for that kind of thinking when he was much younger and had found nothing. When that belief became adaptively processed in EMDR, and Buddy could emotionally accept that the divorce was not his fault, I asked him how long he had believed that. He replied that it had been about two years, since he attended a divorce class in school where he was told the divorce was not his fault. That statement got him thinking that maybe it had been his fault. He imagined a scenario where he had been a whiny baby, requiring a lot of attention from his mother, which his dad resented. His parents fought, got divorced, and it was his fault. The result of this thinking was anger toward his parents, as well as a sense that he was a bad kid.

Over the past two years then, he was not able to tell his parents about his anger and self-blame, but his grades declined in school, he was not motivated to pay attention, and he became sullen and minimally cooperative at home. He experienced immense relief in the EMDR session when he let go of those ideas. His mother was brought into the session, and told him what an easy, happy baby he was, and even if he hadn't been, the divorce would not have been his fault, that her difficulties with his dad had begun before Buddy was born and even preexisted the marriage.

Through EMDR, Buddy had improved his behavior several times, most recently bringing his grades up dramatically and becoming more cooperative at home. Would the situation have been much worse without the intervention of EMDR? There is no way to know for sure, but if Buddy's relationships had been unceasingly difficult from ages 7 to 12, how would his parents have viewed him? Would they see him as angry for no reason, uncooperative, not smart, not motivated, needing medication, perhaps incorrigible? Such are the attributions on which identities are formed.

What we have learned from this case is that EMDR can be relatively successful with cases where there are behavioral problems related to emotions (primarily anger), without clear traumas. The word "relatively" is used because, although EMDR was rapidly effective, it did not prevent Buddy from having additional related problems later on. Later, I will discuss a child with behavioral problems related to extreme anger, with no clear trauma, where EMDR produced more enduring changes.

These two very different cases illustrate the broad range of applicability of EMDR with children. While EMDR seems to be most effective with children who have been traumatized, it can also be effective when no traumas are readily apparent, and the focus is on ESPs (as in Buddy's case). A conceptual framework was presented that suggests when traumas are clearly involved, the nature of the traumas has a significant impact on EMDR treatment duration and outcome (as in Julie's case).

In the next chapter we'll look at conducting the first session with the child, including such topics as setting up the safe place and handling dissociation—both crucial in using EMDR with children.

*three*

# The First Session with the Child

"I'm in my safe place."

—SEAN, AGE 11

## PARENT-CHILD INTERACTION

After meeting with the parents, it is often useful to start the first session with the child by having the child and the parents together in the office. This gives the child a sense of security when he or she meets the therapist, and allows the child to take cues from the parent(s). It also allows the therapist to observe the behavior of the child with his parents, which is especially important if there are conflicts in the family or abuse is occurring. The same kinds of observations can be made with respect to the parents' behaviors. The therapist can get a conception of how the child views the problem situation. Referring to a "problem situation" allows the child to externalize the problem, as, for example, a problem situation at school, at day care, or with a mean brother. Sometimes, prior to EMDR, the child reports, "My teacher hates me." After EMDR, the externalization allows the child to say, "My teacher is nicer to me now." (EMDR thus helps teachers improve their behavior even when they don't come in for therapy!) If the child is at a loss to explain why he is there, a parent can be called upon to assist in the discussion. Generally, from this discussion the therapist can obtain a good idea of the problem areas, the areas of strength and confidence, likes and dislikes of the child, and how the child understands the problem situation.

If parent-child interaction seems to be an issue (and even if it's not), a useful approach is to ask the parents and the child to discuss the problem areas with each other. Careful observation of the discussion can reveal patterns of hostility, blaming, frustration, escalation, and stalemates at certain points. It is important for the EMDR therapist to determine the nature of the home environment, especially the interactional environment. Does an angry child provoke the parents to disagree about discipline? Does the child recognize this? Do the parents form cross-generational alliances; for example, does the dad favor the daughter, and the mother the son? Does the fearful child elicit irritation from his dad and overprotection from his mom? Is the situation abusive? The possibilities for interactional difficulties are manifold, and they often come to light with observation, appropriate questioning from the therapist, and openness from the parent(s).

Interactional analyses are important in order to determine if the present environment is playing a role in the child's problems. Again, EMDR is most effective when there is a healthy family that can be supportive and helpful to the traumatized child. A child whose parents argue over, for example, whose fault the accident was, whether the child is really traumatized, or whether the child is being aggressive in school for no good reason after the accident, will possibly require additional interventions. The child's immediate improvement in EMDR could defuse the disagreement; however, if the child improves more slowly because, in addition to feeling guilty for the accident, he is fearful that his parents might divorce from their arguments over him (and thinks that it would then be his fault), other interventions, such as marital or family therapy, might be needed.

After the therapist has a good sense of the dynamics of the family interaction, he can decide how to proceed: deal with the family interaction before employing EMDR with the child, deal with it later—or not at all, or take a wait-and-see approach. Our discussion here will assume that the family dynamics are such that we can begin with EMDR. The major point is that in many cases EMDR is not a stand-alone treatment, but requires fitting into an overall treatment plan. There will always be one-, two- or three-session EMDR successes, but these most likely occur with acute-simple and chronic-simple traumas without many complicating factors (as mentioned in the previous chapter). With ongoing problems, multiple traumas, and complex situations, EMDR becomes part of an overarching treatment plan where it speeds up the therapy by being judiciously applied to traumas and emotional stuck points.

Table 3.1 indicates the child protocol that we'll be using in this chapter. It is also relevant when obtaining developmental and trauma histories, among other topics (which will be discussed in chapter 4).

## THERAPIST-CHILD RELATIONSHIP

Once the clinician has completed the initial assessments, he can then go about the process of establishing a relationship with the child, which is sometimes easy, sometimes difficult. Typically, the parents are banished from the office to languish in the waiting room, reading old copies of *People* magazine. Meanwhile, the ther-

## TABLE 3.1
### The EMDR Protocol Phases

PHASE 1. CLIENT HISTORY AND TREATMENT PLANNING

Obtain a developmental history

Obtain a trauma history

Assess the current family or psychological environment

Select targets to desensitize

Explain EMDR to parents or caregivers

PHASE 2: PREPARATION

Establish a therapeutic relationship with the child

Address the child's concerns

Establish safety procedures (safe place)

PHASE 3: ASSESSMENT

Obtain a target image

Obtain a negative cognition

Obtain a positive cognition

Obtain a validity of cognition rating (VOC)

Obtain emotions associated with the target image

Obtain a rating of emotional disturbance (SUDS)

Obtain the physical sensations associated with the emotions

Obtain the locations of the physical sensations

PHASE 4: DESENSITIZATION

Follow the child's chain of associations, using eye movements (or other forms of patterned, repetitive stimulation) until the SUDS is diminished to 0, 1, or 2.

PHASE 5: INSTALLATION

Pair the target memory with the positive cognition and do a set of eye movements. If the VOC is at 7, go on to phase 6. If the VOC is < 7, process further until the SUDS is at 0 and the VOC is up to 7.

PHASE 6: BODY SCAN

Ask the child to hold the installation elements in mind and scan her body for sensations.

Process positive or negative sensations.

Generally, children aged 9+ can complete a body scan. If the child is not able to understand the body scan, do sets of eye movements with the safe place until the child feels safe and relaxed.

PHASE 7: CLOSURE

Give closing comments to the child or the child and parents together.

PHASE 8: REEVALUATION

At the beginning of the next session, review progress and decide on the next course of action.

apist spends time with the child, initiating therapeutically-oriented activities that
are fun for the child. The therapist may talk with the child, play games, use
nondirective play therapy, sand tray activities, drawing, coloring, modeling with
clay, go for a walk, play catch, use puppets, role play, tell stories, make up
metaphors, have a snack, tell jokes, look at family albums (requested ahead of
time), or whatever else he has found to be therapeutically useful and interesting
to the child.

## THE SAFE PLACE

It is extremely important for a child to feel safe in the therapist's office; ensur-
ing safety in the therapeutic session is the central task of beginning therapy
(Herman, 1992). At some point in the process of establishing a setting that
feels safe to the child, the clinician can introduce EMDR by using the safe
place. With some children, the safe place can be introduced within the first five
minutes, but with others it may be months before it can be introduced. For
example, an infant who has been neglected or abused for two years, then
placed in a series of foster homes, and finally adopted, could be a child with
whom it takes months before employing the safe place. Such a child might not
feel safe anywhere and initially not be able to trust or feel safe in the therapeutic setting.

Introducing the safe place can be a simple as, "Let's try something. Can you
think of a special place where you feel safe and happy? Can you get a picture of
that in your mind? Describe what that picture looks like (and sounds, smells,
and feels like). When you picture that place in your mind, what does it make
you feel like right now? Where do you have those feelings in your body? Now
hold that picture in your mind, along with those feelings and where they are in
your body, and follow my fingers with your eyes (or tap my hands with yours)."
Or have the child draw a picture of the safe place, in addition to or instead of
just visualizing it. After going through one to four sets of eye movements (more
on that later), and the safe place has been installed, the clinician can say something like, "That is your safe place. We'll use it in three ways: First, if your feelings get too upsetting in the rest of what we do, give me a signal to stop
(demonstrate hand signal) and we'll stop and have you bring up your safe place;
second, we'll use it at the end of our meeting to make sure you feel good before
you leave; and third, you can use it on your own, in between our meetings if
something makes you feel bad."

For most children, one set of eye movements or hand taps will be enough to
"install" the safe place, but if the child is apprehensive, additional sets may be
necessary to help her feel more comfortable. By "installing" the safe place I mean
to have the child pair the sounds, smells, feelings, and memories of the safe

place with a set of eye movements or hand taps, which seems to enhance and strengthen the positive effects of the safe place.* Sometimes children obtain an immediate positive effect from the safe place, which lasts after the session, even if no other EMDR is attempted.

Once the safe place is installed, the clinician can initiate further EMDR when clinically relevant material comes up by asking, "Do you remember what we did with the safe place? Let's try that when you think about the accident. Can you get a picture of that in your mind?" Of course, once the safe place has been set up, the clinician can immediately proceed with the next EMDR protocol step, rather than waiting, if the child seems receptive, willing, and relaxed.

Sometimes receptive and willing is enough. I remember working with an overly anxious 11-year-old girl, who was unable to sleep much for four months after seeing a horror movie, due to anxiety and panic activated by the movie. She had previously seen a psychologist, who had attempted to help her with an array of cognitive-behavioral approaches, to no avail. He then referred her to me as he knew that I specialized in EMDR. During the entire EMDR session, she sat huddled in the corner of my couch, unable to relax due to the intensity of her anxiety. I thought that if she couldn't relax any more than that, there was no way that the session would be effective. However, after using EMDR, I was quite surprised when she slept four out of the next seven nights in her own bed without awakening. After the next EMDR session, she slept through all seven nights.

Clinically, I have found that the safe place is an extremely important part of the EMDR protocol for several reasons:

- It helps the child feel safe in the session prior to EMDR processing of what may be difficult events.
- It introduces the EMDR format to the child and helps the clinician see how the child responds to it; for example, the clinician can see if hand taps would work better than eye movements and if the child can identify and localize feelings in the body.
- It helps the clinician anticipate modifications in the EMDR procedure that might be necessary.
- It provides a safe training ground for the therapist to teach the elements of the EMDR procedure without upsetting the child.
- It helps the clinician identify how traumatized the child has been, which

---

*This raises an interesting theoretical question: Why do the eye movements alleviate emotional pain but solidify the emotional effects of the safe place? One possible explanation is that once barriers to emotional health are removed, there is a natural movement in that direction. Maslow (1968) postulated such a drive in his hierarchy of motives. Interestingly, he also postulated that safety and survival motives were the most basic and had to be satisfied first or they would remain dominant.

can become evident if the child can't identify a safe place—then the intermediate therapeutic goal becomes to establish a safe place, real or imaginary.

Perhaps most important of all, the safe place provides an escape from the EMDR procedure when it is emotionally overwhelming. The EMDR desensitization phase can be stopped and the child can retreat to the security of the safe place and engage in sets of eye movements or hand taps until she is in enough control to return to the target image. The safe place can be considered a form of controlled dissociation that is consciously regulated and helps give a sense of mastery to the child. Even though the child has been to hold up her hand to indicate that she wants to stop to bring up her safe place, what happens most often (and this is reassuring), is that instead of the child holding up her hand, she simply says at the end of a set of eye movements, "I'm in my safe place." Thus, the safe place often comes up naturally, without conscious or deliberate forethought. It then becomes easy for the therapist to conduct sets of eye movements with the child, continuing to image the safe place until the child feels comfortable in returning to the target (starting) image.

Here is a clinical example that illustrates the use of safe place. Linda, age 10, was traumatized by the Oklahoma City bombing. Although she was not in the bombed building, and no member of her immediate family was hurt, her father worked downtown, close to the site. In addition, a close friend of the family was badly injured. A month after the bombing, Linda was still highly apprehensive. She had trouble sleeping and was unwilling to go upstairs or downstairs in her house without someone going with her. During EMDR, Linda held up her hand to go to her safe place when she visualized the friend who had sustained a severe neck laceration, nearly bleeding to death. Linda then needed a number of sets of eye movements in the safe place before she was ready to return to the original target. Following that, the EMDR session was successfully completed and Linda required no further sessions. She was less anxious after the session, more lighthearted, slept better, and was able to go upstairs and downstairs by herself.

## Dissociation

Managing dissociation is extremely important in EMDR. Therapists who use EMDR with children must learn to watch carefully for signs of dissociation and take steps to minimize it. If a child dissociates in EMDR, the way she did in the actual trauma, the effectiveness of the EMDR will be compromised.

Frank Putnam (1997), who has thoroughly explored the nature and development of dissociation in children, states, "Dissociation involves a failure to integrate or associate information and experience in a normally expectable fashion" (p. 7). In developing a "discrete behavioral states" theory of dissociation, he regards pathological dissociations as extreme examples of "discrete behavioral states of consciousness." That is, when a child is traumatized, the memory is stored in an encapsulated fashion as a discrete behavioral state of consciousness, making it inaccessible for normal mental processing.

> Trauma creates specific states that are very different from normal states along many state-defining variables, such as arousal, affect, and physiological milieu. Trauma interferes with associative pathways between states. Trauma also interferes with the acquisition of control over behavioral states, often leading the individual to seek external controls over mental state (e.g., alcohol and drugs). . . . Pathological dissociation . . . is defined as a category of trauma-induced discrete behavioral states that are widely separated from more normal states of consciousness in multidimensional state space. The degree of the separation is influenced by four processes: differences in physiological arousal and other state-defining variables; state dependency of the accessibility of specific information, particularly autobiographical information; architecture of the pathways connecting the states; and differences in the metacognitive integration of sense of self. (p. 179)

Using Putnam's definitions of dissociation and pathological dissociation, I would suggest that something in the EMDR treatment package causes the breakdown of the state-specific barriers, allowing dissociated material to be incorporated into more normal mental processing. Although Putnam's definitions are useful in postulating internal events (in the brain), in our discussion I will refer to its classical definition, as used by Janet, Freud, and others (Wekerle & Wolfe, 1996). That is, dissociation is perceived as a defense against overwhelming trauma or emotion, where the child alters her usual level of self-awareness to escape an overwhelming event or feeling. Here, dissociation is defined in terms of an action, rather than an internal state. Although I'll go into greater detail later on, here are a few ideas about recognizing and dealing with dissociation.

In some cases, dissociation is easy to recognize. For example, let's say a 9-year-old child is manifesting PTSD symptoms months after a severe automobile accident. In EMDR he shows intense affect during the time that the image is being obtained along with the negative and positive cognitions, the emotions, and the physical sensations. Then, when the eye movements are about to start, all the affect, which has been quite noticeable from behaviors such as tearing up, rapid breathing, squirming, and grimacing, suddenly disappears. The clinician can infer that dissociation has occurred, and suggest that the child bring up his safe place. Or, if during the eye movements, despite intense affect, the child begins to show signs of falling asleep, dissociation is likely occurring. This behavior must be a quite primitive defense; it is quite striking to observe. Here the child is thinking and talking about something that seems intense and over-whelming, and he seems to be dozing off! At this point, the clinician can suggest returning to the safe place, saying something like, "I can see that this is very upsetting to you. This is a good time to bring up your safe place," thus reinstructing the child in using the safe place, when he might have momentarily forgotten, due to the intensity of emotions coming up. The clinician can also suggest they return to the initial memory or engage in progressive relaxation procedures, such as deep breathing. He can also simply hold the child's hands (with his permission) to give him a tactile connection to the present situation.

## SELECTION OF TARGET

The selection of a starting target, or memory or image, is important with adults and can be even more important with children. For example, if an adult has been referred for emotional trauma related to an automobile accident, and the adult has not been multiply traumatized by prior events, chances are the accident will be targeted as a starting point. On the other hand, a child may be too traumatized to start with the accident and object to starting with that focus. For example, his nightmares or fear of riding in cars might be targeted instead.

Nightmares are especially good starting points, as the child is likely to experience immediate relief, both in the session and later that night, when no nightmares occur. Then the child can see a clear reason for using EMDR and is likely to be motivated to use it with other targets. It is interesting to speculate as to why nightmares are usually so quickly resolved with EMDR. It may be that both dreams and EMDR activate the right hemisphere; both seem to be associated with emotional processing and often-changing and metaphoric visual images. Or, EMDR, with its alternating left-right stimulation, activates the same neurophysiological structures in the brain as does REM sleep, which is associated with processing the events of the day and has recently been found to be related to new learning. It may be that alternating left-right stimulation simply stimulates the exchange of information between the two hemispheres. Or, patterned, repetitive stimulation may activate the brainstem. Or, the eye movements may boost the functioning of the right hemisphere, as Ramachandran (1995) suggested in his work with anosognosic patients. Perhaps the above hypotheses are not mutually exclusive, but rather overlapping explanations. At any rate, nightmares are excellent first targets for children.

If the child is apprehensive about focusing on a trauma or problem, it is sometimes a good idea to start with positive situations to enhance self-esteem and a sense of self-efficacy and build a sense of trust in the therapist and in the EMDR procedure. With adults in EMDR, the focus on these positive targets is referred to as "resource installation" but I prefer the less obscure terminology of self-efficacy targets, self-esteem targets, or positive targets. Using the terminology of self-esteem and self-efficacy ties in the practice of EMDR with the large bodies of psychotherapeutic literature on self-esteem and self-efficacy.

An example of using self-efficacy targets is the case of a 12-year-old boy, diagnosed with ADD, who was referred to me for treatment. He seemed so beaten down by repetitive failures that I used only positive targets and positive self-cognitions in the first session. Changes were so dramatic after the first session that we continued to target positive images for the next five sessions, with improvements being noted each week. When those improvements slowed down, we began targeting negative incidents, with good results; the boy was able to tolerate the negative focus at that point, which would have been difficult in the first session. If the child is so abused or neglected that no self-efficacy images can be evoked, then happy images (without a sense of personal accomplishment) might be elicited. If the child still cannot access positive incidents of any kind and does not seem ready to focus on problem areas, other approaches are warranted which go beyond the scope of this chapter (see chapter 8).

Sometimes the target that the therapist chooses is not relevant to the child and goes nowhere. The child may be too defended against the more salient target, but willing to work on something else. For example, Buddy, who pulled down his pants on the playground, was initially unwilling to target that event. Another child, age 7, following many deaths in his extended family, stated that the worst thing that ever happened to him was falling off the trampoline five times in a row, and his biggest worry was getting his homework completed. Yet this child developed symptoms of encopresis and enuresis after his father threatened suicide.

If the target goes nowhere, it is often useful to ask the child about the worst feelings he has and whether he would like to get rid of or lessen those feelings. The therapist can also ask about the things that trouble him the most or the worst things that have happened to him. As those things become resolved through EMDR, the child may become more receptive to the issues the therapist targets. Actually, this interplay is no different from other therapies with children, where issues dealt with are the result of interaction between the child and the therapist. Table 3.2 lists possible starting points for using EMDR.

Children who have been sexually abused are often understandably reluctant to target the abuse itself, or they may not remember it. A case in point is that of Jackie (referred to in the previous chapter), who was 6 years old when I first saw her. She had been severely sexually abused when she was 18 months old. She had no apparent memory of the abuse; she never talked about it, even when her mother encouraged her to do so. However, the abuse had been so severe that Jackie had required medical attention for vaginal and rectal tearing, and she now had a depressed immune response, for which she required blood testing

## TABLE 3.2
### *Possible Starting Targets for Children*

The traumatic event

Nightmares

Self-esteem targets (events where the child felt good about herself)

Self-efficacy targets (events where the child felt good about something she accomplished)

Happy events in the past

Exciting events in the past

Wearing favorite clothes

Something the child would like to do in the future

Something that would make the child happy in the future

A special birthday in the past

A special Christmas in the past

An ideal birthday celebration

An event that made the child feel sad

An event that made the child feel angry

An event that made the child feel scared

An event that made the child feel guilty

An event that made the child feel hated

An event that made the child feel worthless

The worst three things that ever happened to the child

The best three things that ever happened to the child

The worst feeling ever (and would you like to get rid of it?)

The best feeling ever

every six months. Her mother's description of Jackie's demeanor fit that of a victim. She was overly passive, dissociated with pain, and rarely smiled or played with other children. She was markedly nonassertive; if another child took the toy she was playing with, she would not protest. She would go willingly with any adult who took her hand. Since there was no sexual abuse target on which to focus, in EMDR we simply targeted things that made her happy. Gradually, her demeanor changed in the session.

Following the session, I talked separately with Jackie's mother, who reiterated her concern about how Jackie didn't laugh, play, or smile much. When we opened the door, Jackie was standing immediately outside the office, and said, laughing, "Ha, ha, I can see you through the keyhole!" Her mother was astonished. She called me a few days later, to tell me that when they left the office,

Jackie was so excited that she had to run up and down the block five times before she would get in the family van. During the week, she began playing with other children and laughed and smiled more. She played with the water in the bathtub for the first time in four years. Her mother said the change was amazing, "It's like you took a magic wand and said, 'Bing! You can live now!' It's like my daughter has been dead to me for four years and she's alive again." I do not know how or why the change occurred so dramatically with Jackie, but I do know that changes like this occur at times with EMDR with children. Such changes are a powerful incentive for the therapist to use EMDR with other children.

## OBTAINING THE COGNITIONS

Children between the ages of 9 and 12 years who are developmentally normal and have not been repetitively traumatized are able to give a negative cognition (NC), positive cognition (PC), validity of cognitions (VOC), subjective units of disturbance scale (SUDS), feelings, and the body location of the feelings. A child's NC and PC are likely to be considerably more concrete than an adult's. For example, while the adult might say, "I'm irresponsible," the child would say, "I'm stupid"; the adult says, "It's my fault," while the child says, "I'm bad"; or the adult might say, "I'm competent," while the child would be more apt to say, "I did good." Thus, standards about negative and positive cognitions can be relaxed a bit with children. If it becomes difficult to obtain an NC or a PC, rather than making it a lengthy or frustrating process it is better to go on and identify the emotions and physical sensations, at which most children are more adept.

However, at times it is possible to "back into" a negative cognition through a positive cognition. If the child can't identify an NC, the clinician can move on to ask what the child would like to think as he or she holds the traumatic image in mind. The child might say something like, "I'm strong" or "I am brave," from which an NC can readily be derived. Also, 9–12-year-olds can usually readily respond to the question about an NC of marginal quality, "What does that say about you as a person?" For example, if the child gives an NC of "I didn't do good on the test," the clinician can inquire, "What does that say about you as a person?" Most children would respond with something like, "I'm stupid" or "I'm a failure," which is a preferable NC, because it is negative, self-referencing, irrational, and generalizable. A negative cognition that is fully rational, such as, "I failed the test," cannot be expected to change, but if the NC is at least partly irrational, it is more likely to change in a positive direction during the EMDR process.

Another way to obtain an NC is to ask the child what she typically says to herself when she is really upset with something she did. The critical internal language can then be used to construct an NC for the targeted image. Eliciting this critical self-talk often brings an intensity of feeling and an openness to the session that wouldn't otherwise be there.

## OBTAINING THE FEELINGS

Children, even very young ones, 4 or 5 years old, can often identify feelings. When the therapist asks, "When you hold that picture in mind, along with the thought, 'It was all my fault,' what feelings does that bring up right now?" she is likely to get a good statement of feelings. She can then go on to obtain the SUDS. Sometimes, however, when the therapist asks for a feeling from the child, she gets a cognition instead. Or, conversely, when asking for a cognition, a feeling is reported. In these cases, it is best to accept the verbalization as given and inquire about the cognition or emotion associated with it. For example, the therapist might say, "That's great! And there's likely a feeling that goes with the thought 'I'm dumb.' What do you feel like when you think 'I'm dumb'?" It is also possible to suggest feelings to the child to help him get the idea, for example, "Is it sad or mad or frustrated or some other feeling that you get when you think that you're dumb?"

## OBTAINING THE SUDS

Most 9–12-years-olds can understand the 0–10 scale (0 = neutral, no disturbance; 10 = the most disturbance imaginable) used with adults to obtain the SUDS. Children younger than 9 may need some modification of either the scale or its presentation. For example, the SUDS could be presented as a happy face drawn on the left side of a sheet of paper, with a line extending to a sad, mad, or scared face on the right side, with the therapist asking the child to mark on the line where her feelings are before EMDR, at various times during EMDR, and then after EMDR. Also, the therapist can have the child draw a big circle on the paper to indicate a big (strong) feeling, and a small circle to indicate a less intense feeling. Another way for the child to indicate the size of the feeling is to hold his hands close together to indicate a little feeling; a foot or two apart to indicate a medium feeling; and arms extended wide apart to indicate a big feeling. The therapist can also use a laminated pictorial VOC/SUDS scale available from EMDR-HAP (for a $10.00 donation) where expressive faces indicate various intensities of feelings and emotional validities (How true does it feel?). The clinician could also design and laminate one from materials at hand.

## OBTAINING THE BODY LOCATION

Most children, even those 4–8 years old, can identify and locate bodily sensations. Younger children, in that same age range, are likely to identify parts of their bodies involved in actions. A 6-year-old boy who identifies the anger in his feet, for example, might verbalize that he wants to kick something. In most cases, the therapist can simply ask, "Where do you feel that in your body?" to get a useful answer from the child.

# DESENSITIZATION PHASE

In this phase of the EMDR protocol, there are major differences between children and adults, which are summarized in table 3.3. Because of the differences shown in table 3.3, the clinician who is experienced in using EMDR with adults may think nothing much has happened in the EMDR session with a child because of its brevity, circumscribed focus, and the child's relative lack of visible emotion. However, this would be a mistake, as the results of EMDR are better judged by the behavioral changes that the child manifests after the session. For example, if the clinician targets nightmares for five minutes of EMDR with a 6-year-old child, it would be reasonable for that clinician to assume that not enough work had been accomplished, even if the associative connections of the child had gone from negative to positive. However, often following such a session the nightmares will have ceased, surprising everybody involved.

## Theme Development

Because the associative connections of children are not as rich or complex as those of adults, theme development, where the therapist helps the child make additional mental connections, becomes important. For example, it is not uncommon for a child to report "nothing" on coming to the end of an associa-

### TABLE 3.3
### Child-Adult Differences in the Desensitization Phase of EMDR

| ADULTS | CHILDREN |
|---|---|
| Abreactions likely | Abreactions unlikely |
| Rich associative connections | Few associative connections |
| Long channels | Short channels |
| Long sets of eye movements | Short sets of eye movements |
| Long sessions (90–120 minutes) | Short sessions (5–20 minutes) |
| Many emotional facial cues | Few emotional facial cues |
| Abstract language and thinking | Concrete language and thinking |
| Frequent use of metaphor | Little use of metaphor |
| Spiritual understandings | Spiritual understandings rare |
| Awareness of change | Less awareness of change |

tive channel. An associative channel is a chain of associations on a single topic, which has gone from negative to positive in emotional content. The child appears to have come to the end of a channel when she no longer has any associations, of a positive or a negative nature. Typically, an adult who comes to the end of an associative channel goes on to another; if he does not, the therapist can often prime the pump by asking, "What does that remind you of?" and the adult will go on to another thought or experience. With a child, however, the prompt often needs to be more specific, with the therapist asking the child to "think of another time when you felt that scared." When that channel has been cleaned out (i.e., the associations have gone from negative to positive and there are no further associations), the therapist can again request that the child "think of another time you felt that scared," continuing in this fashion until the child has no further associations on that theme of feeling scared. Then, if time allows and the child's attention span permits, the therapist can go on to another theme, or end the EMDR part of the session.

Themes can be emotional ("Think about another time you felt that mad"), behavioral ("Think of another time when you got in that much trouble"), cognitive ("Think of another time that you thought you were that stupid"), physiological ("Think of another time when your stomach hurt that bad"), or event-related ("What's another part of the accident you remember?"). With a child, when the theme development is event-related, it becomes analogous to the protocol for a recent event with adults (Shapiro, 1995), when different elements of the trauma seem not to have generalized and the therapist needs to encourage the adult client to associate to each part of the event. Further, even with adults, theme development is required at times, but not as commonly as in children.

The purpose of theme development is to ensure adequate processing of the trauma. As children's behavioral cues are more subtle than adults', it is more difficult to determine within the session if adequate processing has been accomplished. Theme development helps to keep the process going in the direction of adaptive resolution, and increases the likelihood that the session will be complete. If the session is not complete, then one of three things may happen. First and most likely, the processing will continue after the child leaves, both on a conscious and an unconscious level, so that when the child returns, there will be less on which to work in the next session. Second, no further processing occurs, so that in the next session the work is merely resumed where the therapist and child left off. Third and least likely, but still a possibility, the child feels "opened up" much as an adult sometimes does after an incomplete session. Since it feels uncomfortable to the child to have such intense, unresolved negative emotions close the surface, the child will be reluctant to resume EMDR in the next session. The use of theme development helps to guard against this outcome, which then requires the therapist to backtrack and do other therapeutic work, prior to resuming EMDR. The younger the child is, the more this third possibility needs to be guarded against. For example, with 9–12-year-old children, such unwillingness to continue rarely occurs; with 5–8-year-olds, it happens occasionally; but with 2–4-year-olds, great care must be taken not to overwhelm the child with intense emotions. It becomes a delicate therapeutic task to continue EMDR long enough to allow for relatively complete processing, but not to continue past the child's tolerance for attending to and dealing with upsetting events.

## INSTALLATION, BODY SCAN, AND CLOSURE

Installation (the pairing of the positive cognition with the target memory after the SUDS has been reduced to 0–2) with children aged 9–12 is much the same as with adults, as most of these children can form a positive cognition and then hold it in mind along with the target memory. Children aged 5–8 often are not able to understand and form positive and negative cognitions, so an installation is possible only with additional assistance, if at all. The therapist might help the child form a very basic positive cognition, such as "good boy" or "good girl" and then think about the original event, holding the positive cognition in mind. However, I'm reminded of one 5-year-old child who responded when asked to hold both in mind, "How can I? I only have one mind!" Thus, developmental level and cognitive development need to be taken into account. Even so, what children can do is often surprising, and it is generally best to encourage as much of the protocol as possible, deleting parts only when necessary. The more completely the protocol elements are brought into play, the more likely EMDR will be effective.

I also adhere to a principle of "minimal creativity." That means I adhere to the full protocol, changing it only if I have to, in order to meet the developmental needs of the child. It also means that during the desensitization part of the protocol, I follow the process as long as it is moving and changing, in order to allow the individual's associative chain to develop as fully as possible. Only when the process gets stuck do I intervene, and then as briefly as possible, to get the process moving again. Generally, it seems that if a child is capable of forming negative and positive cognitions, he will be able to complete an installation.

With 2–4-year-old children, negative and positive cognitions are not possible, so again no installation is possible without assistance from the therapist. If the child can be helped to form a very basic positive cognition, an installation can then be attempted. One reason an installation is important is that it makes use of the Premack Principle, which postulates that if an event with a negative emotional valence is paired with event with a stronger positive emotional valence, the negative event will come to be seen as more positive. For example, if a child hates to get up in the morning, but loves to ski more than she hates to get up, then on mornings when the family is going skiing, getting up will be perceived as less negative by the child. The important part is that the positive valence has to be stronger than the negative valence, or else the child will still hate to get up in the morning, and skiing will be viewed as less positive, instead of the other way around. Applying this to EMDR, only when the negative valence of the target memory has been significantly reduced (SUDS = 0–2), should an installation be attempted. Then the negative event can be experienced as more positive, as it is being associated with something with a strong positive valence (e.g., I am good, capable, strong, worthwhile, important, loved). If the installation is attempted without the SUDS being lowered sufficiently, then instead of the target memory moving in a positive direction, the positive cognition could move in a negative direction, and be seen as less believable.

The body scan, where the client holds the positive cognition and the original memory in mind while scanning the body for sensations, is too complex for most children, and perhaps less pertinent than for adults. It is possible that EMDR can be effective with children before their physiological responses to stress have become highly repetitive and ingrained. On the other hand, adults who were traumatized in childhood and never treated have had for most of their lives somatosensory representations of trauma encapsulated in their bodies and minds. Therefore, they respond over and over to reminders of trauma in the same physiological response patterns, and are likely to have a much greater need for the body scan. As van der Kolk (1994) put it, "the body keeps the score," even when the person is not consciously aware of disturbances. Thus, it makes more sense for adults than children to use a body scan, partly because it is often too complex for children and partly because their physiological responses are less entrenched than adults'.

For children, closure in a session is fairly easy to achieve by using the safe place or repetitions of the safe place. Closing comments for children aged 9–12 are similar to those for adults: "We have started something that will keep on going after you leave, both on a conscious and an unconscious level. It may affect your dreams, thoughts, ideas, pictures in your mind, feelings in your mind or body, or what you understand about yourself. Just notice what comes up for you. Write down or draw a picture of what seems important and bring that with you when you come in next time. If you don't write things down, take a mental snapshot of whatever seems important." With children aged 5–8, I'll make it simpler, something like, "We've started something that will keep on going in your mind after you leave. Just notice what it's like for you and we'll talk about that next time at the start." With children aged 2–4, I'll omit closing statements. With all children, I'll inform the parents about what to watch for in their children's behavior and emotions.

The next session begins with the reevaluation phase of the EMDR protocol, where I typically start with both the child and the parent(s) in the room. Here, I inquire about the situations and the behaviors that were targeted. If, for example, the child had been in a car accident and we had decided to target the postaccident nightmares, I would ask about those. I would also check on SUDS ratings when the child brings up the target memory. If it appeared that there was improvement behaviorally and the SUDS was low, I would help the child select another target memory. If not, we would continue in EMDR on the same image as before.

Now that we have examined the overall parameters of the typical EMDR protocol for children, in the next chapter we will begin to look at the specific modifications that can be made for children at different age and developmental levels. These modifications make EMDR a highly flexible approach for almost any child.

*four*

# Developmental Modifications of the EMDR Protocol for Children

"My lip hurt."
—DAVY, AGE 2 YEARS, 9 MONTHS

THE MODIFICATIONS NECESSARY to apply the EMDR protocol (see table 3.1) to children can be simplified into four major age groupings: 9–12, 6–8, 4–5, and 2–3 years old. Of course, these are only general guidelines, as there are, for example, developmentally delayed children aged 9–12 who will require modifications that would usually be appropriate for a younger child, and there are precocious 7-year-olds who can respond well to the protocol for 9–12-year-olds.

It may seem rather unusual to be talking about a psychotherapeutic approach that can be used with 2-year-old (and younger) children who have been psychologically traumatized, but on a clinical basis there are many therapists who have been able to obtain successful outcomes with such young traumatized children. The implications of having a psychotherapeutic approach that can be used, across cultures, with traumatized individuals from infancy through old age are far-reaching and have hardly begun to be explored. It appears that the EMDR procedure taps into aspects of brain functioning that are present early in life, and that develop in a number of ways throughout the life span. How EMDR taps into these capacities of the mind, arouses intense curiosity in many.

At this point, we don't know what the effective ingredients of the procedure are, but I am reminded of an analogy: A woman who was a gifted cook combined some ingredients in a unique fashion that produced a bread that was delicious and healthy. Although she could teach others how to follow the recipe, she herself was not sure what made her bread so superior. It even took less time to cook than other kinds of bread. Because such intense interest was aroused in her baking, others sought to discover just what it was which made the bread superior. One chef omitted the baking aspect of the recipe, and since the result was inferior, announced that it was the baking which was the crucial aspect of the procedure. Another chef left out the flour, and finding that the results were disastrous, deduced that it was not the baking that was important, but rather the flour. Yet another left out spices and seasonings and produced a bland, tasteless product, and others left out sugar, or yeast, or eggs, all obtaining unsavory outcomes. Each one concluded that he or she had discovered the essential ingredient. Unfortunately, however, many children grew up malnourished while the bakers were arguing over which ingredient was the most important.

Any analogy is false when taken to its limits, and any metaphor has utility only insofar as it stimulates us to think more clearly. What I wish to suggest with the preceding story is that it is more important to investigate the range of application of EMDR rather than to discover its essential ingredients—although both are important. This seems especially true, as research into which part is most effective (dismantling research) is likely to be time-consuming, difficult, and perhaps misleading, as I suggested in chapter 1. In the meantime, investigating the range of application of EMDR with children is likely to benefit many children who otherwise might not be assisted in recovering from traumas.

## THE PRINCIPLE OF MINIMAL CREATIVITY

Because the EMDR treatment package has great effectiveness without extensive modification for children, I encourage a principle of "minimal creativity" (briefly referred to in chapter 3). This means the clinician modifies the standard adult protocol only as much as she has to, in order to accommodate the developmental level of the child. It doesn't mean the therapist isn't creative—at times she will be highly creative in making modifications—but only that modifications are made one step at a time, and only as necessary to keep the process moving. This is similar to the principle in working with adults: The clinician always follows the client's processing unless the processing gets stuck. In this sense, EMDR is the ultimate person-centered therapy: Within the EMDR framework, the clinician always follows (the associative chains of) the client.

One overall goal of the EMDR protocol is to have as many sensory modes involved as possible (visual, cognitive, emotional, and kinesthetic) so that the processing proceeds more quickly. A second goal is to have the initial part of the procedure be as emotionally evocative as possible without overwhelming the child. Thus, the clinician increases his chance of success by following as much as possible of the full protocol.

# ASSOCIATIVE CHAINING

Having conducted many EMDR sessions with children and adults, I have found that associative chaining is frequently productive, even if unpredictable. That is, the client's chain of associations follows a course that in retrospect makes sense and leads to emotional resolution. At times the chaining surprises the therapist because he espouses a theory that suggests a different direction or because he has worked with a person who had a similar experience or issue, and the chain of associations resolved differently. Milton Erickson's adage to make a new theory for each new client fits very well here. Perhaps one reason EMDR works as well as it does is because the therapist is more constrained from intruding on the client's thought processes than in other therapies, allowing for a natural unfolding of mental processes that are linked in important ways. EMDR illustrates that healing and self-actualization (Maslow, 1968) can occur when the mental blockages from trauma are removed. Thus, an interesting question arises: If, as we see in EMDR, the mind goes where it needs to go, what do we call that directing force? Words like "spirit" or "soul" spring to mind, but those words are hard to fit into contemporary psychological theory. Perhaps our theories need broadening.

In many ways, EMDR raises more questions than it answers. An apparent aspect of that directing force is that in EMDR, adults often come to highly spiritual understandings of their lives, or events in their lives. While this seems less true of children, I have become much more aware of the depth, intensity, and complexity of children's feelings through EMDR. Children take the process seriously and often communicate more openly, less defensively, and more productively in EMDR than in other forms of communication or therapy. I often see agitated children settle down when we start EMDR. When I conduct trainings, a frequent question that comes up is, "What do you do with an uncooperative child?" You can start EMDR to capitalize on this quieting and attentional factor and see what happens.

As adults, we often tend to minimize or ignore the emotional lives of children. I find that EMDR helps me to be much more conscious of the emotional underpinnings of children's behavior, in a way that goes beyond what I was capable of before. This may be due to how children find it easier to cooperate in EMDR, or it may be due to the way emotions surface with children in EMDR, so that the emotional connections become more obvious to the therapist. While the emotions may not be as evident in children's faces, their verbalizations, attentional focus, and behavioral changes indicate to the therapist that core emotional issues are being accessed. Children do not need to be "interviewed" about feelings, as they are more likely to spontaneously verbalize their emotions. This "cooperation" makes it much easier for the therapist to understand how a child is responding to an upsetting event. For, example, when a child who was in a car accident says, "I thought my mommy was going to die" and the child did not verbalize that before EMDR, the therapist (and probably the child) has a much clearer sense of the emotional impact the accident.

# DEVELOPMENTAL MODIFICATIONS FOR CHILDREN AGED 9–12 YEARS

## The Safe Place

For most children aged 9–12, few modifications to the adult protocol are necessary. I must once again, however, stress the great importance of the safe place. The issues of safety, responsibility, choice, boundaries, and empowerment, which are important in EMDR with adults, are also important in EMDR with children. Use of the safe place helps the child feel safe, establish boundaries, feel empowered, and able to have some control in the EMDR procedure. I find that I cannot anticipate when a child will signal a desire to go to his safe place; rather, I am often surprised by a raised hand or a verbal request to bring up the safe place. Other times, I may be the one to suggest imaging the safe place, because I suspect that the child is feeling overwhelmed, or because I wish to demonstrate permission for the safe place to be used so that the child can be more likely to bring it up later on, if needed.

The safe place can also be more effective than the body scan in ending the session, as the latter is too complicated for most 9–12-year-old children.

## Recognizing and Dealing with Dissociation

If a child dissociates during EMDR, it will interfere with the effectiveness of the procedure. As mentioned in chapter 3, dissociation refers to the defensive act of gaining distance from emotions by shutting them out in some way. The child might shut out either the feelings connected to the original traumatic event or the feelings related to the entire present situation. When this happens, the therapist can intervene in a number of ways to minimize or eliminate the dissociation:

- Use verbal encouragers to help the child stay present, for example, "Stay here; stay present; stay with me."
- Use touch, for example, the therapist might (with permission) take one of the child's hands and hold on to it while using his free hand to conduct the eye movements.
- Use hand taps, which maintain the physical immediacy better than eye movements.

- Suggest a return to the safe place.
- Return to the target more frequently.
- Use shorter sets of eye movements, so that the child has shorter chains of association.
- Use imaginal techniques to minimize or eliminate dissociation, for example, "What might you put in that picture to help you feel safe (strong, bigger, smarter)?" Perhaps the child's favorite hero can intervene; the technique of envisioning the hero in the picture, with the child putting his hands on the hero's shoulders and then stepping into the hero's body can work very well.
- Make a distinct change in the environment, for example, have the child get up and walk around, ask the child's parent to come back into the room, put on some music, or turn the lights up or down.

## The Use of Target Imagery to Control the Session

Although the clinician follows the EMDR process as long as it does not get stuck, she has to exert some control over such things as when to start EMDR, when to stop, and how to manage the process. Managing the chains of association that are generated in EMDR is one aspect of this. Most children in this age group may be able to make a number of associative connections, such as remembering one part of a trauma, and then another part, and so on, or one traumatic incident, and then another, and yet another. The higher the number of associative connections that can be made, the more likely it is that the original incident will be completely desensitized and reprocessed. However, on some occasions, the chain of associations may lead further and further away from the original incident. The clinician can exert control over this process by going back to the original target when the associative chain seems to be getting off track or allowing it to branch out when there is time, the associations are relevant in some way, and the child is not becoming fatigued or overwhelmed. These are important clinical decisions in the EMDR process, and mistakes can be made in either direction (allowing too much branching or not allowing enough). For example, one clinician may think the child is straying too far afield from the original trauma and choose to divert him, but another clinician might choose to let the chain of associations develop to see where they go.

Sometimes these decisions are made on the basis of how much time remains in the session. The therapist can go back to the target memory more frequently toward the end of a session or less frequently at the beginning of the session. If, at the end of a session, a child brings up another earlier trauma, the therapist could say, "We'll come back to that memory next time," and use appropriate closure techniques. Sometimes decisions are made on the basis of the fatigue level or attention span of the child, with the therapist saying, "You seem pretty tired and you have done a lot of good work today. Let's deal with that the next time you come in."

I once made the mistake of overloading a 13-year-old preadolescent boy when he had completed the processing of an event where he had shot and killed his 8-year-old cousin. It was at the beginning of the second EMDR session when the processing of this event had been completed, and we had more than an hour left in the session. I then suggested that we go on to process three years of sexual abuse that this boy had suffered at the hands of his stepfather several years earlier. Although he verbally agreed to it, and the processing went in the right direction, afterward both he and I recognized that he had been overtaxed by focusing on the additional series of painful events. (See chapter 9 for a detailed case description.)

## Case Example

Eleven-year-old Sean had been referred for problems with encopresis and anger. When Sean was 8, a group of older boys restrained him under a picnic table and raped him. Since that time, Sean would, on a daily basis, insert his fingers up his rectum, causing him to soil his underpants. At times, he would do this in a hypnogogic state as he was falling asleep, and not be fully conscious of what he was doing. In his initial EMDR session, which lasted only about 10 minutes, we set up a safe place and then targeted the memory of the sexual abuse (see chapter 10 for a transcript of the session). Sean's image was of being under a picnic table with a blanket over him, with the other boys being on top of him, "sticking their penis in my butt." His negative cognition was that he was "weird" and his positive cognition was that he was "normal" (VOC = 1). He felt afraid, with the SUDS being at 10. Within a few sets of eye movements, the VOC ("I'm normal") had risen to 7 and the SUDS (fear) had dropped to 0, with Sean reporting that he felt relaxed. However, not much time had elapsed, and Sean still remained impassive, not smiling, and not showing much outward change.

During the short session, Sean went to the safe place spontaneously, without raising his hand or requesting to go there. What happened instead is that when we completed a set of eye movements, and I asked Sean what he was getting, he stated, "I'm in my safe place." He completed a set of eye movements in his safe place and then returned to the target memory. Despite the brevity of the session and the lack of apparent emotional changes, Sean soiled himself one additional time after that session, but had no further encopresis over the next six months. He remained in therapy during this time to work on issues related to anger, especially at his stepfather, who refused to be involved in family therapy.

Six months later, Sean's mother reported an incident of physical abuse to

Sean and the family became involved with another therapist, who was employed by the Department of Social Services. Sean began soiling himself again, only this time it was for current issues, not for a traumatic incident in the past. While this might seem like a minute distinction, it may have pertinence for other cases as well. At times, a symptom rooted in past experiences will be eliminated in EMDR, only to recur due to new upsetting events. It is as if a certain vulnerability for a particular form of symptom has occurred, which can be activated by new events. While this can be viewed negatively, it can also be seen as a positive situation: If EMDR eliminated the prior symptom, it is highly likely that it can eliminate the more recent one. How vulnerable the individual remains to symptom formation from future traumas continues to be an open question, but a model of EMDR therapy emerges that calls for short-term interventions if and when an individual becomes retraumatized. Thus, the person does not engage in continuous therapy; only therapy as the need emerges episodically, if at all.

Sean's case illustrates for several aspects of EMDR for children: the brevity of the EMDR treatment; the importance of the safe place; the recurrence of symptoms, but for different reasons than originally; and the lack of dramatic change within the session, accompanied by dramatic changes outside the session. This final observation is important because it frequently occurs with children. (Sean's case is also presented in more detail in chapter 10, including a transcript of the initial EMDR session).

## DEVELOPMENTAL MODIFICATIONS FOR CHILDREN AGED 6–8 YEARS

The first elements of the protocol to disappear are negative and positive cognitions, because most children between the ages of 6 and 8 years have trouble developing them, and the VOC, which is derived from cognitions. Thus, for many 6–8-year-olds, the standard protocol is most likely to involve a target memory, an image, an emotion, and a body sensation, but no cognitions. However, with some additional guidance, many children this age can "back into" a negative cognition. The clinician can assist the child in forming a positive cognition, even one of a rudimentary nature, such as "good boy" or "good girl," and then help the child formulate what he wouldn't want to believe about himself in that situation, such as "I was bad." When this can be accomplished, the protocol is then not much different from the one for 9–12-year-olds, although the cognitions tend to be more simple and concrete. If the negative cognition cannot be obtained, even by "backing into" it, the clinician still may have elicited a positive cognition, which helps as a goal for the child to work toward.

Most 6–8-year-olds can identify feelings associated with the targeted image and then use some system to rate the feelings associated with the image. Many will be able to use the 0–10 rating scale while others will be able to understand "small," "medium," and "large," depicted by holding hands close together, mid-range, or far apart, or drawn on a piece of paper in some fashion, as, for example, a big circle depicting a big feeling and a small circle denoting a small feeling. The scale could also be presented graphically, such as a drawing of a happy face and a sad face with a horizontal line connecting them. The idea is to find a way for the child to communicate about the size of the feeling; as long as the child understands the concept of size, something can generally be established.

Most children this age can identify body locations for the feelings. Since I have been using EMDR with children, I have been quite surprised at how clearly children can identify body locations for their distressed or happy feelings.

## Short Channels

With this age group, channels are likely to be very short with only one to ten sets of eye movements involved before the child is reporting positive images, thoughts, or feelings. It seems so quick that it is tempting for the clinician to infer that nothing much has happened. The best thing to do at that point, is to go back to the target, check SUDS, and then if that has been lowered, go on to another aspect of the trauma. Please note that this is a departure from the adult protocol, which indicates that an installation would be attempted here. While changes have occurred (the channel has gone from negative to positive), it is not likely that the entire trauma has been reprocessed, and reprocessing of other channels is now necessary. The adult is more likely to go on spontaneously to other channels, but the child of this age more typically comes to a stop at the end of the channel. After the child has reprocessed as many different channels as can be elicited, then an installation can be completed. While it might be possible to complete an installation after clearing out a single channel, behavioral changes would not be as likely after the session, due to the incompleteness of the work. Generally, the younger the child is, the more active a role the therapist must take to ensure that the therapeutic work is complete. The active role consists of interventions that maximize associative chaining, such as theme development, story-telling, future projection, and the child's use of imagination.

## Conducting an Installation

When the processing of a number of channels is complete (when the VOC of the original target = 7 and the SUDS = 0), conduct an installation by having the child hold the positive cognition (which may have changed by now) along with the memory of the original incident (not the picture, as the image may have changed) and go through a set of eye movements. If positive changes occur, continue processing the positive associations until they stop and then complete the session with the safe place. If the installation doesn't "take," go back to the target and process some more. This will occur when the negative aspects of the event remain stronger than the positive cognition (e.g., the child says, "What happened seems true, but the words don't") or the child indicates that the two parts are incompatible ("They're different; they don't go together"). Such an occurrence is highly unusual if a number of channels have been reprocessed, with their SUDS declining to 1 or 0.

Sometimes if the child gets "stuck" with a SUDS of 3 or 4, it's possible to attempt an installation, which will often get the process moving again. If an "early" installation doesn't work, simply return to the target and process some more. Note that the early installation is an alternative to a cognitive interweave (where the therapist supplies a new cognition to help the client get unstuck; Shapiro, 1995). The early installation is somewhat less intrusive than a cognitive interweave, and thus very useful with children.

If the clinician has not been able to obtain a positive cognition or a VOC, then no installation is possible. However, at this point in the protocol, after a good deal of processing has occurred, it is sometimes possible to obtain a late positive cognition. For example, the clinician can ask, "Now can you think of something good about yourself that you would like to go with what happened? Okay. Hold those words in mind along with the memory of that event and follow my fingers with your eyes."

After these steps, the therapist can close the session with the safe place and closing information about how the process will continue after the session.

## Case Example

Buddy first started therapy with me when he was 7 years old, as he was getting in trouble for fighting and acting out in school, and his grades were poor (his case was described in chapter 2). I terminated therapy with Buddy after 13 sessions of evaluation and treatment, three of which had been EMDR. He showed so much progress with the EMDR that there seemed no further need for therapy. However, after a year, similar problems began to recur and his parents sought therapy for him again, this time before the problems got so severe. Therapy had been so helpful previously that they were optimistic that additional EMDR would be as productive.

Buddy was now 8 years old. The following segment illustrates how much of the standard protocol an 8-year-old can follow (in fact, Buddy had been able to comprehend the different steps in the protocol very well even at age 7). A year had elapsed since his prior EMDR sessions, so he did not remember details of the protocol. In the following account, note that Buddy has no difficulty establishing a safe place, forming negative and positive cognitions, identifying feelings and describing their physical location, and using scaling techniques to describe intensity or validity. The body scan is the only part of the adult protocol not attempted, with closure in the session being achieved with the safe place.

I began the session by helping Buddy set up a safe place.

"Well, Buddy, to start with, can you think of a place that's a safe place for you? A safe place is a place where you feel safe and happy and calm and just real good."

Buddy replies, "Boardwalk," which is a video game arcade, and went on to explain, "playing my favorite game."

"What's your favorite game?"

"Traveling Mutants. It's sort of like Mortal Combat, but it's not. But it's even funner."

"Oh, yeah?"

"You can like cut off their arms and then cut off both their arms. What you want to do is you want to cut off their legs and then cut off their heads so they don't do an 'air blow-out.'" Here it's possible to see the aggressive nature of the games he is attracted to, which may be therapeutically relevant, but it's also easy to see how young boys are socialized into aggressive fantasy with video games, among other things. What are we teaching our children?

"So get a picture in your mind of your being at Boardwalk playing your favorite game and think about how happy that makes you feel and where you feel that happy feeling in your body. Where do you feel it?"

"Brain and my face and my hands."

"Okay, so hold that picture in your mind and the good feelings and follow my fingers and we'll install those good feelings." Buddy completes a set of eye movements. (Eye movements will be designated with EM and hand taps with HT). "That's good. Okay, and then blank it out and take a deep breath and just notice the good feelings. . . . Okay, now that's your safe place, and if you get upset sometime you can go to your safe place.

"Uhuh, if my dad will take me."

"I mean in your *mind*, that you can just picture your safe place in your mind and it'll help you feel better. (Unlike me, remember that children's thinking is usually more concrete than adults.) We might use it in here too—if you get real upset in here about something, I'll have you think of your safe place and follow my fingers again, okay?"

"Okay."

"All right, let's take a situation where you have felt real unhappy, real sad, or real mad. Do you want to think of the one on the playground? No? Okay, picture another one." Here I am targeting the dysphoric or aggressive feelings that I think underlie his aggressive behavior at school. Initially, he rejects dealing with the incident on the playground where he pulled down his pants after his peers excluded him from participating in athletic activities. It is likely too embarrassing for him to deal with at first. Although I am establishing an agenda for EMDR based on the referring issues, I need to be flexible with him.

Buddy is willing to target a related incident and says, "When kids bother me a lot and don't let me play football."

"Can you get a picture in your mind of that?"

"Uhuh."

"And as you hold that picture in your mind, what's it make you think about *you*?"

"Unwanted." This startles me. I had expected to have to do quite a bit of digging to get an acceptable negative cognition, but this this one is a great start.

"Okay, and if you feel unwanted, what does that mean about you?" Here I'm probing to see if he can come up with a deeper core belief about himself, such as "I'm a failure" or "I'm no good." The question of a negative belief, "What does that *mean* about you?" or "What does that *say* about you?" often gets at the core negative beliefs quickly and effectively, but here it doesn't lead to a better negative cognition.

"People don't like me most of the time."

"Okay, and what would you rather believe about yourself?"

"That people like me."

"Okay, and as you hold that picture in your mind about kids bothering you and not letting you play football, how true does that seem to you, 'that people like me,' from 1 to 7, where 1 feels not true at all and 7 feels completely true?"

"Between 5 and 4." Eight-year-old Buddy has no trouble applying the numeric VOC scale.

"Okay. Then holding the picture in your mind, kids bothering you and not letting you play football, and the bad, unhappy thought that goes with that, that people don't like you, what kind of feelings go with that?" Here I want Buddy to be emotionally aroused to a significant degree by holding the image and the negative thought in mind while identifying his feelings.

"Sad."

"Okay. How strong is that sad feeling right now as you think about it, from 0 to 10, where 0 is just nothing, and 10 is the worst it could be?"

"Ten." Again I am surprised. I cannot tell from Buddy's facial expression or body movements that his feelings are that intense. Also note that he has no trouble with the numeric scale for the SUDS, just as he had no trouble with the VOC scale.

"Oh, real strong then. Okay. So, now what I'm going to ask you to do is to bring up the picture in your mind and the thoughts and feelings that go with that, feeling unwanted and sad and that people don't like you, and then to follow my fingers. Your job is to just let anything come to mind that comes to mind. Okay, got the picture?"

"Uhuh."

"And the thoughts and feelings . . . unwanted and sad . . . not liked. (Here, by stating each part and pausing briefly, I give him time to bring up each element of the protocol, image, thoughts, feelings and body location, so the procedure is as emotionally evocative as possible.) Follow my fingers. (EM) That's good, real good. (EM) Okay, now blank out your mind, take a deep breath. . . . What comes to mind now?"

"Being all-time quarterback, 'cause I usually am if the other kids let me."

"And how does that make you feel?"

"Happy."

"Okay. Hold that picture and the happy feeling that goes with it and follow my fingers. (EM) Real good. (EM) Okay, blank it out. Take a deep breath, and what do you get now?"

"Being Barry Sanders."

"Okay. And what's that like?"

"Happy." Apparently this was a very short channel, as it went from negative to positive emotions very quickly and stayed there. With children, this rapid change in emotions with only one set of eye movements is quite frequent, and often strains credulity. However, it doesn't mean the work is complete. This is where theme development becomes important.

"Can you think of another time when you felt unwanted or left out or other kids bothering you, not letting you play?"

"No."

"Can you get a picture in your mind of the time when you got real upset and pulled down your pants?"

"Uhuh."

"Hold *that* picture in your mind and do you remember how you felt?"

"Sad and mad."

"Hold that picture and those feelings. Where did you feel those feelings in your body?"

"Everywhere."

"Hold that picture and the sad and mad feelings and follow my fingers. (EM) That's good, real good. (EM) Okay, blank it out, take a deep breath. You're doing real good. What do you get now?"

"Me not going to the principal's office."

"Okay, you're *not* going to the principal's office?"

Buddy agrees with a nod of his head.

"Okay, think about that. (EM) Okay, blank it out, take a deep breath. And what do you get now?"

"Me going to Tyler's birthday party." Again, apparently this was a short channel, as it has rapidly gone from negative to positive ideation. This happened so rapidly that it is difficult to imagine that much of consequence has transpired. The best stance is to be skeptical; to wait to see what happens in the days after the session.

"Okay. Now let's do a check. Let's go back to that original situation on the playground where kids bug you, don't play with you, don't let you play football. Bring that up again. What do you get now when you bring that up?"

"Me playing football." Now the starting image has changed in a positive direction, as Buddy sees himself being included in the activity.

"Okay, and that thought that you'd like to have, 'that people like me,' how true does that feel right now, from 1 to 7, where 1 feels not true at all and 7 feels completely true?" As the starting image has changed in a positive direction, I'm checking the VOC to see if it has become more positive.

"Seven."

"Okay, and then the feelings of sad that go with that; how strong are those sad feelings right now, 0 to 10? Zero is nothing; 10 is the worst." Now I'm checking the SUDS to see if they have also declined. If so, I can then attempt an installation. More recently, I only check SUDS before going on to an installation.

"Zero."

"Okay, now I want you to hold two things in your mind: the thought that 'people like me' and that original situation where kids bugged you."

"Okay."

"Got both? Follow my fingers. (EM) You're doing a great job. . . . Real good. . . . Real good. (EM) Okay, blank it out, take a deep breath. . . . What do you get now?"

"Me playing football." Apparently the starting event has been desensitized.

"Okay, now bring up that incident in your mind where you got mad and sad and pulled down your pants. What do you get now when you bring that up?" After checking on the starting event, I want to check on the second incident we worked on.

"Nothing."

"Okay. Now Buddy, we're going to have to stop in a minute, but let's go back to your safe place. Can you bring up a picture of your safe place?" Here, as previously discussed, I'm using the safe place for closure in the session, and not the body scan.

"Yeah."

"Hold that in mind; follow my fingers. (EM) Okay, blank it out, take a deep breath. . . . Good. What kind of feelings do you have now?"

"Happy."

"Okay, and where do you feel those happy feelings?"

"Everywhere."

"Good. Now let's talk for just a minute about what you'd like to do this week, if things go better. Let's start with being at home. What can you do at home to make things go better?" This is not the standard closure. It would have been better to let him know that the processing is likely to continue, and in what ways, and how to keep track of it. After that, I could have added these comments.

"Play with my friends and maybe go to the penny arcade or go to the Boardwalk, taking Tyler."

"And if your mom asks you to do things or your dad asks you to do things, what can you do?"

"I would do them."

"Can you do that?" I'm skeptical, too. I'm not sure we've covered enough ground to get behavioral changes after this session.

"Uhuh."

"Well, let's see how things go. I will see you in two weeks and we'll see how things go in the meantime. How do you feel right now?"

"Happy!"

After this session (where the EMDR portion was about 15 minutes), Buddy did show dramatic behavioral changes. He received two more EMDR sessions over the next six weeks to increase and stabilize the changes. Therapy was then terminated, as there were no additional issues on which to continue to work.

There are a number of issues that this session illustrates. Most important is that most of the full adult protocol can be used with children as young as Buddy. Also important is the shortness of the channels and how quickly the chain of associations went from negative to positive. As is typical with children this age, Buddy would have no further associations when he reached the end of a channel. I don't look at this as resistance, partly because it happens so frequently, but rather as an indication that children don't form associative connections in the complex fashion that adults do. Therefore, the therapist needs to assist the child in making further associations, and can do so by implementing the theme development described earlier. Theme development was attempted with Buddy when I asked him if he could think of another time when he felt unwanted or left out or bothered by other kids. Although Buddy responded negatively, he was able to continue by processing the more painful or embarrassing memory of pulling down his pants on the playground. This EMDR session is also notable in illustrating how intensely a child can feel something without the feeling being obvious on the surface: for Buddy the initial feeling was a 10.

Finally, it doesn't look like a lot was accomplished in this session, but the behavioral changes that occurred *after* the session belie that. Buddy went on to improve his grades and his peer relationships and he became more cooperative at home and at school. After two more EMDR sessions, we had run out of issues on which to work.

## DEVELOPMENTAL CONSIDERATIONS FOR CHILDREN AGED 4–5 YEARS

With this age group the general format is to establish a safe place, then evoke a description of the event, followed by a described image of it. Most 4–5-year-olds can then describe their feelings associated with it. If the child cannot describe current feelings, it is often helpful to have the child recall the feelings that occurred at the time of the event and then inquire if the child can feel those emotions "a little bit" in the present. If the child can, then it is possible to encourage her to amplify the feelings while she holds the image of the event in mind. Body location for the physical sensations can then be ascertained, followed by having the child think about the image of the event, the feelings, and the physical sensations. The therapist can then have the child engage in eye movements or hand taps with the child tapping. Again, the general principle in setting up the EMDR protocol is to use as much of the full protocol as possible and modify it only as necessary.

### Eye Movements

Most children this age will not be able to use eye movements. Therefore, if a child cannot track with his eyes, the therapist can use alternating left-right stimulation in kinesthetic or auditory form (or a combination of these). If trying hand taps, I think it works better to have the child tap the hands of the therapist, as in pattycake. It is a game many children are familiar with, and it can be very playful. Also, it involves use of the child's large-muscle groups, so she becomes actively involved rather than sitting passively while the therapist taps. If eye movements and hand taps are not effective, left-right auditory stimulation can be used; finger snaps, clickers, rattles, and drums are all good alternatives.

Although it is far from proven, it is my impression that eye movements are the most effective of the different forms of stimulation, so it makes sense to try various forms of ocular pursuit before going to other forms of stimulation. I have worked with a number of children who did not track well with their eyes, but when we attempted tactile or auditory stimulation, it was less effective, and we returned to the eye movements, even though poorly executed by the child. Interestingly, in those cases, the children stated a preference for the eye movements, as they could apparently sense a difference.

Some variations on the traditional eye movement stimulation include: use finger puppets; have full-size puppets pop up from behind a barrier, first on one side, then on the other; draw smiley faces on the end of your fingers, and have the child follow those. Another technique is to hold up a right-hand finger on the right side, then a left-hand finger on the left side, so that the child looks alternately right and left. Children incapable of ocular pursuit often can respond to this approach, as it does not involve visual tracking, but just looking back and forth. It can also easily be made into a game by asking the child to tell which finger, or how many fingers, is being held up, or to point to the finger(s) being held up. A laser pointer also makes an effective game: The clinician puts two targets on the wall, spaced as far apart as possible, and has the child "shoot" first one and then the other (thanks to A. J. Popky for this contribution). Magic wands can be purchased in toy stores, and can engender additional interest in back-and-forth movement.

## Cognitions and Emotions

Most children this age are not capable of coming up with negative and positive cognitions. In most cases it is better to elicit feelings after the target memory and image has been selected. Most 4–5-year-olds can identify feelings and rate them from 0–10 or from small to large verbally or visually.

## The Use of Board Games

EMDR can be incorporated into board games that a 4–5-year-old can play. An example is the "Talking, Feeling, Doing Game" or the "Family Happenings Game" in which the child rolls the dice, moves his piece the corresponding number of spaces on the board, and takes a card appropriate for the space that the piece landed on. If the child can do what the card says (e.g., talk about a time he felt sad) the child gets a token for discussing the request on the card. The person who gets the most tokens wins the game. If the child is able to read (not frequent in this age group), blank cards provided with the game can be written to incorporate elements of EMDR in an incremental fashion (e.g., "Move your eyes back and forth"; "Move your eyes back and forth and think of something sad"). Of course the therapist can help the child with the activity so that the child can get a token. If the child doesn't read, card content can be made up on an ad hoc basis by the therapist.

## Case Example

Shirley was a highly oppositional 5-year-old child in a family with fairly strong-minded and oppositional parents. She was referred for, among other things, refusing to have bowel movements in the toilet although in the past she had been willing to do so. When Shirley figured out what I wanted her to do in EMDR, she refused to do it. Instead of doing EMDR, then, we played a game. When I realized that Shirley couldn't read, I began disregarding what the card actually said and making up content. I "read" the next card as, "Move your eyes back and forth." As she had some difficulty doing that on her own, she was willing to let me help her move her eyes back and forth by following my fingers so she could get a token. Other cards "read" "Move your eyes back and forth and think of something happy," ". . . something sad," and eventually, "Move your eyes back and forth and think about having a bowel movement in the toilet." After two sessions she proudly told me she was now having "BMs in the toilet."

## DEVELOPMENTAL MODIFICATIONS FOR CHILDREN AGED 2–3 YEARS

There are not many psychotherapeutic approaches geared to 2–3-year-olds. The question can be raised as to why anyone is applying EMDR to children this young, as there is nothing that suggests that EMDR could or should be applied to this age group. However, I can think of three reasons that this application has come about:

1. EMDR is simple enough to start with so that further modifications allow a child to be capable of following the sequence.
2. The clinician follows the associative lead of the child; in this way, EMDR is similar to other therapeutic interventions with children this young, such as nondirective play therapy. In both approaches, the therapist provides the overall structure for the child, and then observes what emerges from the child. The child does not have to rely on adult verbalizations for the therapy to work, and the clinician can deduce much of what is going on with the child through nonverbal and behavioral clues inside and outside of the sessions.
3. Clinical serendipity. That is, as EMDR-trained therapists have been thrust into working with very young traumatized children, they have approached the traumatized children with a tentative let's-see-if-this-works stance. The protocol gets modified and simplified so that even a very young child can accomplish the steps involved, and the clinician and the parents wait to see what happens.

What has happened is that in some cases EMDR seems to have led to a cessation of, or improvement in, the symptoms of the child, such as bed-wetting, nightmares, anxiety, and PTSD symptoms of intrusion, avoidance, and hyperarousal. These results get communicated to other EMDR therapists at work-shops and conferences, who then apply the same or similar modifications to children they have been treating. As they, too, obtain positive results, a body of knowledge grows up on an anecdotal basis of how to use EMDR to treat a 2–3-year-old. If there had been no successes, this part of the chapter would not be included in this book.

## Parental Assistance

Whereas many 5-year-olds can identify feelings and rate them on a scale, most 2- and 3-year-olds cannot. This means the therapist brings up the event in some way and has the child engage in alternating left-right stimulation while think-ing or talking about the event. Often enough, information can be obtained from the parents about the trauma (with this age group the traumas are most likely to be specific events) so that the therapist can evoke the memory by asking about it. Of course, it is preferable to have the child describe what happened, what was scary, and what was the worst part. If the child is unable to do so, it's possible to have the parents in the room to evoke the memory by describing the event, while the child engages in hand taps or left-right auditory stimulation.

Joan Lovett (1997), a behavioral pediatrician practicing in California, described a procedure where the parents write an account of what happened, then read it to the child while the child is engaged in left-right stimulation. This is an excellent approach when the very young child is unable to describe the experience but the parents know what happened, as in an automobile accident in which they all were involved. It is less useful when the parents don't know what happened or when the child is unable to think about what happened. Again, it is the associative chaining of the child which needs to be tapped into, if it can be elicited at all. If it can't be, narrative descriptions by the parents or other adults can be used to stimulate the associative chaining, as described above.

Frankie Klaff (1998), a child psychologist practicing on the east coast, described a similar procedure, in which she makes a narrative from information that she has obtained from the parents and the child, and then tells it to the child as the child engages in left-right stimulation. Again, while this is less opti-mal than the child's own chain of associations, it is more direct than using metaphors with children (as Richard Gardner [1986] advocates). Perhaps a hierarchy could be constructed of postulated clinical effectiveness, ranging from the child's own chain of associations as most effective, followed by a narrative constructed by an informed adult as moderately effective, and metaphors as least effective. In fact, it would be possible to assess the comparative effective-ness of metaphors, narratives, or associative chaining, with and without left-right stimulation.

Sometimes other methods, especially nonverbal ones, of eliciting the child's memory of the event are more useful. For example, even very young children love to draw and paint. If the child can draw an image of the event, the drawing can serve as a stimulus for the EMDR, especially if the child can look at it while hand taps are used. Linda Cohn, an art therapist, has pioneered the use of this approach (Cohn, 1993).

The use of drums with small children is an involving and exciting way to gain attention and provide alternate left-right stimulation. Montessori methods of learning advocate multisensory stimulation to promote learning in young children. This principle can be employed with young children in EMDR. Would the session be more effective if the traumatized child observed a photograph of an aspect of the trauma (e.g., a picture of an automobile accident) or his own drawing or painting of the trauma while the therapist drummed with two drums, one on the left side and one on the right side of the child? Would it be more effective if a narration or verbal cues were added, or would this prove to be overstimulating? Could the child do the drumming while the therapist or the parents held the picture and provided verbal cues?

Good therapy is always geared to the needs and interests of the child. I have used drumming with a young girl with Down's syndrome whose measured language development was at about a 2-year-old level (although chronologically she was 6 years old). She found the drumming involving, and could sustain an interest in it for 10–15 minutes at a time. I have also used it with an Alaskan Indian 10-year-old boy who had been adopted at age 5½, after being given up first by his mother and then his grandmother. Understandably, the boy had attachment difficulties with his adoptive parents. These difficulties were greatly improved by the use of EMDR, where he drummed with two drumsticks on a single drum (low-budget version). He became friendlier and happier both inside and outside his family, establishing friendships, which he did not have before. His cooperation with and attachment to his adoptive parents also improved. He showed tearfulness and grief when his adoptive mother's grandfather died, although he had not shown grief before.

There are other ways that parents can be helpful in the EMDR treatment of 2–3-year-old children. For example, a parent could play the role of the child in EMDR with the child watching. In this way, the child can learn through observation what is expected from her. Then the child could either perform the actions with the therapist, if the child is ready, or go through the motions with her parent first. The parent could teach the child hand taps or have her draw a picture, or play a therapeutic board game with her. These are useful approaches if the child seems frightened or shy around the therapist. Another possibility is to have the child sit in the parent's lap, with the parent guiding the child's hand taps or narrating the event while guiding the child's hands. It might seem merely like a conversation between parent and child, with alternating left-right stimulation added, with additional guidance given the parent by the therapist. As these suggestions infer, there are a wide range of possibilities that can be employed. The reward for these efforts is seeing the child lose her symptoms or improve in her functioning. While this doesn't always happen with a child this young, it happens enough that a trial of EMDR with a traumatized child is worth the effort.

## Additional Considerations

With this age group, extra caution is warranted for two primary reasons. First, it is not usually possible to set up a safe place, so there is no way for the child to have a built-in safeguard in the EMDR procedure. Hence, it is even more important for the therapist to monitor the younger child's affective state, but the emotional cues may be harder to discern. The therapist, then, is justified in being cautious, watching the child closely to avoid overstimulating him, and in having brief EMDR encounters, interspersed with many other involving activities such as games, art, and play.

Second, in my experience, children this age are more likely to feel overwhelmed by their feelings and seek to avoid thinking about them. For example, if a 3-year-old child has been molested by the baby-sitter's husband, who has told her that he will hurt her or kill her family if she tells, that child may be much more terrified than a 10-year-old who has experienced and been told the same thing. The 3-year-old may panic each time the man's name is mentioned and hide under the table, refusing to participate in anything until the fear goes away. Even after engaging in different forms of play until she is relaxed, the child may again hide or refuse to talk when the man's name is mentioned again. Such a reaction can happen repeatedly. This kind of therapeutic impasse can also occur with an 8- or 9-year-old, but it is more difficult to resolve with a 2- or 3-year-old, as the younger child typically has less well-developed cognitive and coping abilities.

To help avoid these difficulties with 2–3-year-olds, the parents can be invaluable allies. They can provide much information before the first session with the child about activities the child enjoys, how to make EMDR into a game for the child, and how to make the child comfortable. Perhaps this advance planning is the most important part of working with a child in this age group. Once a plan (and contingency plans) have been laid out ahead of time, the actual session with the child is more likely to be successful.

Theme development can be used with this age group, with the therapist striking a careful balance between developing themes and continuing the EMDR too long. If EMDR is continued too long with a child of this age, it is likely that she will be reluctant or avoidant about participating in the future. Again, good parents can be powerful allies in this form of work, as they are likely to recognize signs of fatigue in the child, and be able to interpret various aspects of the child's behavior to the therapist.

## Case Example

Davy was 2 years, 9 months old when I first saw him. He was born with fetal alcohol effect from his mother's drug and alcohol usage during her pregnancy. As a result, he had developmental delays in his speech and language development, as well as the typical facial features of a child with fetal alcohol effect. He had also been born with a cleft palate. When he was 14 months old, he underwent a second surgery to repair the cleft palate, and "came to" during the surgery (see Shapiro & Forrest, 1997, for a detailed description of this case). Following the surgery, he had night terrors for the next 18 months (more than half of his life) before he was referred to me. Night terrors are like nightmares, only more severe, as they are akin to sleep walking, where the individual is not conscious, but appears to be awake and engaging in various activities. In night terrors, however, the fear is extreme, as the name implies, and, unlike nightmares, the child has amnesia afterward. At first, the night terrors occurred nightly for Davy, but over time they diminished to three to four times per week, until he moved to Colorado Springs with his maternal grandparents, who were raising him in lieu of his mother. At that time, the night terrors increased to nightly, often two to three times per night. The neighbors across the street turned them in for child abuse, as they would hear him screaming at night. When the grandfather, Jack, had to be away from home on training for an eight-week stint, all of the burden of handling Davy fell to his grandmother, Claire. As the night terrors lasted about 45 minutes, and it took another 45 minutes to calm Davy afterward, and with this occurring two or three times per night, nobody was getting much sleep.

In desperation, Claire sought medical help, and was referred to a child psychiatrist, who diagnosed Davy as having posttraumatic stress disorder, fetal alcohol effect, and attention-deficit/hyperactivity disorder. The child psychiatrist referred Davy to me, wondering if EMDR might help. After I saw Davy the first time (with Claire), I called the psychiatrist back, telling him that I saw no way to use EMDR, as Davy couldn't even give me eye contact, let alone follow my fingers back and forth. At the time, I had not used alternating hand taps with children. In fact, I had never worked in EMDR with any child this young, developmentally delayed or otherwise. Even play therapy could not be used with Davy, as he was too hyperactive and traumatized, and too young chronologically and developmentally for that approach.

As I was in the middle of telling the psychiatrist on the phone that I didn't think there was anything I could do, I thought about the possibility of using hand taps with Davy. I changed my mind midstream, and said that I'd see him another time, as there was one other thing I'd like to try. If Davy couldn't respond to eye movements, perhaps he could respond to hand taps.

At this time, Davy was in speech therapy and physical therapy and he had undergone medication changes, but none of these approaches had seemed to affect the night terrors. The medication cut down his hyperactivity during the day, but Davy still had the hyperarousal characteristic of PTSD, which may have exacerbated his already-existing ADHD symptoms. The situation was so desperate, with very little sleep for Claire and Davy, that he was being considered for rehospitalization, so that Claire could get some respite. Of course, that would likely magnify Davy's terror, to be ripped away from his only source of security, and placed in a hospital setting, similar to where he had originally been traumatized. Chances are that he would have been put on even stronger doses of medication to contain his terror in that setting.

In the second session with Davy, I allowed him to get used to the setting again and to play with the toys that were available in the playroom. I also spent about five minutes teaching him to play pattycake, which I had decided was the way to handle hand taps—not the form that is most frequently used with adults, where the therapist does the tapping. I wanted to make sure that Davy's attention was fully engaged in the task at hand and I wanted to involve him in as much patterned left-right stimulation as possible. Although it was clear that he would rather play with the toys, he was able to engage in five minutes of hand tapping, and laughed through most of it, as we made it a game. His grandmother videotaped the session.

Because Davy's language development was delayed (standardized testing indicated that he was functioning at about the 18-month level for both receptive and expressive skills), in the next session I decided to have him repeat after me emotionally evocative words related to the surgery while doing hand taps. I knew a number of possibilities for words from background information provided to me by Claire. For example, Davy would panic, scream, and cry when his grandparents took him to the hospital or when he saw a doctor in a green surgical gown. In his night terrors, he would cry out, "It hurts!" When they had taken him to the mall to get his picture taken, he had panicked when he saw the large photographic lights turned on, as they were similar to the large surgical lights in the hospital. I thought that words like hospital, doctor, big lights, bright lights, mouth hurts, lip hurts, it hurts, would prompt him to think about the pain and trauma of awakening during the surgery and would be words that he could repeat after me, despite his limited language and speech skills.

In the third session with Davy, he was willing to sit in a chair and hand-tap with me. He had not been willing to do so in the second session. We began the hand taps, and I had him repeat words after me. We started with "bright light." Davy responded with something that sounded like "bright light." I said, "Okay. Hit my hands. That's it. This one. Say it again." This time Davy responded, "Big light." I was surprised. Was he already making mental connections between my words and the experience he had had in surgery? Again, I asked him to say, "Bright light." He responded, "Bright light." Then I said, "Okay. Say 'big light.'" Davy responded, as he tapped my hands, "Big light."

"Okay. Hit my hands."

"Big light," Davy repeated.

"Big light," I repeated.

"Big light," he responded.

"Big light. Big light. Big light. Say it."

"Big light," Davy repeated again. He continued to tap my hands and at this point seemed to become very thoughtful.

I continued, "That's it. . . . Again. . . . Big light. . . . Hit my hand. . . . Big light. Big light. Big light. You say it. . . . Can you say 'hurt'?"

"Hurt."

"Hit my hand. Hit my hand. That's it. That's it. That's it (as Davy continued tapping). That's it. That's it. Okay, say 'Lip hurt.'"

This time, to my astonishment, Davy said, "*My* lip hurt." Again I wondered, could he be making a mental connection between these words and the memory of the surgery?

"That's it. Say it again. Say it again."

"My lip hurt," Davy responded again.

"Now say, 'Mouth hurt.'"

"My mouth hurt."

"Mouth hurt."

"My mouth hurt."

"That's it. That's it. That's it. That's it (as Davy continued tapping). That's it. Good. Good. Good. Good. Harder. Harder. Harder. Good. Good. Now, can you say 'Doctor'?"

"Doctor."

Davy's attention began to wander. I asked him to look at me and to watch my fingers as I moved them back and forth. His attention wandered more and we stopped the EMDR. Davy was now free to play with the toys, while Claire and I pondered what had happened. It didn't look like much. Davy had engaged in left-right alternating stimulation with hand taps, and at the same time had repeated words after me, which seemed to evoke thoughtfulness on his part about the surgery.

I was incredulous when, a few days later, Claire called me and told me that the night terrors had stopped. She recounted how she and her husband had awakened the next morning after the EMDR and suddenly panicked when they realized that Davy had not awakened them during the night. They rushed into his room and found him still sleeping soundly.

The night terrors didn't return, despite two subsequent hospitalizations over the next two years for Davy. He began to sleep better, he did not have to be immediately hospitalized to give his grandparents respite, and his medication was reduced. Davy continued in speech therapy, physical therapy, and other approaches appropriate for a child with developmental delays, but he no longer manifested the symptoms of having been traumatized: no more night terrors or terror from bright lights, hospitals, or doctor's green scrub gowns.

More recently, Claire and Jack were concerned about how Davy would react as he experienced mouth pain and bleeding when his adult teeth started coming in. Would that cause regression, recurrence of memories from the surgery? Davy now has his first two adult teeth, and there have been no night terrors, no regression, and no increased preoccupation about the traumatic surgery. He continues to progress through the specialized services he receives to enhance his development. And he no longer has PTSD from the trauma. He says to his grandparents, "Remember when my mouth hurt when I was a baby? It's better now."

Davy's case is instructive for a number of reasons. First, it indicates that EMDR can be applied even to very young children. Although Davy was 2 years, 9 months old chronologically, he was more like an 18-month-old child in his language development, as measured by standardized tests. His case, then, suggests how much the EMDR protocol can be adapted to apply to very young children. Whereas the case of Buddy demonstrates how little EMDR often *needs* to be modified to be applicable to children, the case of Davy illustrates how much EMDR *can* be modified and still be effective treatment.

Second, these results are not unusual. I have talked to other therapists who have achieved similar results with young children who have been traumatized by medical procedures, car accidents, sexual or physical abuse, or natural disasters.

Also, other therapists have recounted their experiences to me about using EMDR with infants. For example, a father described to me how his 6-month-old infant seemed to be afraid to move for several hours after rolling off a changing table. His father, noting his apparent fearfulness, gently rocked him from side to side for a period of time. After that, his child went back to rolling over again, and did not seem fearful of moving around. Another therapist told me how she had treated an infant who, after a long and difficult birth, was fussy and colicky for the next few months. She engaged the child in alternated left-right stimulation (gently tapping the child's shoulders, arms, and legs), after which the child was no longer fussy and colicky. Yet another therapist told me, after hearing my presentation on children at an EMDR training, that her granddaughter often seemed in pain, arching her back, screaming, and crying. The grandmother and her son had discovered that the only thing that soothed the child was to alternately pat the buttocks and the back of the infant's legs, sometimes for hours at a time. She had not thought of this as being related to EMDR until she heard me speak.

Are these different examples actually EMDR? I hesitate to draw too much from these cases, as the information could be distorted by any number of factors. However, we have seen how EMDR might fit in with other examples of left-right or patterned stimulation, and the ability to respond to these patterns might be present in very young children. There is much to be explored here. For example, could many colicky babies be soothed through patterned stimulation of a left-right nature? Could parents be trained to use this? Would it be especially helpful to train at-risk parents to use this to deal with a child, otherwise unresponsive to parental input? Would it cut down on child abuse? Infant massage has been shown to be soothing and beneficial. Would patterned stimulation be even more beneficial? Could the two be combined? Some of the spin-offs from EMDR with children may go beyond the immediately obvious.

Davy's case also has implications for children diagnosed with ADHD. As mentioned earlier, he was diagnosed with fetal alcohol effect, posttraumatic stress disorder, and attention-deficit/hyperactivity disorder. After EMDR, his night terrors ceased and he was able to sleep through the night. His medication for hyperactivity (Dexedrine) was reduced. These results provide a model for what can happen with other children who have developmental delays, been traumatized, or diagnosed with ADHD. Thus, some children like Davy, with the ADHD diagnosis, will become less hyperactive after EMDR, as they are no longer hyperaroused from the trauma, and their medication can be reduced or eliminated. In these cases, we are not curing ADHD, but reducing or eliminating the reactions to trauma. The ADHD remains. In other cases, after EMDR, no hyperactivity remains. In these cases, it is likely that the original diagnosis was incorrect, with the child having PTSD from a trauma, but not ADHD.

Developmentally delayed children can also benefit from EMDR. Many of these children have been traumatized by ordinary events of daily life, as have children with ADHD. As their understandings of ordinary events is different or less well-developed, they may be more likely to be traumatized by a dog or cat, being left at a nursery school, or yelled at by a teacher or a neighbor who doesn't understand their more limited or different comprehension of a situation. Even parents may not fully appreciate their child's disabilities. Having worked with parents of autistic children, I have sometimes seen how their desire to see their autistic child as normal causes them to put their child in situations that are beyond the capacities of the child. The child then experiences failures and criticism to which they otherwise would not be subjected. The parents are well-intentioned, but the child experiences additional difficulties. Here again, the EMDR does not modify the developmental disabilities, but reduces or eliminates the reactions to big traumas (e.g., the car accident) or little traumas (e.g., being left at nursery school with no preparation), thus assisting the child in achieving developmental trajectories closer to normal.

In other cases that are similar to Davy, where there are multiple diagnoses, it is difficult to know ahead of time what the response to EMDR will be, as it is impossible to know for certain what each condition is contributing. In these situations, EMDR can be used on a trial basis, with the idea that only a few sessions would be necessary to find out if it would be beneficial. For example, I recently had a 5-year-old boy referred to me after he was severely burned in an auto accident. Following the accident he had lost much of his speech and it was not known how much of his impairment was due to trauma and how much was due to a possible brain injury. After three initial EMDR sessions, he talks more, sleeps better, has stopped grinding his teeth at night in his sleep, and seems more relaxed during the day, but his progress has been slowed by additional hospitalizations for continued medical treatment of his burns. EMDR will be undertaken after he returns from his most recent hospitalization, but it remains to be seen how much improvement will obtained through EMDR in the long run. In the meantime, he has experienced definite benefit.

Now that we have covered the developmental modifications necessary to work with children of various ages, we can turn to other aspects of using EMDR with children, such as the characteristics of and the kinds of traumas that children are subjected to, the symptoms children exhibit, and the emotional disorders of childhood with which EMDR can be used. In the next chapter, we will examine the role that different characteristics of trauma can play in the success of EMDR therapy.

# five

# Simple Traumas: Automobile Accidents, Lightning Strikes

"It cleared out of my brain."

—STAN, AGE 7

ALTHOUGH THERE ARE A NUMBER of ways to organize case material with EMDR, I have chosen to organize cases by the characteristics of trauma discussed in chapter 2. These characteristics allow for an integrated system of diagnosis and treatment, permitting relatively accurate prediction of treatment duration and outcome. For example, children with difficulties from a singular trauma have more in common with each other in terms of their symptoms and their response to EMDR than they do with children who have been multiply traumatized, regardless of the kinds of trauma or their diagnoses. Likewise, children who have been multiply traumatized have more in common in regard to their response to EMDR and their symptoms than they do with children who have experienced a singular trauma.

How a child responds to a natural disaster, for example, depends on the severity of the trauma, including whether he had been previously traumatized, whether previous traumas were similar to the present one, and how supportive his family and school environments are, among other things. The most useful grouping of cases is not by the kind of trauma (e.g., automobile accident), *DSM-IV* diagnosis (we have seen how misleading that can be with children), or symptoms (e.g., treatment duration depends on how many times the child was traumatized and how many ongoing elements are presently causing her current fear). However, the practicing clinician might find it useful to be able to look up cases by diagnosis, type of trauma (e.g., assault, accident, bereavement, natural disaster), or symptoms. Therefore, cases are presented in this and later chapters using those three characteristics as organizing frameworks.

EMDR seems to work most quickly and effectively with simple traumas, whether they are acute or chronic. A simple trauma is a singular occurrence, completed in the past, or a series of occurrences of the same type that are no longer occurring. Good examples of simple traumas are an automobile accident, a dog bite, a sudden bereavement, or a one-time molestation by the baby-sitter. It happened once, is now over, but has left behind PTSD symptoms. With regard to the efficacy of EMDR, it doesn't seem to matter whether the simple trauma is acute or chronic. Our research with adults has shown that the length of time since the occurrence is not related to EMDR outcome. The median length of time that the adults in our study had suffered PTSD symptoms that interfered with their lives was 13.5 years. Those who had suffered the longest improved as much and as quickly as those who had been traumatized more recently. This was certainly an exciting finding. However, those who had had PTSD symptoms for longer periods of time had endured negative psychological effects for longer periods. My clinical experience and that of other child therapists suggest that this is also the case with children: It doesn't matter whether the trauma was one month or three years ago, in terms of the effectiveness of EMDR. However, if children are diminished in their emotional, social, and cognitive growth due to the trauma, they may have a lot of catch-up development to accomplish after losing their symptoms.

Most parents, however, wait to see if the PTSD symptoms will disappear or improve on their own, and thus are more likely to bring their child in only after a significant period of time has elapsed and the symptoms haven't improved, have returned, or have worsened. Therefore, many childhood traumas are no longer acute by the time the child is referred for treatment. While this does not impair the effectiveness of EMDR, it does mean that the child has had to live with the emotional pain of the symptoms for a longer period of time and the child's developmental trajectories have been more significantly distorted. As EMDR becomes better known to the public, more children may be referred while their symptoms are still acute, shortening the length of time that they have to suffer. Then, less reparative work restoring or improving the child's self-esteem or parent-child relationships will be necessary, and there will be less remedial work in school, as the child would have a shorter period of time in which to experience failures with parents, peers, and teachers.

At this point, we will take a look at some of the most common simple traumas (and some unusual ones) that children face, and examine how EMDR can be applied in those situations. Because EMDR is so quickly effective with simple traumas, we can present actual transcripts of entire EMDR sessions, or a series of EMDR sessions, so that change points can be identified, along with aspects of therapeutic choice. Such a microscopic approach is relatively unusual in writing about psychotherapy, but is possible here because of the brevity and clarity of change possible with EMDR.

## AUTOMOBILE ACCIDENTS

Thousands of children are involved in car accidents every year, and afterward many of them develop symptoms. In discussing the prevalence of PTSD following serious motor vehicle accidents (i.e., requiring medical attention after the accident) with adults and children combined, Blanchard and Hickling (1997) state, "We believe the lifetime prevalence values [of PTSD following serious motor vehicle accidents], multiplied by the population of the United States from the last three studies (1% to 3%) gives some indication of the size of the potential problem, 2.5 to 7 million cases in the United States alone. Thus, we have a sizable mental health problem in this country that has been all but ignored by American researchers and perhaps by the mental health treatment community" (p. 19). If only 25% of those 2.5–7 million cases were children, then it would appear that 625,000–1.75 million children could have PTSD symptoms from motor vehicle accidents alone.

In fact, the National Highway Transportation and Safety Administration (NHTSA) provides yearly figures for motor vehicle accidents by age. For 1996, NHTSA indicated that 52,000 children under age 5 were injured; 122,000 between ages 5 and 9; and 204,000 between ages 10 and 15, for a total of 413,000 injured children (NHTSA, 1996). Preliminary statistics from 1997 are not very different (Cerrelli, 1997). It is likely that many of these children develop some PTSD symptoms, and if one-third develop full-blown PTSD, then more than 130,000 children are developing PTSD each year from motor vehicle accidents alone. Using these incidence rates, we can estimate a prevalence rate (i.e., multiply 130,000 children developing PTSD each year for 10 years) of 1.3 million children in the U.S. with PTSD. This figure is not too far off from the 1.75 million upper limit estimate from Blanchard and Hickling (1997). Such incidence and prevalence rates suggest a sizable PTSD problem involving children following motor vehicle accidents.

## Thunder Breaks the Sun

Five-year-old Julie had been in two car accidents (she was briefly discussed in chapter 2). After the second accident, she began crying hysterically and subsequently developed nightmares and fearfulness in many different situations.

In the first EMDR session, we focused on the last accident, and in the second and third sessions we focused on the nightmares and phobias. Julie drew a pic-

*Figure 5.1*

ture of one of the nightmares where "the thunder broke the sun" (figure 5.1) and of the tornado that she feared so much (figure 5.2). After three sessions of EMDR, Julie's behavior had returned to normal. Instead of clinging to her mother and being afraid to leave her side when they went grocery shopping, she again engaged in appropriate exploratory behavior on her own. She no longer had nightmares or preoccupations with tornadoes.

In Julie's family, it is clear that other problems existed besides Julie's PTSD for the two accidents in which she had been involved. However, Julie's symptoms could improve, even though the family setting was not perfect for her. What was

*Figure 5.2*

important, was that she was supported and nurtured by her concerned parents, despite their other problems.

Here's how the EMDR part of those three sessions transpired. Note that in the first session, because of Julie's age (5 years), I didn't attempt to obtain negative and positive cognitions, nor did I attempt an installation or a body scan. As the emotional changes were so profoundly positive, we ended the session with her enthusiastic happiness. Theme development plays an important role in this session, as I encourage her to remember every aspect of the accident and the subsequent events. Also notice how quickly the emotional content changes from negative to positive in each channel.

## Session 1

T: Julie, can you think of a place that you can go to in your mind, where you feel safe and happy?

J: Where I feel safe and happy? I feel safe and happy in my home.

T: Is there a room in the house where you feel especially safe and happy? (If the child mentions the family home as the safe place, it is often useful to see if a particular room in the house can be the safe place, as it is easier to obtain a mental image of a single room and regard it as especially safe.)

J: In my bed.

T: Okay. And can you get a picture of that bed and bedroom in your mind?

J: Yes.

T: As you hold that picture in your mind, tell me what it looks like.

J: It looks like it has two bedrooms in it, and two beds in it, and it has a lot of books in it, and it got a lot of stuffed animals in it, and it has a Pocahontas, and a piece of paper with a picture of Pocahontas.

T: When you're in that room, how do you feel?

J: How do I feel?

T: How's it make you feel when you're in that room?

J: Bad. (I don't understand this answer after her previous responses of a positive nature, so I question it).

T: It makes you feel bad?

J: Mmhm.

T: It doesn't make you feel safe and happy?

J: It does.

T: Well, I want your safe place to be a safe place where you feel really happy. Do you feel really happy in your room?

J: Yeah.

T: And do you feel safe?

J: Yeah.

T: When you hold that picture of the room in your mind, can you feel some of those safe and happy feelings right now?

J: Yeah.

T: Where do you feel them in your body?

J: In my hands.

T: Where else do you feel those safe and happy feelings in your body?

J: In my arms.

T: Uhuh. Anywhere else?

J: No.

T: What I'd like you to do now is hold that picture of your safe place, your room, along with the safe and happy feelings that you feel in your hands and your arms, all in your mind and then follow my fingers with your eyes. Is it okay if I hold my fingers this far away and move them this way and that way?

J: (Nods)

T: Now, bring up that picture. Got that picture? Okay, and the safe and happy feelings? . . . And where you feel them in your hands and arms? Okay, now follow my fingers. (EM) Hold your head still and just move your eyes. . . . That's it, that's good. . . . Real good. . . . You're doing a good job. . . . Real good. . . . Okay, now stop and take a deep breath (demonstrates) and then blow out the air (demonstrates). You do it. Take a deep breath and then just relax as you breathe out. . . . That's good. And that's your safe place. And when we're thinking about scary things in here, if you get too scared, you can give me a hand signal to stop. You can hold up your hand like this (demonstrates) to tell me to stop and then we'll stop and we'll have you go to your safe place. Okay?

J: Okay.

T: What I'd like for you to do is tell me what about the car accident was most scary for you.

J: Was most scary for me? I thought when Mommy was going to die. (This is the first time that she had indicated directly that this fear was behind her screaming and crying.)

T: Was that why you were screaming?

J: (Nods)

T: Can you get a picture of that car accident in your mind?

J: Yeah.

T: When you thought your mommy was going to die? Tell me what that picture looks like.

J: It looks like it was a black car and it looks so pretty and it looks kind of ugly now. And now when it's all broken, it makes me sad.

T: And is your mom in that picture?

J: Yeah.

T: And what does she look like in that picture?

J: She looks like in that picture? She's laying down in the ambulance out there.

T: Okay. As you think about that picture, with the black car and it's all broken and it makes you sad and you see your mom laying down and the ambulance is there, how does it make you feel right now?

J: How does it make me feel right now? It makes me feel sad.

T: Is that sad feeling right now this big? Or is it this big? Or is it this big (moves hands from close together to wide apart)?

J: That big (holds her hands wide apart).

T: That big. . . . Julie, what I'm going to ask you to do now is to hold that picture in your mind of the car accident where you thought your mommy was going to die and she's lying on the ground . . .

J: She's laying on the bed.

T: Oh, she's laying on the bed? Okay, and she's laying down and you thought she was going to die; hold that picture along with the sad feelings and follow my fingers. (EM) That's good. . . . Real good. . . . Doing a good job. . . . Okay, now stop and let the picture go away. And then take a deep breath and blow away all the bad feelings! . . . And what do you think of now? ("Blowing away the bad feelings" engages the child in a playful way and helps to reduce fearfulness about the negative feelings.)

J: What do I think of now? Nothing's not coming. (This may indicate a change has occurred or just that the child is drawing a blank. Either way, I go back to the target image.)

T: Now bring up that picture again of the car accident.

J: It's back now.

T: And what? It's back now? And tell me what that picture looks like now.

J: It looks like now? It looks like now it all turned up. And the back's turned up. (Although this description is not entirely clear, inquiry is not necessary.)

T: Okay, and think about that and follow my fingers. (EM) Blank out the picture. Take a deep breath. . . . Blow away the bad feelings. . . . And what do you think of now?

J: Think of now? I think now everything's okay. (Can this be true? Have the emotions really shifted so quickly? I decide to check on her SUDS.)

T: Do you remember that sad feeling? How big is that sad feeling now? Like this or like this or . . . (shows with hands).

J: Like that (holds her hands close together).

T: What else do you remember about that car accident? (I think it's too soon for an installation, so I focus on theme development instead.)

J: I remember we went to the hospital. And I remember I saw her laying in the bed.

T: In the hospital?

J: Uhuh.

T: Did you think she was going to die then?

J: (Shakes her head no)

T: Well, hold that picture in your mind of going to the hospital, and see your mom lying on the bed, and what kind of feelings does that make you have right now?

J: Make me have right now? Make me have right now? Bad.

T: Bad how? Is it sad or mad or scared?

J: Sad.

T: Sad. Okay, and how big is that sad feeling right now?

J: That (holds her hands about a foot apart). (Thus, although Julie felt a rapid shift in feelings associated with the initial target, another channel is not yet desensitized.)

T: Okay, so hold that sad feeling and that picture of being in the hospital, seeing your mom on the bed. Follow my fingers. (EM) That's good; that's real good. . . . Okay, now let the picture go. . . . Take a deep breath and blow away that sad feeling! . . . That's good; and what do you think of now?

J: Think of now? Everything's going to be fine (another positive shift in emotions).

T: Okay. . . . Think about that, how everything's going to be fine, and follow my fingers. (EM) That's good. . . . Doing a good job. . . . Really good. . . . Okay, now stop. Take a deep breath. . . . Good. What do you think of now?

J: Think of now? Everything's all right.

T: Can you think of another part of the accident (theme development again)?

J: 'Nother part of the accident?

T: Mmhm.

J: My dad was at the hospital. But he didn't got hurt cause he was at his work.

T: Think about how you saw your dad at the hospital and he didn't get hurt. Okay? Think about that. (EM) Doing a good job. . . . Now stop, take a deep breath. . . . Good. What do you think of now?

J: Think of now? Everything is okay.

T: Just think about that: Everything's okay. And what kind of feeling do you have when you think, "Everything's okay"?

J: Happy feeling.

T: Think about that happy feeling and how everything's okay. (EM) That's good, real good. . . . Okay, now stop, take a deep breath and relax as you breathe out. You're doing such a good job. Now, can you think of another part of the accident?

J: 'Nother part of the accident.

T: Like maybe when it first happened?

J: When it first happened? Lost all my toys. Some stuff were hanging in the car. Some evidence guy gave it to me.

T: So what happened?

J: What happened.

T: To that stuff in the car.

J: What happened to that stuff of the car? My stuff? Somebody gave it to me in the evidence.

T: And when you got in the accident, what happened to that stuff?

J: Fell all over; fell out.

T: Think about that. (EM) Now stop, take a deep breath. . . . Blow away the bad feelings. And what do you think of now?

J: Think of now? It's all right.

T: Okay. And just think of that; how it's all right now. (EM) Good job, really good. . . . Now stop. Take a deep breath. . . . In that accident, do you remember how you were screaming and crying (further theme development)?

J: I remember when I was screaming and crying. I was screaming 'cause I wanted to go home and I was crying 'cause I wanted to go home.

T: When you were screaming and crying, do you remember what the feelings were like?

J: Sad. Broken.

T: Can you get a picture in your mind of your screaming and crying? Hold that picture in your mind along with the sad and broken feelings. (EM) Blank it out, take a deep breath, blow away the bad feelings! And what do you think of now?

J: Think of now? Everything is all right.

T: How big are the sad and broken feelings now?

J: That (holds her hands together).

T: So just think about how everything is all right. (EM) Now stop. Take a deep breath. . . . And what do you think about now?

J: Think about now? Everything is okay and all right.

T: That's nice. And how do you feel right now?

J: Feel right now? Okay.

T: Okay. Do you feel happy or sad?

J: Happy.

T: Happy. How big is the happy feeling right now? Is it big or is it little?

J: Big (throws her arms back)!

T: Good. And you know, you did such a nice job with this that I think we should play a game. Would you like to play a game?

In this session, I made a game out of blowing away the bad feelings, showing Julie how to take a deep breath and then blow it out fiercely, expelling all the bad feelings. She seemed to delight in this form of animation, and it helped to hold her attention as we went through the theme development on the accident.

### Session 2

In the second session, five days later, Julie's mother reported that Julie was doing somewhat better since the last session, and was less whiny. However, she had had a single nightmare since the last session, so we targeted nightmares. I had asked Julie to draw pictures of two nightmares that she remembered. We then used the pictures as targets in EMDR.

T: When you look at this picture, tell me what happens in the picture.

J: Me and my brother run into the house and the sun turns into pieces.

T: What turns into pieces?

J: The sun.

T: The sun turns into pieces. Okay, and when that happened in that nightmare, what did it make you think about you? (This time I decided to see if I could elicit negative and positive cognitions.)

J: Think about me? Bad.

T: Bad? Did you think, "I am in danger," or did you think, "I need help"?

J: In danger.

T: I am in danger. Okay. And what would you rather think about yourself than "I am in danger"? What would you like to think instead?

J: I would like to think . . . (long pause).

T: What would you really like to think about you?

J: I would like to think, I would like to think, think about getting in the house real quickly. (This is probably a good enough positive cognition for a 5-year-old.)

T: You would like to think, "I can get in the house real quickly." All right. When you are having this nightmare, did you think, "I can get in the house really quickly," or did you think, "I can't get in the house really quickly"?

J: I think, "I cannot get in the house really quickly."

T: And then as you are thinking about the nightmare, what kind of feelings does it make you have right now?

J: Bad!

T: Bad feelings. And what kind of bad feelings? Are they sad, scared, mad, surprised, or happy? What kind of feelings do you have when you think about this nightmare picture?

J: Bad.

T: Bad how? Is it scared or sad?

J: Scared.

T: In this picture, how scared are you? Like, if you are really scared right now, mark an X right there, and if you are not scared at all, mark an X right there, and if you are a little bit scared, mark it in here. (I show her a sheet of paper on which I have drawn a happy face on the right side of the page and a sad face on the left, with a horizontal line connecting the two faces. In this session, I am interested in finding out if she can visually depict on paper the strength of her feelings, rather than showing me with her hands. If this approach doesn't work as well, we'll go back to the previous method.)

J: Really scared.

T: So would it be over here?

J: Yes.

T: You mark it on there, over there.

T: That's good. Julie, I am going to ask you to hold this picture of the nightmare in your mind along with the scared feelings and the thought "I am in danger," and then follow my fingers back and forth with your eyes the way you did last time. You did a really good job with that. I want to remind you of your safe place, too. If you get really, really scared in thinking about the nightmare, you can hold up your hand to tell me to stop and we will stop and have you go to your safe place. Okay?

J: Okay.

T: So what you can do is look at this picture. Will you hold up this picture so the camera can see it? Okay. And in the picture you can see, tell me what is in the picture.

J: In the picture, my brother, me, and the sun, and the thunder.

T: And you can hold the picture or I will hold it for you. As you hold this picture in your mind, where do you feel the scared feelings in your body?

J: In my arm.

T: Where else?

J: In my other arm.

T: Okay, and where else do you feel the scared feelings?

J: In my shoulder.

T: Anywhere else?

J: My head.

T: Anywhere else you feel it?

J: No.

T: So now hold the picture of the nightmare in your mind. Got that picture in your mind? And how it makes you think, "I am in danger," and how it makes you feel scared and you have that scared feeling a lot in your arms, in your shoulders, and in your head. Got all that? Now follow my fingers. (EM) Good job. . . . Real good. . . . Just notice whatever you think of. . . . Now stop. . . . Take a deep breath and blow away the bad feelings. . . . And what do you think of now?

J: Think of now?

T: Do you feel the same or different? (With children about Julie's age, it is often useful to ask if something is the same or different, to help them notice and verbalize changes that occur.)

J: Different.

T: How do you feel different?

J: Bad.

T: You feel bad? Where do you feel that bad feeling?

J: In my head.

T: Think about that bad feeling and think about the picture, the nightmare, and follow my fingers. (EM) Okay. . . . Blank it out. . . . Take a deep breath and blow away the bad feelings. . . . And what do you think of now?

J: Think of now?

T: Do you feel the same or different?

J: Different.

T: And how do you feel different?

J: Bad.

T: How bad do you feel now? Show me on this picture. Do you feel really scared or not very scared? (Julie marks on the picture.) That means you don't feel scared at all. Do you feel scared?

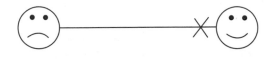

J: No.

T: How else do you feel?

J: How else do I feel? Fine. (As we seem to have another shift in emotions, I decide to conduct some theme development before attempting an installation.)

T: Can you think of the other accident you were in; the other car accident?

J: Yes.

T: Tell me about that accident.

J: That was scary.

T: What happened?

J: What happened?

T: What happened in that accident?

J: There was a man and he was hitting us and the police came and took us to the apartments.

T: Can you get a picture of that in mind? Tell me what that picture looks like.

J: It looks like the policeman was driving in the car and the man was in there and then he locked him in the jail.

T: As you think of that picture in your mind, what does it make you think about you?

J: Think about me? Bad. (This may be about the best negative cognition that Julie, a 5-year-old, can give. Because it is so general, and may be just a feeling instead of a cognition, I decide to go on to clarify feelings rather than a positive cognition.)

T: And how does it make you feel?

J: Bad.

T: Bad how? Like bad sad, scary, or happy?

J: Scary.

T: Show me where that scary feeling is right now. Over here is the most scared you could be and over here is not scared at all. Can you mark in there how you feel right now as you hold that picture in your mind? (Julie indicates a moderate level of fear.) Okay. Mark it right there. And where do you feel that scary feeling in your body?

J: In my hands.
T: So hold that scary picture in your mind of the accident and the police taking the man and locking him in jail and think about that and follow my fingers. (EM) That's good. . . . Now stop and take a deep breath and blow away the bad feelings. What do you think of now?
J: Think of now? Okay.
T: Think about something else that happened in that accident. (Again, I'm not doing an installation here, but rather continuing with theme development. Later, after desensitizing as many channels as possible, I may attempt an installation.) What else do you remember about that accident?
J: About that accident. Bad.
T: Tell me what else you remember.
J: What else I remember? I am okay.
T: What else happened in that accident?
J: My mommy and daddy hurt their head and necks.
T: Think about how your mommy and daddy hurt their heads and their necks, and think about how that makes you feel. Does that make you feel scared?
J: Yes.
T: Okay, think about that. (EM) Blank out your mind, take a deep breath and blow away the scared feelings. And what do you think of now?
J: It's fine. It's all right.
T: What else do you remember about that accident?
J: There is nothing else about the accident I remember.
T: Was there anything else you remember? Were you hurt in that accident? Where were you sitting?
J: In the back.
T: Why didn't you get hurt?
J: Because I am a big girl (a positive cognition turns up).
T: Okay, think about that: "I am a big girl." (EM) Okay, now stop take a deep breath and blow it out. And what do you think of now?
J: Okay.
T: Can you think of another nightmare?
J: No.
T: Can you think of something else that makes you scared?

J: No.

T: Do you want to draw me another picture?

J: Yes.

T: What would you like to draw me a picture of?

J: Another nightmare.

T: Okay. (She draws.) We will hold this up so we can show the camera the picture of this nightmare. Will you tell what happened in the nightmare?

J: What happened in nightmare? Everything was bad.

T: And what's in this picture?

J: Me and the tornado.

T: As you think about you and the tornado, how does it make you feel right now?

J: Bad.

T: Bad. How?

J: Very bad.

T: Okay, think about that.

Unfortunately, the session was interrupted at this point, as Julie's mother had to return to work, and there was a misunderstanding about when our session would end. I closed the session with several sets of eye movements in the safe place, but did not conduct an installation.

## Session 3

T: Julie, do you remember the nightmares you had this week?

J: I didn't have any nightmare this week.

T: I thought you said you had nightmares about the tornado.

J: I had a nightmare the other day. (Maybe she doesn't understand what a week is.)

T: Tell me about that one.

J: There was a tornado coming and we was at the park and there was some sticky sand and they were washing it down.

T: And what was the scary part?

J: When the tornado is there.

T: And what happened when the tornado came?

J: It laid on the sand and was picking all the kids up but we were pushing it down and the kids felled off. (It's hard to tell what this means, but again it's not necessary to pursue the content.)

T: Okay. And can you get a picture of that in your mind?

J: Yep.

T: Tell me what the picture looks like.

J: The picture looks like I look out the window, and there the guys look out the window too, and when it comes, we go down and we push it.

T: And when you hold that picture in your mind, about that tornado and the dream, how does it make you feel? (Because of Julie's previous difficulties in obtaining negative and positive cognitions, I've decided to use only the image, feelings, and physical sensations in this session.)

J: Bad.

T: And does it made you feel a little bit bad like this? Or this bad? Or this bad (shows with hands)?

J: This bad (holds her arms out wide).

T: And where do you feel that bad feeling in your body?

J: My leg.

T: I am going to ask to hold that picture from that bad dream, of the tornado. Got that picture in your mind? Okay. Then the bad feelings. And how you feel them in your hands and legs. Think about all of that and follow my fingers. (EM) Okay, now stop and take a deep breath, and blow the bad feelings away. And what do you think of now?

J: A little bit bad.

T: A little bit bad. Show me with your hands: Is it this much? this much? or this much?

J: This much (holds her hands about a foot apart).

T: So, we will see if we can make it smaller. Think about those bad feelings. And think about how you feel them this much. Where do you feel them in your body?

J: On my other leg, on my other arm, and that's it.

T: Bring up that picture of the tornado. Got that picture in your mind? And the bad feelings? Okay, follow my fingers, and notice the picture and the bad feelings. (EM) That's good. . . . That's good. . . . Doing a good job. . . . Now stop, take a deep breath, and blow the bad feelings away. . . . What do you think of now?

J: All right now.

T: How big are the bad feelings now?

J: (Puts her two hands together)

T: Are they all gone?

J: (Nods)

T: Good for you. Can you think of another nightmare that you have had?

J: I don't have no other nightmares.

T: Do you remember the nightmare you drew me a picture of last time? Tell me what that picture looks like.

J: I remember the sun was breaking.

T: Yeah. What was breaking the sun?

J: The thunder.

T: When you think of that nightmare, can you get that picture in your mind?

J: Yes.

T: When you think of that picture, how does it make you feel?

J: Bad.

T: Show me how big that bad feeling is. How big is that bad feeling right now?

J: This bad (holds her hands about a foot apart).

T: Shall we make that bad feeling smaller?

J: Okay.

T: Want me to show you the picture of the nightmare you drew for me?

J: Okay.

T: See, here's that picture you drew me last time. Tell me what is happening in the picture.

J: The thunder is breaking the sun and we are trying to run.

T: And as you look at that picture, how big is that scared feeling right now? Show me with your hands.

J: This big (holds her hands about a foot apart).

T: Okay. And where do you feel that scared feeling in your body?

J: In my both legs and both arms and that's it.

T: Think about that picture of the nightmare. And how the thunder is breaking the sun and how you and your brother are running. Think about all that and follow my fingers. (EM) That's good. . . . Notice the bad feelings and where you feel them. . . . That's good. . . . Now blank out your mind and take a deep breath and blow away the bad feelings. Good. What do you think of now? (Again, we are going with just the image, feelings, and physical sensations—no cognitions.)

J: Fine.

T: How big is the bad feeling?

J: This big (holds her hands about six inches apart).

T: Want to see if we can make is smaller?

J: Okay.

T: Hold the picture in your mind. Is the picture the same or different?

J: Different.

T: How does it look different?

J: They run over there and he was in the house, and there were some more houses over there. (Perhaps the houses represent safety and security to Julie.)

T: So hold that picture in your mind—about the nightmare about the thunder breaking the sun and notice the bad feelings—and notice the scared feelings in your arms and legs. Think about all that and follow my fingers. (EM) Now stop, take a deep breath, and blow away the bad feelings. How big are the scared feelings now?

J: (Holds her hands two inches apart)

T: Want to make them smaller?

J: Yep.

T: What's the picture of the nightmare look like now?

J: The house is over there and we are running again.

T: Hold that picture in your mind. And where are the bad feelings now in your body?

J: In my head, in my elbow, in my leg, and both shoulders, and that's it.

T: Think about the bad feelings and where you feel them in your body. Get the picture of the nightmare and follow my fingers. (EM) Now stop, take a deep breath, and blow away the bad feelings. . . . Where are the bad feelings now?

J: (Holds her hands close together)

T: Good. Do you have any bad feelings left when you think of that picture?

J: No.

T: Good for you. You have done a really good job. And how do you feel right now?

J: Better.

T: When you feel better, what's that like? Is that happy or relaxed? Or what's that feel like?

J: Happy.

T: Think about that better, happy feeling you feel right now. Where do you feel that in your body?

J: In my both legs, my both elbows, and my both shoulders, and my both arms.

T: Think about that happy feeling and where you feel it in your body and follow my fingers. (EM) Blank it out, take a deep breath, and let out your breath slowly and notice the good feelings. How big are those good feelings now? Are they this big? This big? Or this big?

J: This big (throws her arms wide open and smiles).

T: Good job. I am glad you feel good. How would it be with you if we work on a time when you felt mad? Can you think of time when you felt mad at somebody? (Julie's mother had indicated that Julie was having trouble with anger prior to our starting EMDR in this session. The three of us had discussed this together in the first ten minutes of the session.)

J: I felt mad with my brother.

T: Tell me about that. When did you feel mad at your brother?

J: When he was taking my candy.

T: Can you get a picture of that in your mind when he was taking your candy?

J: (Nods)

T: What does that picture look like?

J: Looks like when we are eating cereal and he got up from the table and then was stealing it.

T: Okay. As you hold that picture in your mind, how does that make you feel when you think about it?

J: Good.

T: Makes you feel good? And it doesn't make you feel bad right now? Can you think of last night when you got mad at your dad?

J: (Nods)

T: Can you get a picture of that?

J: (Nods)

T: What does that picture look like?

J: It looks like, the bed was a queen-size bed and we was yelling and the light was on.

T: And why were you mad?

J: Because I wanted play.

T: And what was your Daddy saying?

J: I don't remember.

T: Why were you mad?

J: Because I didn't want him putting them away.

T: So he wanted to put your toys away and you didn't want him to. And what did you say?

J: I said that he hurt me and he said, "Yeah, right" and he thinks I am lying about . . .

T: So he thought you were lying; does that make you feel mad right now?

J: Yep.

T: Show me how big that mad feeling is right now.

J: A little bit mad.

T: Show me with your hands. Is it this? Or this? Or like this?

J: (Holds her hands one inch apart)

T: A little bit mad. Where do you feel that mad feeling in your body?

J: In my hand, on my shoulder, and in my head.

T: Think about that mad feeling where you feel it all over: hands, shoulder, and in your head. Hold the picture in your mind of last night when he put the toys away and you didn't want him to and you were mad. Think about that. (EM) That's good. . . . Real good. . . . Now stop, take a deep breath, and blow away the bad feelings. . . . What do you think of now?

J: Okay.

T: What's that mad feeling like now?

J: Not too bad.

T: Not too bad. Is it still there some?

J: (Nods)

T: Where do you feel it now in your body?

J: In my finger.

T: Okay. Think about that mad feeling in your finger and think about the pic-ture about last night when you were mad at your dad. Got that picture? Got that mad feeling, the anger? Okay. Follow my fingers. (EM) Okay, blank it out, take a deep breath, and blow away the mad feelings. . . . What are those mad feelings like now?

J: All right.

T: Show me how big those mad feelings are right now.

J: (Holds her hands together)

T: Is it all gone?

J: (Nods)

T: How do you feel now?

J: Happy.

T: Just think about that happy feeling. Follow my fingers. (EM) Okay, let it go, take a deep breath, and let it out slow, and notice those happy feelings. You did a really good job. Do you think you will have any nightmares this week?

J: No.

T: I hope you are right. Would you like to play a game?

The next session was missed (her mother was hospitalized for psychiatric reasons, in part related to PTSD from the three automobile accidents she herself had been in), with the result that Julie didn't come in until almost four weeks later. She and her mom indicated that Julie had not had any nightmares since the last session. In addition, Julie was no longer obsessively preoccupied with tornadoes, now saying that they were "stuck in the mountains" and she didn't have to worry about them anymore. She no longer timidly clung to her mother's side when shopping, but, rather, when her mother needed something, would say, "I'll go get it." Further, her mother said that Julie seemed happy with herself again and once more was able to function independently. Although there had been definite improvement, I wanted to check on the work we had done and determine if there were any additional areas on which to work. We started by checking on the previous nightmares.

T: Julie, do you remember those nightmares you were having?

J: Yes.

T: Are you still scared of tornadoes?

J: No.

T: Why aren't you scared of tornadoes anymore?

J: Because I don't want to be scared anymore. I am praying to God that they be nice dreams.

T: And are they nice dreams?

J: Yes.

T: Do you have nightmares?

J: No.

T: How long has it been since you have had nightmares?

J: A long time.

T: Are you scared of tornadoes?

J: No.

T: Why aren't you scared?

J: Because I am not scared.

T: Where are the tornadoes?

J: They are stuck in the mountains.

T: So if they are stuck in mountains, can they come down here?

J: No.

T: Do you remember the car accidents you were in?

J: No.

T: Do you remember you were in an accident?

J: No.

T: Do you remember that we talked about those accidents?

J: Yes.

T: Do they still scare you?

J: No.

T Can you get a picture in your mind of one of those accidents?

J: Yes.

T: Tell me what that looks like.

J: It looks like we were going to the dentist and then a car hit us. It was a clean car and it shot behind us.

T: And when you think of that picture, how does that make you feel right now?

J: I don't know.

T: Does it make you scared?

J: No.

T: What was the other accident?

J: The other accident? I didn't been in the other accident. I been in the first one.

T: When you ride in a car now, are you ever afraid that you might be in another accident?

J: No.

T: Are you scared when you ride in a car?

J: Yes.

T: What's that scared feeling like?

J: Bad.

T: Should we work on making that bad, scared feeling go away?

J: Yes.

T: Can you get a picture in your mind of riding in that car and feeling scared?

J: Yes.

T: What does that picture look like?

J: It looks like we are driving and the washed car comes and the car behind hit us.

T: As you think about that, does that make you feel scared right now?

J: No.

T: When you are riding in a car, do you feel scared sometimes?

J: (Nods)

T: Think about that when you ride in a car and feel scared sometimes. Where do you feel that scared feeling in your body?

J: In my hands.

T: So hold that picture in your mind: Riding in a car and feeling scared, and where you feel the scared feeling in your hands. Follow my fingers. (EM) That's good. . . . That's really good. . . . Now stop, take a deep breath, and blow the scared feelings away. . . . What do you think of now?

J: It is okay.

T: Think about how it is okay and follow my fingers. (EM) Let it go, take a deep breath, and blow the scared feelings even farther away. What do you think of now?

J: It is okay.

T: Think of something else that makes you feel scared.

J: Nightmares make me scared.

T: Can you think of a nightmare?

J: No.

T: What else makes you scared?

J: Scary movies.

T: Can you think of a scary movie?

J: Yes.

T: What is the scary movie?

J: It is on TV and it is called *X-Files*. (At the time, I had not seen that program. Having subsequently seen the show, I would say that it is too frightening a program for a traumatized 5-year-old child to watch, and I would advise her parents of that.)

T: Think about *X-Files* and how it makes you feel scared. And where do you feel that scared feeling?

J: In my head, in my both legs, and my both arms.

T: Can you get a picture of the *X-Files* in your mind? What does it look like?

J: It looks like monsters and they are all over the town and hurting everybody.

T: Hold that picture in your mind and that scared feeling in your head and in your arms and in your legs. Just think about that. (EM) Blank it out, take a deep breath, and blow those scared feelings away. What do you think of now?

J: I am happy.

T: Think about that happy feeling. (EM) Blank out your mind, take a deep breath, and let it out slow and notice the happy feeling.

J: Happy feeling is still there.

T: Where is it?

J: Everywhere.

T: Think about that happy feeling everywhere. . . . Just notice where you feel it all over. (EM) Blank it out, take a deep breath, and let it out slow. . . . And keep the happy feeling.

J: It is still everywhere.

T: It is still everywhere. That is wonderful! Think of something else that makes you feel scared.

J: Sharks make me feel scared.

T: Sharks do? Can you get a picture in your mind of sharks?

J: (Nods)

T: What does that look like?

J: It looks like sharks in the water eating all the fishes.

T: How does that make you feel?

J: Scared.

T: Where do you feel that scared feeling?

J: Everywhere.

T: Hold that scared feeling and the picture of the shark very deep under water and eating all the other fish. (EM) Okay, let it go. . . . Take a deep breath and blow away that scared feeling.

J: Do you know what kind of movie I have? I have *E.T.* I saw E.T. phone home.

T: Is that a scary movie?

J: No.

T: How does that movie make you feel?

J: That makes me feel happy. And it brings all my bad dreams away.

T: Think about that about how that movie makes you feel happy and makes your bad dreams, your scary dreams, go away. (EM) Let it go, take a deep breath, and just notice the happy feelings. Where do you notice the happy feelings?

J: Everywhere.

At this point, we spend a few more minutes making sure the shark images are desensitized and close the session with the safe place. Of particular note in these sessions is the necessary interplay between thoroughness (activating as many aspects of the associative network as possible) and the need for sensitivity to both the child's ability to handle the emotional material without becoming overwhelmed and the child's attention span.

We scheduled no further sessions, but Julie's mother called me a month later to let me know that Julie was continuing to do well. While this was good news, it was my impression that both parents were suffering from PTSD symptoms from the three accidents in which they had been involved. They continued in treatment with the referring psychiatrist for marital therapy and those PTSD symptoms. Although Julie responded very well to her individual treatment, the amount of apparent disturbance in the family raises the possibility that she might need additional treatment due to the family issues. This case is a good example of a young girl who has suffered two simple, acute traumas and who recovers well with EMDR, but who may need additional interventions due to the other family dynamics.

## Happy Joy, Joy, Joy

The following case is one where the child's symptoms from an automobile accident were not as extreme as Julie's and the treatment was even briefer. It is also a case of a simple trauma, although after one year the symptoms might be considered on the verge of becoming chronic.

Stan, 7 years old, came in with his mother about a year after he and his dad were involved in a car-pedestrian accident. He had been on a walk with his father and a male friend of his father, when they were hit by a car making a right turn. He was pinned against a tree by the car and was unable to move. Stan was taken to the hospital by ambulance, treated, and released, as he had only minor injuries, such as abrasions. Initially, on returning home, Stan seemed to think that the accident was "no big deal," but he began to have nightmares, which continued episodically through most of the next year. These nightmares occurred once or twice a week. On a developmental history form, Stan's mother, Mary, wrote, "Throughout (the last year) there were incidents of nightmares that woke Stan, who would be crying. I would also hear Stan speaking loudly while he was asleep. The nightmares, according to Stan, involved his attempting to run away from someone who was trying to kill him. Though I felt Stan was having residual effects of some sort from this incident, I decided to consult you due to the art (enclosed) that Stan drew his first day of school this year."

The first picture showed Stan helping up a girl who had been run over by a car (figure 5.3, page 122), with a second one depicting a girl crushed under a car that had run over her (figure 5.4, page 123). In the same picture, a plane flying overhead crashed and destroyed a boy who had been walking outside. Of course, Stan's mother became concerned that the accident was having more severe residual effects on Stan's functioning than had been immediately obvious to her.

I have noticed, from working with children who have been traumatized, that if the child thinks what happened will cause him or a loved one to die, the memory of the trauma becomes "fixed" or "stuck" in the mind without changing over time. Joseph LeDoux (1996) wrote that a primitive part of the brain

*Figure 5.3*

(the reptilian brain), which is involved in self-preservation, becomes activated when the individual thinks that the issue is one of survival or death. This primitive and subcortical area of the brain then exerts a stronger influence on behavior than does the cortex with its rational analyses. In fact, he found that in animals, these traumatic memories seemed to be indelible and could not be modified over time. Thus, if EMDR helps to change the thought "I'm in danger of death" or "I'm going to die" or "My daddy's going to die," it is most likely having subcortical effects. If traditional therapies deal primarily with cortical thoughts, they are probably less effective in trauma-related therapy issues, as they have greater difficulty reaching the subcortical representations that likely exist concerning life-and-death issues.

While the above is an oversimplification of the findings regarding the differences between traumatic memories and ordinary memories, a good deal of current research supports the fact that traumatic memories are quite different from nontraumatic memories (e.g., van der Kolk, 1997). Further, the more we under-

*Figure 5.4*

stand about those differences, the better we can make educated guesses about what it is that EMDR does in causing a traumatic memory to be transformed into an ordinary memory.

Several studies have found decreased hippocampal volume in individuals with PTSD, indicating subcortical effects (Bremner et al., 1995; Paige, Reid, Allen, & Newton, 1990; Rauch et al., 1996). Others have found increased activation of the amygdala and related structures in individuals with PTSD (LeDoux, 1992; Pitman, Orr, Forgue, de Jong, & Clairborn, 1987), again implicating subcortical structures in traumatic memory.

Hemispheric lateralization also appears to be involved, in that persons with PTSD respond to traumatic memories with increased activation of the right hemisphere and decreased activation of the left (van der Kolk, 1997). Brain-imaging research (Rauch et al., 1996) has indicated that individuals with PTSD respond to their traumatic memories with heightened activity only in the right hemisphere and in the areas associated with heightened emotional arousal (the amygdala, insula, and the medial temporal lobe). In addition, there is a decrease in the left-hemisphere activity, specifically Broca's area, which is thought to play a role in translating personal experiences into communicable language.

There is evidence that children who have been abused manifest a variety of neurodevelopmental abnormalities with different behavioral sequelae (Teicher, 1997). Especially vulnerable in brain development is the hippocampus, which is involved in memory storage and retrieval, as well as behavioral inhibition and anxiety. Abuse-induced abnormalities in hippocampal development may lead to problems in handling anxiety, as well as producing somatic and dissociative effects (Teicher, 1997). Further, severe early abuse is associated with deficient left-hemisphere development as determined by EEG studies (Teicher, 1997).

Other neuroimaging studies have implicated the role of the anterior cingulate gyrus, in that non-PTSD participants activated their anterior cingulate only in response to traumatic reminders, while PTSD participants activated the anterior cingulate indiscriminately. Brain scans recorded before and after successful EMDR treatment on a small number of persons with PTSD (van der Kolk, 1997) indicate that their improvement is related to increased activation of the cingulate area and of the left prefrontal cortex. This suggests that successful treatment with EMDR allows traumatized individuals to now discriminate between real threats and traumatic reminders that are no longer threatening. While much of this evidence is recent and tentative, it is helpful in suggesting ideas about what is happening in the brain during EMDR treatment.

The evidence is that EMDR causes changes in traumatic memory to occur more quickly and more predictably than anything else we know (van Etten & Taylor, in press; Wilson, Becker, & Tinker, 1995; Wilson, Becker, & Tinker, 1997). Thus, children who have been traumatized, who have thought that they were going to die, who act as if the danger is not over, then develop symptoms that indicate they are still in acute fear of imminent death. Julie's symptoms demonstrate that fear. Stan's nightmares indicate that at some subcortical level, he thought he was still in danger of being killed, and, indeed, that someone was trying to kill him. If he was asked in a rational way if he thought someone was attempting to kill him, he probably would have said no. But his nightmares and his drawings indicated that at some level he felt differently. It was as if the danger was still present and imminent each day, instead of being an unusual event. LeDoux, Romanski, and Xagoraris (1991) suggest that matters of life and death activate the brainstem, with vital information being indelibly and immutably recorded in the brain (at least in other species). It may be that EMDR in some way changes this learning that is "indelible." What happened in a single session of EMDR apparently allowed Stan to get beyond his underlying fear of impending death. Here's how that session transpired, along with notations about my interventions.

After Stan seemed to feel comfortable in the session and we had set up a safe place, I asked Stan to recall the accident in which he had been involved.

"What I'm going to ask you to do is remember that accident we were just talking about. Bring up that picture that you got in your mind of the accident. Remember, you told me about the car? Tell me what that picture looks like."

"It's me under a car." Instantly, Stan's hands cover his eyes.

"As you hold that picture in your mind, what's it make you think about yourself?"

"Under a car."

As this is not exactly a good negative cognition, I am interested in probing for a better one. Stan is a good example of a boy who needs additional help in developing the elements of the EMDR protocol, due to his young age.

"Okay, and if you're under a car, what's that mean about you?"
"That I'm bleeding." This is not really a negative self-concept, but a further description of the event. Since my probe to improve the negative cognition has not led to much improvement, I decide to provide some more direct help.

"Do you think something like, 'I'm in danger' or 'I can't protect myself'?"
"Yeah."

"Which of those thoughts do you have?"

"Both of them."

"Both of them? Okay, what words would you rather put with that picture about yourself?"

"Well, I don't know."

"Here's an idea. You tell me what fits. One thought you might have is, 'It's over now' or 'I'm safe now.'"

"Okay."

"Which of those would you rather think about?"

"It's over now." Although Stan has required assistance with negative and positive cognitions, he has been able to make choices with the possibilities I have presented to him.

"As you hold that picture in your mind, how does it make you feel?" Note that I neglected to obtain a VOC for "It's over now." However, when I probe for a feeling associated with the memory, Stan again gives me a description of the event—not unusual for this age child.

"Me standing on the ground."

"Think about the picture where the car's on top of you and you're bleeding. Think of that. And as you think about that, how does it make you feel—happy or sad or scared? How does it make you feel *right now* as you hold that picture with the car: You're under the car and you're bleeding." Here, I'm making the statement as emotionally evocative as possible.

"I'm crying."

"You're crying? And what feelings are there when you cry?" I'm still probing for feelings. Tears have many different feelings associated with them, and it's good practice to inquire about which ones might be there.

"I don't know."

"Are you sad or scared?"

"Scared!" Now we finally have an identified feeling.

"How strong is that scared feeling right now, from 0 to 10, where 0 is not there at all and 10 is the worst it could be? How strong is it right now as you think about that accident?"

"Eight."

"Now Stan, what I'm going to ask you to do is hold that picture in your mind, being under the car and bleeding and being scared and thinking, 'I'm in danger, I can't protect myself.' Hold all of that in mind and follow my fingers with your eyes, back and forth. Okay? Got the picture and the scared feelings? Where do you feel those scared feelings in your body?"

"Everywhere again."

"Hold that and follow my fingers with your eyes. Now open your eyes and hold the picture (Stan's hands were still covering his eyes). (EM) That's it. . . . Real good. . . . You're doing a good job. . . . Real good. . . . That's it. . . . Just notice the picture, notice the feelings. Blank out the picture. Take a deep breath and blow the bad feelings away. What do you think of now?"

"Happy."

"Okay, hold that happy feeling and follow my fingers. (EM) Just move your eyes. Hold your head still and just move your eyes. . . . That's it. . . . Real good. . . . Okay, let it fade. Take a deep breath and let it out. What do you get now?"

"I don't know."

"Bring up that picture again of being under the car and bleeding and tell me what that picture looks like now. Is it the same or different?" (I'm going back to target as Stan is unable to report anything.)

"The same."

"And that scared feeling. Is that the same or different?"

"The same."

"How strong is that scared feeling right now, from 0 to 10, where 0 is not there and 10 is the worst it could be? How bad is that scared feeling right now?"

"Six." (It was 8 a moment ago.)

"Okay. Bring up that picture of the accident. Have you got that picture of the accident? . . . Okay. And the scared feelings? Okay. And the thought "I'm in danger; I can't protect myself.' Think about all of that and follow my fingers. (EM) You're doing good. Just let whatever comes to mind come to mind. . . . That's good. . . . Just think about anything that comes to mind. Follow my fingers. . . . Keep following my fingers. . . . Now stop. . . . Blank it out. . . . Take a deep breath.

. . . Blow out the bad feelings. . . . What do you think of now?"

Stan shrugs.

"What are the feelings like now?"

"I don't know."

"After the last time you did this you felt happy. Do you feel happy now?"

Stan nods.

"Think about that happy feeling and follow my fingers. Just think about the happy feelings. (EM) Doing good. . . . That's it. . . . And just let whatever comes up, come up. . . . Follow my fingers. . . . That's it. . . . Blank it out. . . . Take a deep breath. . . . Blow out the bad feelings. . . . What do you think of now?"

"Happy. Happy joy."

"Wow."

"I can sing a song to you."

"Okay, sing a song."

"I have to get on the ground."

"Sing it right there so I can get you on TV."

"Actually it's kind of crazy. That's why I need to be on the ground."

"Okay, I'll turn the camera then." Stan does a completely unrecognizable version of "Johnny Be Good" on air guitar. "Okay, sit back where you were. Now, let's do a check. Stan, can you bring up the picture again of the accident?"

"I don't think I can."

"What's happened to it?"

"It cleared out of my brain."

"And how do you feel right now?"

"Happy joy."

"Happy joy," I restate.

"Happy joy, joy, joy."

"Can you think of another part of the accident? Sit up again so I can get you on TV. Think of anther part of the accident."

"I'm thinking that I'm knocking over a tree with my head and that's how I got my scars."

"Okay, hold that picture."

"That's when I was 6, too."

"Was it?"

"That was two years ago." (Although Stan said he was 6, he now says it was two years ago. I took this to indicate that it was a separate incident when he got his scars.)

"Think of that and follow my fingers. (EM) Good . . . good . . . good job. . . . You're doing a good job. Just let whatever comes to mind, come to mind. Now stop, take a deep breath, let it out."

"You've got games? Can we play one?"

"Maybe later. And what do you think of now?"

"Happy."

"Think of another part of the accident."

"There is no other part."

"There is no other part?"

"No."

"How do you feel right now?"

"Happy."

"I think we better play a game."

Again, in this segment, we can see the rapid resolution of the trauma, as well as an earlier one (two years ago). As Stan required more help than some other children in understanding the protocol, at times I asked more leading questions than what is optimal. Did these leading questions distort the process? Perhaps they did to some degree, but the leading questions can also be construed as low-level inferences, which did not heavily distort the therapeutic process. If the leading questions are valid, they further the EMDR process; if not, the process continues until resolution occurs. As a general rule, however, it is better to avoid leading questions or to use them minimally.

Stan's emotions changed dramatically during this short session, as he went from showing a surprising amount of anxiety nonverbally, with his hands immediately covering his eyes, to joy so intense that he did a song and dance. I have been surprised by how many children who, like Stan, mention the word "joy" after they resolve a frightening situation. These dramatic changes seem to outweigh the impact of helping the process along through a minimal use of leading questions.

## Dad, Don't Go So Fast

EMDR can be helpful to children even younger than Stan and Julie who have been traumatized by car accidents. Mike was barely 3 years old when involved in an accident where a garbage truck collided with the van in which his family was riding. His father became disabled due to a back injury sustained in the accident, and Mike was momentarily unconscious, pinned underneath the back seat in the van. Although Mike had been sleeping by himself prior to the accident, afterward he felt unable to do so, because of severe anxiety. Also, following the accident he experienced nightmares about once or twice a week. He would say, "Daddy, it scares me," when talking about a nightmare. In addition, during the nighttime, he would frequently wake up and go into his parents' bedroom and sleep on the floor by their bed. He would also sleep in the living room on a couch that was near their bedroom door so he was not as far away from them as he would have been in his own bed. In the weeks immediately following the accident, Mike wet his pants a number of times, which was unusual for him. However, these daytime accidents had ceased about a month prior to his first appointment. When riding in the car with his father, Mike seemed apprehensive and would keep watching for cars behind them. He scanned the environment for garbage trucks and vans and would anxiously point them out to his father whenever he would see them. He also frequently admonished his father, "Dad, don't go so fast." Overall, it was clear that Mike's behavior had been altered by the accident.

After an initial session with Mike and his father, I conducted two EMDR sessions with Mike, about nine days apart. These sessions seemed to go well, and when his mother brought him in for an appointment three weeks later, she reported that he was doing much better: He was no longer having nightmares, he exhibited no tension when riding in the car with his mother or his father, he no longer paid undue attention to garbage trucks and vans, and he now slept in his own bed once again, not outside his parents' bedroom door. Whereas I intended to see him for one or two follow-up sessions, his parents missed the next session and did not reschedule further appointments. By phone contact they indicated that Mike was doing well and that they would bring him back if further problems ensued.

If Mike were an adult or a young adult, it might be argued that the results could be due to placebo effects. That is, the adult treated with EMDR would recognize that what was accomplished in therapy might have some effect on his PTSD symptoms, and the expectations themselves would eliminate the symptoms. However, with a child as young as Mike, it is less likely that he would form an expectation that the EMDR would affect his anxiety while riding in a car, his nightmares, or where he slept at night. Of course, his parents could convey that those were their expectations, and Mike might rise to their expectations. Mike's parents, though, were like many parents; they just brought him in and allowed me to administer a treatment. Then they took him back home and waited to see what would happen. Thus, it seems that placebo effects would operate less with a very young child like Mike, who would be less aware of cause-and-effect relationships between therapy and behavioral outcomes, and would not be watching to see how EMDR affected his nightmares or riding in a car.

Generally, the role of expectations on the part of the child is so reduced that it is difficult to see how they would be a major influence for the child, especially if the parents are skeptical. Even if the parents are not skeptical, why would their expectations about EMDR be more powerful than their expectations and hopes that the child will "just get over it"? Those "just get over it" expectations were likely operative for months prior to the EMDR treatment, but did not produce positive effects.

If EMDR is effective with young children, where placebo effects and exposure effects are likely minimal, it increases the likelihood that the effectiveness of EMDR with adults is not primarily due to those factors, but rather to intrinsic aspects of the procedure itself. And, in fact, our 15-month follow-up research with adults shows that the EMDR results hold over that 15 months (Wilson, Becker, & Tinker, 1997). Out of a total of 67 participants, no participant reliably deteriorated ("reliable" deterioration is a technical term that takes into account the reliability of the test being used to measure the deterioration). This finding is in contrast to a recent study of reliable change (Lunnen & Ogles, 1998) that found in a sample of 52 outpatients at a mental health clinic, 13 out of the 52 reliably deteriorated. While the two rates cannot be directly compared because of differences between the samples, it can be seen that EMDR has a low rate of reliable deterioration. Further, Chemtob and Nakashima (1996) reported that not only did they find EMDR to be effective with children traumatized by Hurricane Iniki, but it also was a relatively benign and enjoyable form of treatment for the children.

## STRUCK BY LIGHTNING

The case of 10-year-old Brent is another example of a simple trauma. Brent was struck by lightning on a sunny day on the eastern plains of Colorado. It was on a summer weekend holiday, and many neighborhood families were outside, enjoying the sunshine with friends and family. A solitary small, dark cloud appeared overhead, and a single bolt of lightning struck Brent as he was playing outside on a small mound. Although he initially was without pulse or respiration, he was revived with CPR and rushed to a regional hospital by helicopter. He survived, but not without residual impairments. He had to relearn how to read and he was impaired in most aspects of his academic functioning. His play with toys a year after being struck was like that of a much younger child. He had no appetite and was slowly losing weight. Other family members would have to remind him to stop playing and to come and eat, for he didn't manifest any interest in food. Even when he was at the table, he had to be urged to eat, for the desire was no longer there. Mealtimes became frustrating for everyone involved, as Brent did not eat willingly. In addition, he became understandably phobic about going outside when there was a cloud to be seen. Even if he was riding in a car and clouds appeared, he became panicky. In the winter, even snow clouds caused him great anxiety.

A year after Brent was struck by lightning, he became a participant in our EMDR children's study (unpublished) and he received five sessions of EMDR with pre- and post-evaluations. No other form of therapy was employed during the course of the study and all sessions were videotaped so that treatment fidelity could be checked. Therefore, therapy results with Brent are a bit more rigorous than those usually obtained in a standard outpatient setting. After five sessions of EMDR, Brent was no longer phobic about playing outside when there was a cloud in the sky. He told us about an "experiment" he did after the first two sessions of EMDR, where he went outside when the sky was cloudy, and stayed outside for 10 minutes without feeling upset. From then on, he was fine playing outside, clouds or no clouds. He also felt comfortable riding in a car during a rainstorm, as long as the windows were up.

Also important was the fact that Brent's appetite came back, due to our focus on that in the EMDR sessions. During the four weeks during which he received EMDR treatment, he gained five pounds. His mother reported that for the first time since he had been struck by lightning, Brent said that he felt hungry. Also, when he came to the table, he was more willing to eat and did not have to be urged to eat as much as before.

In EMDR, knowing that he had little or no appetite, I deliberately had him focus on his favorite foods as he moved his eyes back and forth. Brent identified pizza, macaroni and cheese, and hot dogs as some of his favorite foods. Prior to his being struck by lightning, spinach had been a preferred food, but he had shown no interest in it since being struck. After the first session in which we targeted favorite foods, he again showed an interest in spinach, listing it as one of his favorites. A few days later, his mother included it in his dinner. Brent liked it and ate it. At the end of the five sessions permitted in the study, Brent's mother indicated that he was showing hunger at breakfast and lunch, and inquired if we would include a few additional sessions so that he would be hungry at dinner. Of course, we had to tell her that dinner was not included.

There are a number of medical conditions where loss of appetite becomes a major problem, such as cancer and AIDS and their treatments. It might be worthwhile to pursue the connection between loss of appetite and the use of EMDR to stimulate interest in food in those medical conditions, much as was done with Brent. Again, we have the suggestion that EMDR might be affecting the lower brain centers, as well as the possibility that EMDR might be involved in stimulating neural connections in the brain.

EMDR treatment of phantom limb pain is another area where EMDR has effects that go beyond what is usually obtained in other therapies. Phantom limb pain is a condition where a person who has had an amputation continues to experience pain in the now-missing limb. Such pain affects 50–80% of all amputees, but less than 1% ever experience complete elimination of pain on a lasting basis (Sherman, 1997). In 1995, Linda Vanderlaan, an EMDR therapist, treated a Colombian girl with phantom limb pain a few days after a leg amputation due to cancer. The girl's phantom limb pain disappeared. This anecdotal report inspired us to conduct a pilot study with seven individuals who suffered from phantom limb pain (Wilson, Tinker, & Becker, 1997). Of the seven individuals, we found that six truly had phantom limb pain—the other had pain in the stump itself, which had been misinterpreted as phantom limb pain. All six remaining participants reduced their phantom limb pain; two eliminated it completely (one after one year of continuous pain, the other after 12 years of pain), and one other (an eighth participant in the pilot study*) eliminated the most severe aspects of it (after 25 years of pain). One of the participants in the pilot study was a 14-year-old girl who had had her leg amputated when she was 10 years old because of cancer. Her phantom limb pain decreased from 4 to 1 on a 0–10 scale, where 0 represented no pain and 10 indicated the worst pain imaginable (all seven participants declined from an average score of 5 to 1.5 after five sessions of EMDR treatment). It is now two years posttreatment and treatment gains have been maintained for the adolescent girl and for the other three who eliminated or almost eliminated their phantom limb pain (we don't yet have follow-up data on the others).

Research in this very interesting application of EMDR is continuing. If these findings are confirmed on other children and adults, it is an indication that EMDR produces an effect that no other therapy, physical or mental, has been able to accomplish. And it once again suggests that EMDR taps aspects of brain functioning that are useful for healing in a unique and rapid fashion.

---

*This person's one-year follow-up data was not available at the 1997 presentation, so she was not included in the data analysis.

*six*

# Simple Traumas:
# Bereavement, Specific Phobias

"I feel like all my problems are gone. . . .
I just flushed them all out."
—JUDY, AGE 10

IN THE PREVIOUS CHAPTER, we looked at the treatment efficacy of EMDR with several kinds of simple traumas. In this chapter, we continue the examination of the effectiveness of EMDR with other simple traumas. What is most notable from these cases is the consistency of treatment effectiveness and the brevity of treatment. In my years as a clinical psychologist prior to using EMDR, I employed a variety of treatment approaches, and if one didn't work, I tried another. Over years of practice, I think I improved my ability to establish an effective treatment relationship and to select approaches that fit the problems of the individual seeking treatment. Becoming an effective therapist seemed to be a melding of several areas: interpersonal skills, knowledge of content areas such as diagnosis and syndromes, and knowledge of specific techniques. Now, however, with EMDR being consistently and predictably effective, I tend to fit other approaches around EMDR, rather than the other way around. This leads to an approach that integrates assessment of trauma characteristics with the initiation of EMDR on specific targets, followed by predictable outcomes.

If the reader is familiar with EMDR, the cases presented will make sense and fit into his or her existing EMDR expertise. The reader is likely to think something like, "I've seen sessions like this with adults; I just didn't know they happened that way with children" or "I've had sessions like that with children, but I've never had a case just like that before" or "I can see now how EMDR can be simplified so children can respond to it."

The reader who has not used EMDR is likely to view the cases as oversimplified or as atypical outcomes or where the therapist presenting the case comes across as so expert, charismatic, or so effective that the average therapist could only hope to emulate the presenting therapist on rare occasions, if at all. However, when EMDR therapists from across the nation (all were trained at the facilitator, or highest, level for practicing EMDR) assisted after the Oklahoma City bombing, a number of individuals were treated in three sessions by three different EMDR therapists. These individuals did as well as those who saw only one therapist for the three sessions. This would seem to be the ultimate level of treatment portability, where one therapist can easily pick up where another therapist has left off, and results are not as dependent upon the therapist as upon the EMDR itself. In the free clinic in Oklahoma City, the way this would happen is that the second therapist would ascertain from the prior therapist's notes the starting image from the previous session as well as the negative and positive cognitions, the VOC, the emotions, the SUDS, and the physical sensations, and then check the current level of VOC and SUDS. If the image had not been fully desensitized, the therapist would continue on the desensitization. If the desensitization was complete for that memory, the therapist would target a new image or memory and proceed with that.

Further, when I have trained other therapists around the country to use EMDR with children, they often report experiences similar to what I describe. Other clinicians are excited about the results they obtain with children using EMDR. This suggests to me that EMDR outcomes are unusually consistent from therapist to therapist.

When I trained therapists in Hawaii to work with treatment-resistant children still diagnosed as PTSD several years after Hurricane Iniki, positive outcomes from EMDR were documented by the different therapists who had been trained (Chemtob & Nakashima, 1996). Thus, a double validation was obtained: one for the application of EMDR to children and one for the training the therapists received.

The point I wish to make is that the EMDR results presented here are reasonable outcomes, achievable by well-trained and conscientious therapists. In the past, most new therapies have been highly dependent upon the personality of the founder: Freud, Jung, Adler, Erickson, Perls, Rogers, Ellis, to name a few. Even cognitive-behavioral therapies are very different, depending on whether it's the approach of Wolpe, Stampfl, Lazarus, Meichenbaum, or Beck being employed. In contrast, EMDR seems to accommodate a variety of personality styles and a variety of theoretical orientations on the part of the therapist. And while the structure of EMDR remains consistent from therapist to therapist, the content from the client is given free rein within that structure.

# BEREAVEMENT

## It Felt Like Someone Just Stabbed Me

While death is difficult for children to understand, the loss of a parent is particularly wrenching and incomprehensible to most. Judy lost her mother to cancer when Judy was 7 years old. Following her mother's death, Judy's behavior deteriorated. Her grades in school declined. She alienated most, if not all, of her friends by her angry outbursts. She goaded her teacher into anger, and did the same thing with her brother. With her brother, however, she often got into physical fights, in addition to taunting him. On one occasion, she jabbed a pencil so hard into his arm that it went into the flesh. On another occasion, she became enraged at a friend, and called her on the phone, leaving a message that she hated her and wished that her friend and her whole family would die. Judy's father was aghast about such behavior and had placed her in grief counseling for 20 sessions, followed by weekly therapy over the next three years. Judy's behavior gradually worsened instead of improving. She was antagonistic toward her father and disruptive when she was cared for by her grandparents. On occasion, they had called Judy's father, begging for assistance, as Judy was out of control and they were at their wits' end in attempting to deal with her. As nothing seemed to be working, Judy's father decided to try another therapist and was referred to me, although he had not heard anything about EMDR. After obtaining background information and a developmental history, I explained to Judy and her father that I would like to use EMDR with her as part of therapy. We discussed the EMDR procedures and what was known about its effectiveness with children and adults. Judy and her father had no objections to another therapeutic approach; in fact, they welcomed it. Judy, however, was skeptical that any new therapist was going to help much. While she had appreciated her previous therapist, at this point she did not expect much from therapy.

In the first session when I attempted to broach the topic of the death of Judy's mother, Judy was clearly reluctant to talk about it, saying that she had discussed that topic more than enough in her previous therapy. Here's how that session went when I asked her what it was like to see her mother in the hospital immediately after her mother's death:

J: I asked if I could be alone with her, so my dad shooed everyone out and he went out himself. And I was 7 and I thought this was a big hoax. And so I started pushing my mother and told her to get up. And I was pushing her more and I kept on telling her to get up. I hadn't cried. When I got to the hospital I didn't cry cause I didn't know what was going on. I'm normally the

youngest in my family, besides my cousins, but they're kind of not my regular family, I guess. So I didn't really know what was going on. My brother
knew what was going on and so did my cousin Ronald 'cause they're three
years older than I am. So they know a little bit more about what disease my
mother had and I didn't 'cause I was in first grade and we're only learning
about how to say no to drugs. I was kind of shocked when my Aunt Julie
came in. She told me to stop pushing my Mom. I said, "Well she's asleep and
I want her to get up." And my aunt started crying and she told me my mom
was dead and I started screaming and crying and I started yelling, "No she
isn't, she's just asleep and I'm going to get her up." And the whole family
came back in again. And I guess that's all about that subject.

I was surprised by the amount of emotion with which Judy recounted this
scene. It was clear that she still intensely felt the pain of her mother's death four
years ago. As I had previously set up a safe place and had discussed EMDR with
Judy, I went ahead with targeting the images and feelings coming up, ignoring,
for the moment, negative and positive cognitions.

T: Okay. What I'd like you to do right now is hold that picture in your mind,
   where you're pushing at your mom and telling her to get up, and also the sad
   feelings that go with that. Can you get that picture?
J: (Nods)
T: And the feelings that go with that?
J: Okay.
T: Okay, follow my fingers. (EM) That's good. . . . That's good. . . . That's it. . . .
   Real good. . . . That's it. . . . Just notice. . . . Just watch. Okay, now blank out
   your mind. Take a deep breath and just relax as you breathe out. What comes
   to mind now?
J: Nothing.
T: Okay. Judy, when you were doing that you looked real sad. Did you feel sad
   when you were moving your eyes back and forth?

Actually, Judy's eyelids had begun to droop, an indication that dissociation was
starting to occur. It is quite strange to see a child apparently start to fall asleep in
the midst of recalling the most awful traumatic memories. It seems to be a very
primitive defense reaction, similar to what happens when other species become
overwhelmed with a dangerous situation (Nijenhuis, Vanderlinden, & Spinhoven,
1998). As I wanted to have Judy fully present emotionally, I attempted to comment on what was going on, by mentioning the very feelings I thought she might
be defending against.

J: (Shakes her head no)

Since that intervention didn't appear to work, I decided to take her back to the original target. Going back to target more frequently when a person begins to dissociate is an approach that can be used to minimize the dissociation.

T: Okay. Bring up that picture again; what's it look like now?

J: The same thing I guess. I can't really picture it.

T: Is it harder to picture it right now?

J: (Nods)

T: Let me have you picture the part where your aunt comes in the room and tells you to stop pushing her and tells you that she's dead and you start screaming. Can you get a picture of that? (As the image had disappeared, I could have had her focus on the memory instead of the image, but I chose to have her focus on an image closely related to the first one.)

J: (Nods)

T: What kind of feelings do you get with that?

J: Sad, mad, confused, and scared.

T: Hold all of that in mind. Follow my fingers. (EM) That's great. . . . That's good. . . . Just watch. . . . Just notice. . . . That's it. . . . That's it. Okay, blank out your mind, take a deep breath. Just let it out slow. Relax as you let it out. And what comes up now?

J: Nothing.

T: Okay. Go back to that picture. Bring that picture up again. What do you get now?

J: I don't know. I can't think of anything. I can't see anything.

T: Can you see anything at all with that picture?

J: (Shakes her head no)

T: How about that picture before when you're pushing and shoving your mom (back to the first image). Can you get that picture?

J: (Nods)

T: What kind of feelings go with that picture?

J: Kind of scared because she didn't wake up, she didn't move on her own, and she was turning blue, and she had eye patches over her eyes. I didn't know why they had those over 'til my dad told me about a year after my mom died. They had those on there because they took out part of her eye. She was donating it to someone who needed it. My mother was a loving person. Whenever she went shopping she only got things for me and my brother. Nothing for her. If she ever got anything she would have to get it from somebody. She never went out and bought it for herself.

T: Judy, hold that picture in your mind where you're pushing and shoving and the feelings that go with it, those scared feelings. Hold that picture and those feelings, follow my fingers. (EM) Okay, blank out your mind, take a deep breath, and then relax as you let it out. Good. And what do you get now?

Here's a good example of therapeutic choice within the EMDR framework. Judy had mentioned feelings associated with the hospital image of her mother, and how her mother was a giving, selfless person. I chose to return to the hospital image, as it seemed likely to have more intense affect associated with it.

J: (Pause) My grandpa. (I was startled by the emergence of this new channel, but realized it was an indication of associative chaining on Judy's part.)
T: Okay.
J: He died in October of this year and I just feel like my whole family is falling apart because my Aunt Jen and my Uncle Roy are divorced. My grandpa and my mom are dead. I just feel like we're falling apart.
T: How's that make you feel?
J: Sad, because sometimes I feel like I'm mostly to blame. When my mom died I was always blaming myself 'cause I ran away from my mom. I've actually packed my bags and run down the street but she would run after me and get me.

Again, I was surprised by what Judy indicated in terms of blame. However, in EMDR, children often bring up a sense of blame or guilt. It happens so often that it makes me wonder if we as humans aren't preprogrammed to feel guilt. Only as we get older and understand cause and effect in logical adult terms, do we more appropriately assign that guilt. Another example: When children's parents get divorced, it is so common that the children involved think that it is their fault, that the therapist must probe for these ideas as a matter of course.

It is highly unlikely that someone told Judy that she was responsible for her mother's death; it is more likely Judy's own construction. She is clearly inaccurate about assigning blame (and guilt) to herself about the breakup of her family, but it is important that these feelings are being expressed, so that they can be reprocessed and change.

T: Okay. Think about that. Follow my fingers. (EM) Okay, blank it out, take a deep breath. What comes up now?
J: Nothing. I feel like all my problems are gone. Just those are it. Probably that's all there was.
T: How does this make you feel, that all your problems are gone?
J: I feel like I just flushed them all out. They're all drained or something.

T: Where do you feel those good feelings right now (probing for physical sensations)?

J: Everywhere.

T: Okay. Think about those good feelings. Notice those good feelings. Follow my fingers. (EM)

One of the most amazing aspects of EMDR is its impact on emotions. It has a way of causing intense emotions to "wash out," leaving the person with the memory but not the intense affect formerly associated with it. Judy's description is similar to that of many adults. However, her facial expression had not changed (not unusual with children), and it's very easy to believe that nothing of much importance happened. Major changes in subsequent behavior typically follow, if the emotional change has really occurred. Therapists experienced in EMDR come to look for these emotional shifts and to welcome them for what they portend. The shift is usually more subtle with children than with adults, but often it is discernible even in very young children. EMDR is most different from other therapies in this particular aspect, as cognitive therapies operate on the basis that if the cognitions are changed, the emotions will tag along; behavioral therapies operate on the basis that if the behaviors are changed, the emotions will follow suit; insight-oriented therapies hold that if new insights are gained, the emotions will subsequently change also. While it is clear that insight-oriented, behavioral, and cognitive therapies are effective at times, it seems that EMDR is the only therapy that directly and consistently impacts the emotions in persons who have been traumatized, thus shortening the therapeutic process and often taking it to a deeper emotional level.

Lipke (1996) has proposed a four-activities heuristic model of psychotherapy, which posits that all therapies engage in the four activities of accessing information, providing information, facilitating information processing, and limiting informational access. He suggests that EMDR is a radical departure from other therapies in that it has a much more profound impact on facilitating information processing, thus speeding the course of therapy. More recently, Hyer and Brandsma (1997) have suggested that even without eye movements, EMDR is good therapy, as it makes use of ten common and sound principles of effective therapy:

1. EMDR accesses associative networks, which are unique to each person.
2. The positive growth motives within the person will ultimately be greater than the negative ones.
3. Therapeutic movement (versus avoidance) is essential for change.
4. The therapist is most effective when nondirective with regard to content.
5. Clarity of treatment expectations is important.

6. "Clean language" is applied, which involves the therapist's use of nonleading language.
7. EMDR supports the use of cognition (especially the use of negative and positive cognitions).
8. Feelings and sensations are even more central than cognitions in EMDR, and they allow the process to unfold naturally and honestly.
9. EMDR reduces the need for security operations on the part of the client.
10. The role of the therapist is liberated: The therapist functions as a "blank screen," but also has a manualized set of rules to create therapeutic movement if the process stalls.

Taken together, these two points of view suggest that EMDR can be effective therapy, with or without eye movement. However, more research will be needed to ascertain whether eye movements really add an additional dimension of effectiveness to EMDR. Perhaps pertinent to this is the observation that EMDR started with noticing the effect of eye movements on negative thoughts; the other stuff was added later to increase the range of effectiveness of EMDR with more difficult clients.

While the first session seemed to produce a major emotional shift for Judy, it needed to be checked in the next session. After what seems to be a good EMDR session, two things must be checked: Did the emotional changes hold (which can be checked at the beginning of the next session) and did behavior change outside of the session (this is more crucial)? If an emotional shift occured, as was apparent with Judy, and her behavior did not change, then more work would need to be done. Perhaps Judy had other traumas that would require desensitization or she may have been caught up in other ongoing situations that would require therapeutic attention. So, in the next session, one week later, we started with a review of the previous session and proceeded from there.

T: Which event seems most upsetting to you right now?
J: When I came in.
T: Okay. Tell me what that picture looks like.
J: I'm sitting or standing and my aunt just arrived and, well she didn't just arrive but she came in the room. She didn't know that I wanted to be alone and she just walked in the room and she saw me pushing and shoving my mom and she told me that she was dead.

A subtle, qualitative change is apparent here: Judy is now talking about the event as if it is in the past. In the previous session, her language and emotions suggested she was reliving the event. This change illustrates van der Kolk's (1997) formulations based on pre- and post-EMDR SPECT brain scans, which showed increased left hemisphere activation, reduced right hemisphere activation, and increased activation of the anterior cingulate cortex after successful EMDR, suggesting that Judy is more able to distinguish the present from what's past.

T: And you remember how it made you feel when she said that?
J: I didn't think it was true.
T: And how does it make you feel right now as you picture that scene in your mind?
J: I don't really have a feeling I guess.
T: Okay. Did you have a feeling last week when you pictured it in your mind? (Often it is useful to obtain prior feelings when current ones are not available.)
J: (Shakes her head no)
T: What was the feeling like at the time (going back further for prior feelings)?
J: It felt like someone just stabbed me.
T: Mmhm. As you picture this in your mind right now, do you get a little bit of that feeling, like someone just stabbed you (bringing feelings to the present)?
J: (Nods)
T: Okay. And where do you feel that in your body?
J: In my heart.
T: How strong is that feeling right now, from 0 to 10, where 0 is not strong at all and 10 is the strongest that feeling could be, the worst it could be?
J: Zero.
T: But you still feel it a little bit? What I'd like you to do, is hold that picture in your mind like before, and the feelings that go with it: being stabbed in the heart. Notice where you feel it physically. Hold both of those in mind and follow my fingers like before.

Although Judy had said the feelings were 0, she had also said that she could get a little of the feeling of having been stabbed in the heart. I decided to do a set of eye movements on the image and memory even though she had said the feeling was now 0. Again, this demonstrates that there is room for clinical decision-making within the EMDR protocol. Focusing on the deepest level of the feeling being expressed is an important part of the EMDR process.

J: Okay.
T: Okay, got the picture? And the feeling? (EM) That's good. . . . Real good. . . . Okay, now blank out your mind, take a deep breath, just relax as you let it out. And what do you get now?

J: Me and her baking cookies. (The positive association that has come up suggests that the channel was or has now been cleaned out, allowing prior memories of an enjoyable nature to now be accessible).

T: What kind of feeling goes with that?

J: Happy.

T: Hold that picture in your mind with you and her baking cookies and the happy feeling that goes with that. Where do you feel that happy feeling?

J: All over.

After the first session, Judy reported that she felt happier, but it was after the second session that major behavioral changes were apparent. She went for a week without having major emotional confrontations at home or at school. Additional EMDR focused on her fears that cancer was contagious, that she might have gotten it from her mother, and on further behavioral improvements. Her father had reported that she had difficulty getting up in time for school, so a behavioral program was instituted in which she would get a star for each day that she got up on time and did her chores prior to leaving for school on time. She chose going to a restaurant as the reward after she had earned five stars. Within two weeks the program was discontinued, as she was behaving so consistently that it was no longer needed. Here are some of the star-chart entries that her father recorded:

| | |
|---|---|
| Thursday: | Up on her own, no problems. Amazing! |
| Friday: | Up on her own, no problems. Amazing! |
| Monday: | Up on her own, no problems. Amazing! |
| Tuesday: | She had a restless night from her brother's coughing, but managed to get up pleasantly. |
| Wednesday: | No problems, up and at 'em. We are going to the restaurant of her choice tonight. |
| Thursday: | No problems. |
| Friday: | Same as yesterday. |
| Monday: | Out the door with time to spare even though she was not feeling well. |
| Tuesday: | Got up late, things were a little hectic until the very end, but made the bus with no arguments. |
| Wednesday | Did not use her time well, but made the bus anyway. I hope she brushed her teeth. |

We terminated therapy after a total of nine sessions (three of them EMDR) over a period of three months. Following termination, Judy wrote me the following note:

Dear Dr. Tinker,

I really miss you, and I want to see you again some time. You made a difference in my life. And I will always think of you and how you helped me. And thank you for all youve (sic) done.

Love ya!

From,

Judy

P.S. I'll write you every month. OK!

Results like this seem truly preventative in nature. Identities form around such negative experiences, becoming a part of who the person is, and a large part of how other persons perceive the individual, and the longer they are maintained, the more they become ingrained. It is likely that our theories about personality development will have to be rewritten to take traumatization into account. A good deal of the disagreement about the nature of child development seems due to failure to consider the differences between normal and traumatized child development. For example, in discussing traumatized child development, concepts such as "fixation" and "repetition compulsion" make some sense (although the language may seem too closely tied to a particular theory), that is, a traumatized child may manifest repetitious play around trauma themes (the child's version of the repetition compulsion) and remain "fixated" at a certain developmental level because the traumatic memories interfere with normal development. Such concepts would make little sense in a discussion of normal child development,

## I Know She's Gone, But She's Really Here With Me

Kevin was the first child with whom I used EMDR in a bereavement situation. I was astonished by the effects it had. His mother died from cancer when she was in her late twenties. She had been a bodybuilder, working out and tanning four to five hours per day, but was also alcoholic and bulimic. I was seeing Kevin, who was 6 years old, around grief and custody issues following his mother's death. His father had not been heavily involved with Kevin, as he and Kevin's mother had separated when Kevin was 2 years old. A maternal uncle and his wife and family had been raising Kevin while his mother was undergoing chemotherapy and after her death. Although the couple had been appointed guardians, Kevin's dad now wanted legal custody. All of this affected Kevin emotionally and he was having great difficulty sorting things out, as might be expected.

Although I saw Kevin about 30 times over 16 months, we only used EMDR on a few occasions. When I initially saw Kevin, we focused on his mother's death, and he seemed to do well after that therapeutic focus. However, about six months later, his aunt, with whom he was living, called me and told me that he had been crying and grieving over the past week. She said that he was carrying around his mother's picture and saying that he missed her. Further, he was asking why she had to die, and what had he done wrong to make her die. He had told his aunt, "I love my mom. I miss her and need her." After I targeted his memories, images, thoughts, and feelings in an EMDR session and I saw the feelings diminish, Kevin patted the couch next to him and said, "I know she's gone, but she's really here with me." He then was thoughtful for a moment and then patted his chest over his heart, saying, "And she's with me here, too." I was incredulous, as I had expected to later talk to him about reaching understandings like that, but there he was, a 6-year-old, telling me about the understandings he had reached on his own. A few days later, I called to see how he was doing, and his aunt said, "I don't know what you did, but he's done a turnaround. He's back to his normal, lovable self again."

## BEREAVEMENT PLUS TRAUMA

When trauma is added to grief, children have more difficulty recovering from that combination than they do from simple bereavement. The following two cases illustrate this point in a rather dramatic way.

## That's for Dad

In this first case, a brother and a sister were traumatized by their father's suicide. There was every indication that the father was planning to take the children along with him in his death, but the mother's intuitions and decisive actions thwarted his apparent plans. As this father had remained home with the children while the mother worked outside of the home, they were quite close to him emotionally. The 10-year-old son was especially devastated because of this closeness, as well as his identification with his father as a role model. His EMDR was much more intensive and difficult than that with his sister.

Five months after her husband committed suicide, Pamela brought her two children, Jim, 10, and Susan, 8, in for EMDR, as they were continuing to blame her, themselves, and their dog for their father's death. Pamela said that their hearts had been broken by their father's death, and they would frequently ask, "Why? What did we do wrong?" In the month prior to his death, he had a "nervous breakdown" and had to quit truck-driving school, ending a long-time dream. Following that, he slept more and more, smashed the TV, walked out on a job interview in a rage. He threatened to kill the family dog if they did not give it away, believing his two children loved the dog more than they loved him. Due to changes in his behavior, and threats of suicide, Pamela refused to let her husband pick their children up from a baby-sitter's after a Christmas party at her place of work. He followed her in his truck, terrifying the kids, and tried to have her arrested for drunk driving (she was not drunk). Later, although he had slashed the tires on her car, Pamela managed to get Jim and Susan out of the house to stay with a baby-sitter overnight. She herself stayed with a friend. When she returned home the next morning, she found her husband in his truck, dead from carbon monoxide poisoning. The back of the truck had been set up to make his two children comfortable for camping. Pamela deduced that he had intended to drive off with the children the previous night, so that he could poison all three of them in the guise of a camping trip.

In the first session with Jim and Susan, Jim started crying as he talked about his dad's death. Susan said it was like her heart broke into little pieces at the funeral. Both children thought they were responsible for his death because they loved their dog and did not want to give it away. Since they, along with their mother, had resisted this, they felt to blame for his suicide.

In the first EMDR session with Jim, his feelings did not fade, but became more intense. Also, the images he had concerning his father's death became more detailed, not less. The same thing happened in the second EMDR session, although Jim said that he had felt better during the week. Jim was a "chronological processor" who, like some other persons in EMDR, engage in sequential accounts of the traumatic event. These two EMDR sessions ran like detailed movies for Jim, as he recounted a chronological sequence, with one image after another following in perfect order. However, in the third session, Jim had many more memories come up about his father, and for the first time some of the memories were positive and pleasant. Also, for the first time his SUDS declined from 8 to 4. I think this type of processing causes anxiety for the therapist (it did for me, and still does when it occurs with other clients), as it requires him to hang on for a number of sessions while nothing much seems to be happening other than a chronological recounting of the trauma.

I have noticed two other forms of reprocessing, which are easier on the therapist. The first is the "bottleneck," where the client reprocesses one memory and the negative affect from all other traumatic memories washes out too. The other is the "construction project" style of processing, where first one memory is reprocessed, then another, and so on, until enough memories have been reprocessed that the client senses that there is now a completed construction. I mention these three styles so that other therapists can watch for them, and perhaps add to this (admittedly crude) typology. Otherwise a beginning EMDR therapist might think something was wrong if the processing wasn't happening in a certain way.

Finally, after this third session, his mother reported that despite Jim retaining strong feelings of anger and sadness, there were periods of time when he seemed happier. She mentioned a family outing where Jim laughed so hard that he fell off his chair. While Jim indicated in the session that his anger and sadness persisted, he also gave evidence that he was much more able to access positive feelings and memories about his dad. His intense anger toward his father had diminished greatly. He regained his appetite and began sleeping better. After his final EMDR session, Jim was able to voice that something had been taken out of his life, but that he could deal with it. He said that his heart didn't hurt so much; that he could get over his dad's death now instead of being stuck on it. Follow-up two years later indicated that Jim was doing well in school and at home.

Jim's sister, Susan, required fewer and less intense EMDR sessions, perhaps because she had not been so closely bonded with her father and was allied more closely with her mother. Unlike Jim, her most intense feelings faded in the first session of EMDR, but we used tactile stimulation after finding that the eye movements were not as effective. It was interesting that she responded better to hand taps, with her feelings changing rapidly with that approach, while with the eye movements, she remained stuck, her feelings not changing. Later, when hand taps were tried with Jim (on the idea that if taps worked better with Susan, they might also work better with Jim), they were found to be less effective than eye movements for him. This was somewhat unusual, as I have more often found that one member of a family will often benefit from the same mode of left-right stimulation as other family members.

After Susan's first EMDR session, her mother reported that she was once again happy and playful, although sensitive to the loss of her father. While watching a Fourth of July fireworks display, she observed a heart-shaped burst of color, and said, "That's for Dad." In her second EMDR session, she focused on the image of her mother kneeling in front of her and her brother on the couch and telling them that their father had killed himself. She also reprocessed seeing her dad in his coffin at the funeral (in this session, her most intense feelings faded more rapidly through eye movements instead of hand taps). In the weeks after this session, she reported missing her dad intensely at times, but she was able to cope with the ordinary demands of life. Two years later, she is doing very well in school, has good friends, gets along well with her mother, and has no major areas of difficulty in her life. Her mother reports that she is a delightful child, who will always remember her father and the time they had together, but the emotional scarring from his suicide seems minimal.

Children of parents who have committed suicide have higher rates of suicide than other children. Perhaps EMDR will help diminish the terrible legacy of a parent's suicide. Only time will tell, but both Jim and Susan are coping well with the awful loss of their father. Their father himself was so traumatized in his adolescence, when a good friend died in his arms, that he changed his own name, and his life seemed on a different course from then on. One wonders, if he could have been treated with EMDR for his prior trauma would things have been much different for himself and his family? The sequelae of trauma seem only to be treated one person at a time, and there are so many traumas. But EMDR gives hope that we can chip away at that wall of trauma and that some intergenerational transmission of trauma can be averted through the power of EMDR.

## A Black Shape on the Ceiling

In the second case, the course of 4-year-old Barry's life was dramatically changed by his father's suicide, which he witnessed on the street in front of their home. However, Barry did not develop overt symptoms until much later. He was treated with EMDR at age 11, shortly after his symptoms appeared following his grandfather's death (Barry's case was briefly discussed in chapter 2).

Although Barry did not have much conscious recall of his father's suicide, he knew the story of it. He knew that when he was 4, his father had held him and his mother hostage at gunpoint. He knew that, in a standoff with a SWAT team, his father had finally released him and his mother, and they crawled out the front door, keeping close to the ground. Moments later, the SWAT team kicked in the front door. His father shot himself, ran out the front door, and died in the street. Barry watched from the inside of a van parked across the street.

When Barry was 11 years old, his grandfather died, and Barry's behavior changed dramatically for the worse. Up until then Barry had been a good student and was even in the gifted and talented program in his fifth grade class. But when his grandfather died in November, his grades dropped so precipitously that in March he was in danger of having to repeat the fifth grade, as he was failing most subjects. His mother noted he seemed increasingly depressed and angry. He had nightmares, and in his waking state he hallucinated a black mass on the ceiling of his bedroom several times per week. His circle of friends narrowed and he seemed more withdrawn.

Certainly Barry seemed in need of psychotherapy and there was a clear emotional basis for his behavioral changes. It is quite possible that Barry could have responded to traditional grief psychotherapy. In Judy's case, presented earlier in this chapter, there was a parallel situation, where her same sex parent died, and then her grandfather also died. After her mother's death, she was unable to respond a combination of grief therapy and conventional therapy. Would Barry have been similarly unable to respond to grief or conventional therapy after his two losses, which might be seen as even more devastating than Judy's? In this case, all we know is that Barry responded very well to short-term EMDR, which focused on the suicide of his father and the death of his grandfather. As he was a participant in our EMDR research with children aged 7–11, we have pre- and post-EMDR measurements of his behavior from himself, his mother, and his teacher, and we know that EMDR was the only method of therapy employed. In all, we have unusually clear-cut information that it was EMDR, and only EMDR, that produced the observed changes in Barry's case.

## SPECIFIC PHOBIAS

Specific phobias in children (formerly called simple phobias) have much in common with simple traumas, in that they are likely to resolve rapidly with EMDR. A specific phobia is diagnosed when there is an irrational fear of an object or situation that produces an immediate anxiety response. It differs from a normal fear response in that the child's fear is out of proportion to the actual danger posed by the object; the fear is extreme, often resulting in an excessive avoidance of certain situations; the fear has a significant negative impact on daily functioning; and the fear is resistant to attempts to eliminate it. Such specific phobias tend to resolve quickly with EMDR treatment unless there are a number of reinforcers or stressors in the child's current environment maintaining the fear. For example, if a child is afraid of snakes and has a nurturing and supportive family, the snake phobia is likely to resolve quickly with EMDR.

Phobias of a more complex nature, on the other hand, are maintained by many elements (stressors and reinforcers) in the present, and it is likely that those complex elements must be dealt with before the phobia improves. Again, this is analogous to complex traumas and we'll call these phobias complex phobias. For example, a child with a vehicle phobia, whose parents are divorcing, whose siblings are making fun of him for his symptoms, and whose parents voice concern and provide extra attention because of his fear of vehicles, may not get over the phobia quickly, or until the supporting elements are improved.

Additional forms of therapy are then required to assist the parents in handling their concerns with the child, in reducing their conflict with each other, and in reducing the siblings' conflict. One way that EMDR may be different from other therapies is that it can provide immediate symptomatic improvement in the phobia, which can then be used to motivate other changes in the family system. For example, the child with the vehicle phobia might show some improvement in riding in cars and in sleeping after EMDR sessions focusing on nightmares about riding in cars and trucks, but the family would then require additional work involving parents and siblings to sustain the improvement.

Specific phobias in children, as in adults, may not have obvious precipitating events. An adult does not have to be in a plane crash to have a flying phobia and, similarly, a child may not have to be attacked, bitten, or chased by a dog to have a phobia of dogs or animals. The child simply has to be imaginative enough to anticipate vividly a horrifying trauma, which can then incubate and generalize. I have often thought that children with vivid imaginations are both cursed and blessed. The curse is the higher likelihood of developing intense fears and phobias. The blessing is that the clarity and intensity of their imaginations makes them more capable of accurate empathy for others and of becoming our most talented artists, writers, artisans, poets, musicians, and muses.

## I Feel Good in My Heart

Kerry was an unusually sensitive and mature 6-year-old girl who had developed a fear of animals in infancy. She had supportive parents, but despite their many attempts to help her with her fears about animals, they deepened and generalized, to the extent that she had become afraid of all animals. By the time Kerry was 6, even kittens, bunnies, puppies, baby chicks, and other infant animals evoked fear responses. More and more family activities were being curtailed because of her fears. Further, her self-esteem was lessening, and she was becoming more timid and less assertive in social situations. She began to be afraid to sleep by herself. In addition, when Kerry was almost 5, her father and her older brother were involved in an automobile accident in which her father was killed and her older brother was given a 10% chance of living. Her brother did survive, with disabilities, but the experience seemed to intensify Kerry's fears. She had to be shielded from newscasts on TV, as reports of disasters seemed to upset her and increase her anxiety.

Kerry did beautifully in her first EMDR session. The EMDR segment lasted for about 30 minutes, which is unusual for a 6-year-old and a tribute to Kerry's attention span. It was thus possible to employ theme development and future projection to help insure that the session would be effective. It was. Not only did Kerry's fear of dogs (her worst phobia and the one we targeted first) fade rapidly, but she was also able to envision playing with a dog that belonged to friends of the family, with whom they were going to stay for a week, almost immediately after the first session.

The following passage is an excerpt from the first session, which illustrates how Kerry processed her fear of dogs. The excerpt begins after a safe place had been set up and installed.

T: I'm going to ask you to think about the worst thing that ever happened to you with dogs. What would that be?

K: When I got chased by my neighbor (dog).

T: Can you get a picture of that in your mind?

K: (Nods)

T: Tell me what that picture looks like.

K: The dog runs around, is white and has brown spots, and he's chasing me.

T: Why is he chasing you?

K: I don't know.

T: Do you think he's mad? (I'm wondering if she is attributing hostile intent to the dog.)

K: (Shakes her head no)

T: But, anyway, he's chasing you. As you hold that picture in your mind where he's chasing you—he's got brown spots and he is running around—what does it make you think about yourself? That's kind of a hard question. What does it make you think about yourself when he's chasing you?

K: Bad.

T: Bad how? Could it be like . . .

K: A little bad.

T: It could be bad because you think "I can't protect myself" or you might think "I'm in danger."

K: Danger.

T: Okay. Kerry, what would you rather think about yourself than "I'm in danger"?

K: The dog's trying to bite.

T: What I want to be asking about is what would you like to think about yourself?

K: Good.

T: You might think "I can protect myself" or "I'm strong" or "I'm good."

K: Protect.

T: Okay. Protect. Now as you hold that picture in your mind of this dog—he's chasing you, he's got brown spots—how true do those words feel to you, that "I can protect myself," as you think about that dog chasing you? From 1 to 7 where 1 feels not true at all and 7 feels completely true?

K: Two.

T: With that picture in your mind, with this dog chasing you, and you're thinking, "I'm in danger," what kind of feelings does that make you have right now as you think about that picture and that thought "I'm in danger"?

K: Sad.

T: How strong is that sad feeling from 0 to 10, where 0 is not there at all and 10 is the worst that feeling could be?

K: Ten.

T: Where do you feel that sad feeling in your body right now?

K: My brain.

T: Is there also a scared feeling there, too, besides the sad feeling?

K: No, just sad.

T: Now I'm going to ask you to do the same kind of thing as before. I'm going to ask you to hold that picture in your mind with the dog chasing you and the thought "I'm in danger" and the sad feeling that's really strong. I'm going to ask you to hold all of that in mind and follow my fingers with your eyes. The main thing here is for you to just let whatever comes to mind, come to mind. You don't have to make anything come to mind or keep anything from coming to mind. Just let whatever comes to mind, come to mind. (This additional instruction is given to help promote associative chaining and to let the child know that it's okay for other images, thoughts, feelings, or physical sensations to arise during or after the eye movements. It also sets up a paradoxical situation, where the child is complying with instructions whether she keeps the original material in mind or whether she doesn't.) Bring up that picture of the dog—white with brown spots and he's chasing you and you're thinking, "I'm in danger," and you have this really, really strong sad feeling— hold that and follow my fingers. (EM) Okay, you're doing good . . . doing good. . . . Now stop, take a deep breath and blow away the bad feelings. And what do you think of now?

K: Really good. (I am tempted to think that this is a case of the child telling me what she thinks I want to hear. However, it happens so frequently and is so often accompanied by behavioral change later on, that I have learned to cautiously trust such a response or at least to hold judgment in abeyance until later. So for now, I just consider it a short channel.)

T: Think about that really good feeling and follow my fingers. (EM) That's good, real good. . . . Okay, blank it out, take a deep breath, let it out slow. You're doing really good. And what do you think of now?

K: The same.

T: Now let's have you go back and bring up that picture of the dog chasing you and tell me what that is like now.

K: I feel good about it.

T: That sad feeling, how strong is that sad feeling right now as you hold that picture from 0 to 10?

K: Not at all.

T: Wow! You're doing great. Now, I want you to hold two things in mind. One is that picture and the other is the words you'd like to have go with that picture, "I can protect myself." Can you hold both of those things in mind: The words "I can protect myself" and the picture? Okay. (EM) Blank it out, take a deep breath. And what do you think of now?

K: The same thing.

T: And what's that?

K: I feel really good about it.

T: Let me have you hold those two things in mind, the picture of the dog chasing you and the thought "I can protect myself" and then just kind of scan down through your body and let me know if you feel anything anywhere. Start at the top of your head and scan down through your body and let me know if you feel anything anywhere. And what do you feel?

K: I feel good in my heart. (Rarely do I hear such a phrase when *not* conducting EMDR. Are children learning in EMDR to trust their senses and intuitions? If so, what are the long-range implications of that learning?)

T: Hold that good feeling in your heart and follow my fingers. (EM) Blank it out, take a deep breath, let it out slow. What do you think of now?

K: Better.

T: Good. Now let's pick another time when you felt scared of dogs or other animals. Can you remember another time? (I don't think enough desensitization of channels has been completed, so I continue with theme development.)

K: My next door neighbor. They have two cats.

T: Can you picture something in your mind where the two cats were scary to you?

K: Uhuh.

T: Tell me what that picture looks like.

K: There's a wall. The cats are by it. I was scared to walk by it.

T: So what did you do if you were scared to walk past it?

K: I ran.

T: Let me have you hold that picture in mind along with what kind of feelings go with that picture as you think about it right now?

K: Bad and kind of good.

T: What are those bad feelings like? Sad or scared or mad?

K: Sad.

T: What are those good feelings? What are those like?

K: Happy.

T: For right now, I'm going to ask you to hold the picture along with just the scared feelings. Where do you feel the scared feelings in your body? (Therapeutic choice: After hearing the negative and positive feelings, I target the negative ones.)

K: My heart.

T: Got the picture? Got the scared feelings? How strong are they from 0 to 10, 10's the worst?

K: Eight.

T: Hold those scared feelings in your heart and the picture in your mind and follow my fingers. (EM) Good, good. . . . You can blink if you want to. . . . Blank it out, take a deep breath and blow away those scared feelings. What do you think of now?

K: Better.

T: Much?

K: Yes.

T: How strong are those scared feelings now, 0 to 10?

K: Zero.

T: Zero already. That's pretty good. Okay, think of another time when you got scared by an animal.

K: I can't think of any.

T: What about in Phoenix? Can you think of that?

K: Uhuh.

T: What's that picture look like?

K: A dog. It's very little and he's lying on the cement.

T: As you think of that picture what kind of feelings does that make you have right now?

K: Scary.

T: How strong are those scary feelings, from 0 to 10, 10's the worst?

K: Nine.

T: Strong. Where do you feel those in your body?

K: Heart.

T: Now this time I'm going to ask you to do something a little bit different. And that is, I'm going to ask you to hold that picture and the scary feelings in your heart and follow my fingers with your eyes until you think of something new, something else, a new picture, a new thought, or a new feeling, and then when you get a new picture—

K: Of the dog and the cat?

T: It could be anything. Whatever you think of. It might be a dog or it might be a cat or it might be something else. Then you can tell me to stop and you can tell me what that is. So bring up that picture of the very little dog on the cement and you're walking over toward it and you have scary feelings in your heart that are pretty strong, about a 9. Think about that and just follow my fingers until you get a new thought or a new picture (EM).(I have found that this change in the standard protocol facilitates associative chaining, especially with children who are having difficulty making associative connections. Kerry is not having difficulty, but she is young and may be getting tired. I thought the change in instructions might help hold her attention.)

K: My mom giving me ice cream.

T: Okay, think about that. Follow my fingers until you get a new thought or a new feeling or a new picture. (EM)

K: My dad buying me a new dress (she's referring to her stepdad).

T: Stop, take a deep breath, let it out slow. That was pretty neat. First you had a picture of your mom buying you ice cream and then your dad buying you a dress. Bring up that picture of the dog on the sidewalk again, and tell me what that picture looks like now.

K: Good.

T: And the scary feelings. How strong are they right now, 0 to 10?

K: Zero.

T: Now what I'd like you to do is get a picture in your mind of . . . Do you know what the dog looks like of the people that you're going to visit?

K: No.

T: Can you get a picture in your mind of being brave and protecting yourself against the dog that lives across the street from you at home?

K: Okay.

T: When you bring up the picture, what would you like to be able to do in the future when you see that dog lying on the sidewalk?

K: Not afraid of him.

T: Can you picture that in your mind, not being afraid of that dog?

K: No.

T: It doesn't have to be something you can do right now, but can you picture, if you weren't afraid of that dog, what you would do, how you would act?

K: I'd just go by him.

T: Would you pet him on the head or just go by him?

K: I'd pet him on the head.

T: Picture that in your mind: going by that dog and petting him on the head. Tell me what that picture looks like.

K: He's lying on the cement and I'm just going by him and I pet him.

T: Picture that in your mind. What are the feelings right now when you picture that in your mind? He's lying on the cement and you're going by him and you pet him on the head.

K: Good.

T: Are you a little bit scared?

K: No.

T: A little bit sad?

K: No.

T: Picture that. You're walking by the dog. He's lying on the cement and you pet him on the head. (EM) Blank it out, take a deep breath, let it out slow. What do you think of now?

K: A little more good.

T: Can you picture in your mind going to the friends' house on this trip that you're going on and picture how you'd like to be around that dog (future projection)?

K: Yeah.

T: Tell me what that picture looks like.

K: The dog playing in the grass. I'm throwing Frisbees at him.

T: What's the dog doing with the Frisbees?

K: Catching them in his mouth.

T: Does that dog do that?

K: (Nods)

T: Picture that: The dog's laying in the grass, you're throwing the Frisbee, and the dog's catching it. Picture that, follow my fingers. (EM) Blank it out, take a deep breath, let it out slow. What do you think of now?

K: Really, really good.

T: Now do you think you could really do that?

K: Yeah.

T: Think about that, how you think you could really do that, and follow my fingers. (EM) Let it go, take a deep breath. Good. And what do you think of now?

K: Better.

T: When you say better, what kind of feelings are those?

K: Good.

T: Have you ever been afraid of other animals besides dogs and cats?

K: Alligators.

T: Alligators! Where have you seen alligators?

K: At the zoo.

T: What happens when you see alligators at the zoo?

K: We just get to look at them and stuff.

T: Does it make you scared when you see alligators?

K: No.

T: Cause they're far away and you're protected (too much leading on my part)?

K: (Nods)

T: Have you ever been afraid of things like kitties or puppies?

K: Yes.

T: Kitties and puppies. Can you think of a time when you were afraid of kitties?

K: No.

T: How about puppies? Can you think of a time when you were afraid of puppies?

K: Yes.

T: Tell me about that.

K: At the store.

T: As you think about that right now, seeing puppies at the store, how does that make you feel right now?

K: Good and bad.

T: What's the bad part?

K: I'm scared when I walk by them.

T: And how strong is that scared feeling right now, from 0 to 10?

K: One.

T: Not too scared. Let's see if we can get that down to 0. So, picture those puppies at the store and you're walking by and you feel that scared feeling. Hold all that and follow my fingers. (EM) Now blank it out, take a deep breath, blow away the rest of the scared feelings. What do you think of now?

K: Zero.

T: Good. You're doing so good. What do you think about all this?

K: Really, really, really good.

T: Can you remember the picture of the first dog that we worked with? Do you remember that?

K: Chasing me?

T: Chasing you. Bring up that picture again and what's that like now that you bring that up?

K: Really good.

T: What do you think you'd do if that dog chased you now?

K: I would just go by and pet him.

T: Now bring up that picture of the dog with this family that you're going to visit. He's lying on the grass. Tell me what that picture is like now.

K: Really good.

T: Do you think you'd be the one throwing Frisbees?

K: Yes.

T: Would it make you laugh?

K: Yes.

T: Can you picture yourself throwing Frisbees and laughing?

K: Yes.

T: Picture that and follow my fingers. (EM) Now stop, take a deep breath. What's that feel like now?

K: Feels good.

T: What do you think will happen when you leave here and you go back home if you see that dog that's white with brown spots? What do you think will happen if you see that dog?

K: I'll still feel better about it.

T: How comfortable do you feel about going to visit your friends who have the dog that chases Frisbees?

K: Really good.

T: Are there any other scary animal feelings that you want us to work on?

K: No.

T: Let's have you bring up your picture of the safe place again and tell me what that looks like.

K: TV, wall with pictures and candles, and the couch and a rug.

T: How do you feel when you're in the safe place?

K: Good.

T: And where do you feel those good feelings in your body?

K: In my heart.

T: Hold that picture and the good feelings in your heart, the safe and happy and good feelings, and follow my fingers. (EM)

Following the first session, Kerry and her family went on two week-long trips, each time staying with a family with a dog. In each instance, she was able to pet, groom, feed, and play with the dog. These trips were ones the family had been dreading, due to Kerry's fear of dogs. However, even though Kerry's mom was impressed with Kerry's ability to be comfortable around the dogs, she was even more impressed with how Kerry had become more outgoing and self-confident around people.

After Kerry returned from her trips, we had a second session, in which we checked the prior work and completed additional future projections. At this point, Kerry wanted her parents to buy her a dog of her own, but her parents demurred, stating that their lifestyle wasn't conducive to having a dog. We then terminated therapy as Kerry had made as much progress as she needed, although I thought she would have benefited from having her own dog.

## Another Animal Phobia

In a very similar kind of case, Jay, who was also 6, was referred for his fear of animals, especially dogs. Jay, however, had a very different kind of personality than Kerry did. While Kerry was timid and cooperative, Jay was characterized by his mother as being "a little type A personality," who was controlling, easily angered, and quickly frustrated. However, at an early age, he had developed a fear of dogs, which then generalized to other animals. As with Kerry, there seemed to be no specific incident that had caused the fearfulness. His mother did recall, however, that when Jay was about 3 years old, they were in a park and two German Shepherds ran up and jumped up on her. After that, she noticed his fear of dogs and other animals. She said that if a dog even looked at him, he would scream and run. Over the last three years, his fear of animals had worsened to the point that cats, rabbits, and other animals also scared him. He would even scream if a rabbit seemed to move toward him. He had stopped riding his bike outdoors, and if he went outside at all, he had to scout the area first. The family was no longer able to go on outings, such as going to a park, because of Jay's fear of animals.

Jay's first EMDR session seemed to go well, and immediately after the session his mom (with Jay's permission) took him to a pet store, where he petted a rabbit and a kitten. More importantly, a few days later, Jay and his mom went to an outdoor fair, where there were a number of dogs running loose. Jay was able to tolerate being there without screaming and running. His mother said that he was calmer around the dogs, and remained at the fair without much apprehension for over two hours.

In the next EMDR session we checked on the previous work, and as the SUDS remained low and the VOC high, we worked on future projections, covering every situation we could conceive of, where a dog might frighten Jay. Imaginally, the only situation that would continue to frighten him was where a big dog (not on a leash, not with an owner) would run directly at him. That fear seemed to be realistic, and we didn't attempt to reduce the SUDS on it. Following this session, Jay spent time with a terrier that belonged to a family that he and his parents knew. He walked the dog on a leash at two outside locations, fed the dog, and brushed him.

Jay and his parents stopped therapy at this point, but I have since learned that after therapy was discontinued, his fearfulness of dogs increased, and he is now fearful of playing outside unless accompanied by an adult. I suspect that therapy was prematurely terminated, but the family is now pursuing other options.

A recent study with children (Muris, Merckelbach, Holdrinet, & Sijsenaar, 1998) has indicated that in vivo desensitization of spiders is effective with children who have spider phobias, but that EMDR is not, when tested by the ability of the children to approach a real spider. How do we reconcile that research with these results with the generally positive (but mixed) clinical results I have seen?

Since Muris and colleagues conducted a controlled study, it's possible that my results are a fluke and would not generalize to other children treated with EMDR. However, that seems unlikely, as other EMDR clinicians report similar results with phobic children. Another possibility is that I may have been more thorough in desensitizing all the channels I could find before doing future projections, which may have been different from what was done in the study. De Jongh, Ten Broeke, and Renssen (in press) point out that Muris and colleagues did not follow vital elements of the EMDR protocol in their research. It could also be that animal or dog phobias are somehow different from spider phobias. For example, EMDR may work better with traumatic phobias than with phobias that do not follow a trauma. Animal phobias may be more likely to be traumatic phobias (e.g., following a dog bite). The emotion involved may be quite different, as nontraumatic spider phobias would primarily involve disgust and revulsion and traumatic phobias would primarily involve fear. Presumably, EMDR would be more effective against the traumatic, fear-based phobias. Also, De Jongh has indicated that snake and spider phobias affect only 1% of the population, while other phobias that affect higher percentages of children and adults tend to be much less researched (personal communication, September

14, 1998). Phobias such as those that follow road accidents, medical and dental procedures, social phobias, blood phobias, and animal phobias affect 40–80% of children and adults (A. De Jongh, personal communication, September 14, 1998). Finally, it may not have been EMDR at all that produced the clinical improvement in these two cases, but rather the in vivo desensitization, which closely followed the sessions. This explanation, however, does not seem likely to me, as the parents of these children had previously tried many times to get their children to approach the feared animals, without any success.

As I have dealt with a number of other children who were phobic (e.g., Julie, tornadoes; Jay, lightning, clouds) with good results, as well as with many adults, I can only say that my clinical results differ from theirs, perhaps because these are phobias following traumas. It is possible that Kerry and Jay were actually traumatized by animals at some point without their parents knowing about it, thus forming the basis for their phobias. At any rate, my clinical experience differs from that of those researchers. De Jongh and his colleagues (in press) point out that there is some evidence that EMDR works better with traumatic phobias and that in vivo desensitization works better with phobias that are not a result of trauma. They conclude, "However, given that there is insufficient research to validate any method for complex or trauma-related phobias, that EMDR is a time-limited procedure, and that it can be used in cases for which an exposure in vivo approach is difficult to administer, the application of EMDR with specific phobias merits further clinical and research attention."

Overall, the effectiveness of EMDR with simple traumas occurring in childhood is unprecedented. One wonders how the course of psychotherapy history might have been changed if Freud's Little Hans (Freud, 1909) had been treated for his phobia of horses with EMDR. It is with these simple traumas that the EMDR "miracles" occur, where the clinician can sense that she is truly accomplishing preventative work with children.

In the next chapter we will begin to examine the use of EMDR with complex traumas. We'll begin to see how different EMDR is in that context, where the total treatment package becomes more important.

*seven*

# Complex Traumas

"Being kind and kind and kind and kind and kind to my sister."
—AARON, AGE 4

IN THE PREVIOUS TWO CHAPTERS, we examined the effectiveness of EMDR for children with simple traumas. It is with the simple traumas that we are most apt to see the EMDR "miracles": the instances where PTSD symptoms disappear in one to three sessions.

In this chapter, we will examine the effectiveness of EMDR with children when the situations are more complex. These are situations where a trauma has occurred, but there are aspects of the trauma that are complex and ongoing so that the child cannot be expected to recover from the trauma without therapeutic interventions other than EMDR. An example would be a child who is molested by an adolescent or adult who remains in the home, or by a neighbor, where there is not enough evidence to prosecute, so the child feels jeopardized on a daily basis. Therefore, in the present chapter, cases will be discussed with attention to the complexity of the entire situation. With complex traumas, EMDR outcomes partially depend upon how quickly other aspects of the situation can be improved.

It seems that children, much more often than adults, are caught up in complex situations over which they have no control. Therefore, clinicians working with children are often required to spend more time assessing the complexity of the situation, than they are with adults. Further, when adults are caught in complex situations they are often able to act as active, volitional agents: They can quit a job, a marriage, a city, a lifestyle, if they so choose; they can initiate a new job, marriage, relationship, lifestyle, geographic location. Children cannot often choose a new family, a new school, a new lifestyle. They get stuck in their situations and society doesn't notice unless the pain is extreme or the abuse or neglect are severe.

This chapter will also consider a case where the child is in a difficult situation, but there is no singular identifiable trauma. Rather, there is a series of upsetting and repetitive events that seem to have a cumulative effect on the child. In a case like that, EMDR can focus on the difficult elements of the situation. For example, the situation might be one where the child's behavior deteriorates (e.g., nightmares, bed-wetting, increased aggression, increased self-hatred, head banging) after visitation with the noncustodial parent. Analysis of the situation might indicate no discrete trauma, but that both parents, custodial and noncustodial, are contributing to the child's distress in different ways. Again, in these situations, EMDR can help to alleviate symptomatic distress, but the overall situation needs modification and likely requires a variety of treatment interventions.

A good example of the first kind of case, where there is a discrete trauma with ongoing elements, is a 10-year-old girl in our children's study who had been molested by an adolescent male sibling, with the adolescent being placed outside the home for a period of time. He was returned home after the study started and the girl had begun EMDR, and her nightmares worsened into night terrors. It turned out that after he returned home, he began verbally attacking his sister, holding her responsible for his being placed outside the home. While he was not being sexually provocative, he was making her feel extremely threatened, and her symptoms worsened. However, when her parents were informed about what was happening, they took immediate action and dealt with the situation in family therapy. When confronted, the brother became contrite and apologetic. He then was less angry and threatening in his behavior toward his sister, with the result that her symptoms improved quite rapidly. If the parents had not taken action to protect her, it is doubtful that EMDR would have provided much benefit. However, with the action they did take, she was able to reprocess the past molestation and the more recent harassment, with the result that her symptoms subsided.

## REACTIVE ATTACHMENT DISORDER

The diagnosis of reactive attachment disorder has been garnering increased attention recently, probably in part because it is difficult to treat, partly because more cases are being diagnosed, and partly because of the perception that it reflects a growing problem in our society. As the diagnosis implies, the child is not attaching because of reactive, not biological, reasons. Many of these children are repeatedly shunted from one caregiver to another, with the end result that they resist attaching to anyone. Despite the impression that the diagnosis is becoming more common, the DSM-IV indicates that in prevalence, the disorder appears to be "very uncommon" (American Psychiatric Association, 1994, p.

117). Perhaps it has been uncommon, but as society changes, and children are kept or moved around in foster care situations for longer periods of time, it becomes more common. Or when institutionalized children from other countries are adopted in the United States, and don't attach, it appears to be more common than previously thought, or at least generates more interest. Onset must be in the first five years of life, and the inappropriate social relatedness across most contexts is thought to be due to "grossly pathological care" (American Psychiatric Association, 1994, p. 116).

"Holding therapy" is sometimes used with children and adolescents. Holding therapy evolved out of an approach developed by Robert Zaslow (1975), who originally applied it with autistic children. He found that when a child with autism was restrained, the child would go into a rage, but immediately afterward would be much more tractable and attentive and better able to form attachments. Later, similar results were found at times with attachment-disordered children who were not autistic. However, the theoretical underpinnings of the two approaches (EMDR and holding therapy) are quite different, with grief processing appearing to be central to EMDR and rage and anger processing central to holding therapy (in fact, holding therapy was initially called rage reduction therapy). Since the theoretical underpinnings and the procedures are so very different, it would be very interesting to compare the efficacy of the two in a rigorously controlled study. Until such a study is completed, we can say that EMDR appears to be less intrusive and coercive, and more focused on resolution of grief than anger.

## I Hid in the Dryer

Kip, 10 years old, came from an Alaskan Indian heritage. He was first raised by his mother, who then turned him over to his maternal grandmother when he was about a year old. His level of attachment was questionable after that. When he was close to 5 years old, his grandmother put him up for adoption after she became ill and felt unable to care for him. He was adopted by a minister and his wife when he was 5 ½ years old. At age 10, his adoptive parents were concerned that he had not attached to them despite their best efforts. He became part of our children's research and received five sessions of EMDR with standardized pre- and posttesting. While the testing indicated there was some improvement from those five sessions, it was minimal. Such a result is not surprising, as reactive attachment disorder indicates a deep disturbance in the ability to relate to others, which is not ordinarily remediated in a short period of time. Thus, when the study was completed, Kip continued in EMDR. At this point, he remains in therapy, and has had 19 additional sessions. While problems remain, he can no longer be diagnosed as having an attachment disorder. He has attached to both of his parents and to his sister in his adoptive family. Here's how the sessions went.

In the first poststudy EMDR session (he had had a different therapist in the study), we set up a safe place. As Kip was monosyllabic and minimally responsive, I began using a modified form of EMDR in which I had him continue his eye movements until he thought of something new. This only produced a slight improvement in his processing. In the next session, therefore, I had him focus on positive targets, so we focused exclusively on times in his life when he had felt proud of himself. For the first time he began to talk about events that had happened before he was adopted at age 5½ (he had refused to do so in the study). After this session, he smiled and indicated that he felt happy.

In the third session, we used drumming and targeted the imminent death of his maternal (adopted) grandfather, a person to whom Kip had begun to get close over the last five years. Although minimally verbal during the session, he became tearful during the drumming. After this session, his adoptive mother indicated that Kip was beginning to be "warmer" in his behavior toward others in the family. In the next session, Kip was highly talkative and responsive in EMDR for the first time. He brought up more memories related to growing up in an Indian village in Alaska and recounted how he had been run over by a bicycle when he was younger and how a neighbor's house had burned down. These were traumatic events for him and we used EMDR to reprocess them. In the following session, Kip was willing to target his memories of adoption in EMDR. These were negative and frightening memories for him.

At this point, Kip had had five sessions of EMDR, in addition to his original five in the study. His parents had begun to notice more affiliative behavior on his part, but other areas remained a problem. He would quickly become passive-resistant when asked to perform in some way, whether it was to answer questions in school, do chores at home, or to hurry up in completing a task. If he himself became angry, he would take it out on his mother or sister. Because of these issues, we began to target anger in his EMDR sessions. He seemed to like tickling games with his dad, but in a recent game he slapped his dad three times. We continued to target anger in the EMDR sessions.

After two more sessions, Kip spontaneously said that his life is getting better. He now enjoys school more, is better about bringing his schoolwork home and completing the work, is making friends for the first time, and says that he is happy. His parents feel that he has attached to them and to his adopted sister. Problems remain, in that Kip is below grade level in school, but he will pass this year (it was in question for a while). He needs to continue working on anger in EMDR, as he is still passive-resistant and doesn't handle his anger well. At times, he behaves in socially inappropriate ways.

In order to detail the changes that began to occur in the EMDR sessions, the following transcripts are from the third and the fifth EMDR sessions following the study. It can be noted how he has gone from being minimally responsive (session 3) to being highly talkative (session 5) in the sessions.

### Excerpt from Session 3

T: Tell me, what makes you like your granddad so much? What kinds of things have you done with him?

K: Not very many things

T: Okay, did you just get to see him? What was it like to see him?

K: (Shrugs)

T: Can you get a picture in your mind of what he looks like?

K: (Nods)

T: Hold that picture in your mind of what he looks like and then just beat the drum. Okay, got the picture?

K: (Nods)

T: What do you feel like when you hold that picture in your mind?

K: (Shrugs)

T: Happy or sad or what?

K: Both.

T: Hold that picture in your mind and hold those feelings in your mind and go ahead and beat the drum like you did before.

K: (Drums)

T: Okay, now stop; take a deep breath, real deep. Just take the deepest breath that you can, let me see your chest come up. That's good, breathe it out slow. Now I want you to do something a little bit different. Can you bring up the picture of your grandpa?

K: (Nods)

T: I would like you to hold that picture in your mind until you think of something else about your grandpa and then just stop and tell me what that is. Hold that picture of your grandpa in your mind and then beat the drum until you get a new picture, feeling, or thought in your mind. Okay go ahead. Got the picture?

K: (Drums)

T: Keep going until you get something new about your grandpa.

K: I do not know anything else about him.

T: That's okay, just keep drumming until you think of something else about him. It might be another picture; it might be something you did together; it might be a memory.

K: (Drums for a lengthy period of time without saying anything)

T: Now stop. Take a deep breath . . . real deep. That's good. Let it out slow. Now you don't have to tell me what this is, but think of a time when you did something with your grandpa that was fun.

K: Nothing.

T: Did you ever do something with him that was fun?

K: (Shakes his head no)

T: Think of a memory about him then.

K: (Long silence)

T: Just anything that you remember. It might be a picture you have in your mind: eating a meal with him, saying hello to him. It might be just spending time with him, fishing with him, just any memory.

K: (Silence)

T: Could be a happy memory.

K: (Remains silent, looks uncomfortable)

T: When you think of something, you don't have to tell me what it is; just tell me you have a memory and I will let you do the drumming.

K: (Remains silent)

T: Did you just visit your grandpa? Did you say anything to him?

K: (Nods)

T: What did you say to him?

K: I said hi and stuff.

T: What else?

K: (Shrugs)

T: Okay, just think about saying hi to him and do the drumming until you think of something else about your grandpa.

K: (Drums)

T: That's good. Nice job. When you think of something else you said or he said, let me know.

K: (Drums, remains silent)

T: Okay, stop. Take a deep breath. That's good. Now Kip, how do you feel about his dying?

K: (Shrugs)

T: Shrugging your shoulders is not a good answer. You have to tell me more than just shrugging your shoulders.

K: (Looks upset but remains silent)

T: Okay, let's try this: Do the drumming until you think about how you feel about his dying. Then stop and tell me how you feel about his dying.

K: (Drums for about one minute)

T: Good job with the drumming.

K: (Drums)

T: That's good with the drumming. That's real good. Okay, now stop. How do you feel right now? Do you feel happy, sad, or what?

K: In between.

T: Now, can you think of something that you and your grandpa have done together that you liked?

K: (Shakes his head no)

T: Did you do anything with your grandpa?

K: (Shakes his head no)

T: What made you like him?

K: I don't know.

T: But you know you liked him?

K: (Nods)

T: Do the drumming and think about how much you liked your grandpa. Do that until you think about something else.

K: (Drums)

T: Good job with the drumming. Just keep drumming until you think of something else.

K: (Drums for about two minutes)

T: Okay that's good. Just keep drumming until something else comes to mind. It doesn't have to be about your grandpa.

K: (Drums)

T: Okay now stop. Take a deep breath. Think about your safe place. Can you get a picture of that?

K: (Nods)

T: Hold that picture; notice the feelings you get from being in your safe place. Go ahead and drum.

K: (Drums)

T: Now stop; take a deep breath. Kip, let me ask you a question: Why do you come here?

K: I don't know.

T: That is not a good enough answer. You can say anything else but that. Why do you come here?

K: (Long silence)

T: Why do you think your mom brings you here?

K: So I can be like other people.

T: That is a good answer. What do *you* think about coming here? Do you want to be like other people?

K: (Nods)

T: In what way do you want to be like other people?

K: So people don't make fun of me. So I can be like them.

T: Do you want to be like other people a little bit or a lot? (By asking this question, I missed an opportunity to have him simply focus on wanting to be like other kids.)

K: A little bit.

T: Are there ways that you do want to be like other people?

K: Kind of.

T: In what way do you want to be like other people? If you were like other people would you be happy, sad, or mad?

K: (Shakes his head no)

T: Do you get happy, sad, mad like other people?

K: (Nods)

T: How *much* would you like to be that way?

K: Just a little.

T: What keeps you from getting happy, mad, sad, and scared? You really don't get happy, mad, sad, and scared at all?

K: Sometimes.

T: Will you miss your grandpa when he is dead?

K: (Nods)

T: How much will you miss him?

K: A little bit.

T: Okay think about that: How you're going to miss him when he is gone and how you're going to miss him a little bit. Hit the drums.

K: (Drums, looks upset)

T: Okay, and just stop when you get a new feeling, thought, or new picture.

K: (Begins wiping at his eyes)

T: Is this making you sad?

K: (Nods, continues drumming, sighs)

T: Just continue thinking about that sadness.

K: (Wipes at his eyes more frequently, sniffles some)

T: Notice these sad feelings. It's okay.

K: I remember him getting married, though. (At this point, not only is Kip experiencing sadness, but he is also engaging in associative chaining. So for the first time in this session, some observable progress is being made.)

T: Okay, think about that. Keep drumming. I will get you a tissue.

K: (Sniffles, wipes his nose)

T: Okay, think about his getting married. When did he get married?

K: (Drums)

T: That's good, really good.

K: And he got some money when he got married, and he got a car.

T: Okay think about that. You're doing great. Think about that and think about the feelings that go with that, and hit the drum.

K: (Drums)

T: That's good; you're doing good.

K: And they got married at lunchtime.

T: Okay, think about that.

K: (Drums)

T: Just notice whatever else you remember.

K: They didn't get married in a church. They just got married in a retirement center, where they get really old and can't take care of themselves anymore.

T: Okay, think about that. You're doing good.

K: (Drums for several minutes)

T: Now stop take a deep breath. Let it out slow. Do you remember what you were thinking about when you felt so sad?

K: (Shakes his head no)

T: What happened to the sad feelings?

K: It went away.

T: What kind of feelings are there now?

K: Nothing.

T: How sad were you: a little bit or a lot?

K: A little bit.

T: Do you think you will feel sad about your grandpa again?

K: (Nods)

T: What else is going to make you feel sad?

K: Nothing.

T: What about when he actually dies? Will that make you sad?

K: (Nods)

T: Think about that: when you hear he is actually dying. Okay, got that? Go ahead, beat the drums and think about how you're going to feel when he actually dies.

K: (Drums, wipes at his eyes)

T: Just tell me when you get a new thought or a new feeling. Are you feeling sad right now?

K: (Shakes his head no)

T: That's good drumming. Just think about what comes into your mind while you drum. Kip, you're doing really good with this: You thought about when you got sad and when you were at the wedding. Did you know the person he was getting married to?

K: (Nods)

T: Did you help out at the wedding?

K: (Shakes head no)

T: You just watched the wedding?

K: (Nods)

T: Did you know the person he was getting married to?

K: (Nods)

T: Did you like her?

K: (Nods)

T: Think about that and how they got married and you liked her, too, and she is already dead. She is already dead and you miss her a little bit. (I had been informed of her death earlier.)

K: (Drums)

T: Okay, now stop. And what do you think of now?

K: Nothing.

T: Who else have you felt sad about?

K: No one.

T: Did you feel sad about your grandpa dying?

K: (Nods)

T: Did you feel sad about your grandma dying?

K: Just a little.

T: How about when you were 5—did you miss people then?

K: (Shakes his head no)

T: What kinds of things make you feel sad?

K: Nothing makes me sad except for just sometimes.

### Excerpt from Session 5

Kip is much more verbal in the second segment, two months later (i.e., he talks about something he is interested in, with associative chaining occurring).

T: Did you think of something new?

K: I sorta did and I sorta didn't.

T: Tell me about when you sorta did.

K: Well, does it have to be something that I want to make better?

T: No, it can be anything.

K: When I went out to walk, he went out to the fence, and the other turtle goes anywhere he wants to and stuff. He can also crawl out of the water.

T: Just think about that.

K: (Drums and then speaks) If you let the turtle walk in the sun, if you let the turtle in the sun for a long time, its shell will fall off.

T: I did not know that. Think about that and drum again.

K: (Drums and then speaks) I know why the dog wants to eat the turtle. It said in the turtle book that dogs like to eat the turtle shells.

T: Okay, think about all that and drum until you think of something new.

K: (Drums and then speaks) Also with . . . turtles, whenever a car goes by in the backyard, the turtles put their heads straight up like they're lying out there in the middle of the street and they don't get run over.

T: Tell you what, now can you think of something that happened when you were much younger?

K: (Shakes his head no)

T: Think of something that we have talked about that happened when you were younger, like the fire, and falling and getting run over by the bike.

K: Well, I was afraid to cross the big open gap where there was no house with my bike because that's because these kids kept riding their bikes through there sometimes. Black kids did. Whenever I went past they rode their bike through. Sometimes when I crossed they would ride by and sometimes they didn't. They picked on my friend. One of them was a nice kid. He wanted to know my name.

T: Think about all that stuff and do the drumming. Can you get a picture of that in your mind?

K: Yup. (Drums)

T: Real good. Tell me when you remember something else.

K: (Drums and then speaks) About when I was little.

T: Uhuh

K: (Drums)

K: I remember when I was asking my grandma Pearl for a bike with a radio on it. All the other kids had one so I wanted one. But she said no. I just had this little small bike, but the ones with the radio on them were cool.

T: Do you remember when she said no?

K: Okay.

T: Just think about that. Can you get a picture of that?

K: Yeah, I can. When I was older I had this friend who had this other friend and his friend did not like me. When he came back he got one of those bikes that had a radio on it and I saw it again and that made me want it even worse.

T: Just remember all of that and do the drumming until you can think of something new.

K: About bikes?

T: It could be about anything.

K: I had this one fort that was made of, built of monster truck tires and you could climb up and jump in and it did not have doors.

T: Okay, think about that and do the drumming.

K: (Drums)

T: Good, really good. Tell me when you think of something new.

K: I just remember this. It was when I had my bike, but I forgot it at my grandma Pearl's best friend's house. She said I could bring it there but I forgot it and when I got it back I tried to ride it again but I almost lost my balance because I hadn't rode it for a long time.

T: Okay, think about that.

K: (Drums and then speaks) And we were playing a game out in the field in the back of the house. I think it was baseball. There were lots of dandelions out there, but my sister wasn't with me. But then I got adopted at my grandma Pearl's best friend's house.

T: Okay, think about that and do some more drumming. Do you remember how that made you feel when you got adopted at that other house?

K: (Drums and then speaks) I didn't want to go. I wasn't afraid of anything, so I ran into the laundry. I answered the door first. I saw that it was my mom, dad, and sister, but I had never saw them before I answered the door. I ran in the laundry room without the lights. My grandma said they are the ones that are going to take me. I hid in the dryer.

T: Think about that. Hold that picture in your mind and begin drumming.

K: (Drums and then speaks) The picture when I got adopted.

T: Yes.

K: Okay.

T: Remember how it made you feel?

K: No.

T: Just hold the picture then, and do the drum—you're doing a good job—until you think of something else.

K: There isn't something else. When I got adopted, I don't remember much about that time.

T: Just hold that picture. What you remember now?

K: But the last time I was here I almost told you everything when I was little and everything that happened when I was little.

T: Now you remember something about being adopted. Hold that picture in your mind and go ahead and drum. Stop when you think of something new.

K: Okay. (Drums)

T: What is the worst part of all of that? When you saw them at the door? When you hid in the dryer?

K: The worst part is when we went with them.

T: Think about that and do the drumming.

K: (Drums and then speaks) Then when I was adopted we stayed at the Smith house because they were in Florida or something. They brought Molly with them. It was their dog before it was the Smith dog. They decided to give it to us for some reason. We slept there all in one room and when we woke up there were these hot air balloons and stuff. And my whole family rode bikes down the hill and the Smiths live in this big house. I went to go look at Andrew's room and he had all these toys in there; also, he had this one stuffed toy. Molly jumped up on his bed and chewed it up so we brought it with us. They gave it to us. They bought a cat, snake, or another dog.

T: Out of all these memories which ones do you most want to think about?

K: The Smith house.

T: Think about that and do some drumming.

K: (Drums) We only stayed there one day. I don't remember that much.

T: Why don't you think about the part where you got adopted?

K: Okay.

T: Think about that and do some drumming.

K: (Drums)

T: What do you think of now?

K: I was sitting there playing with some of my toys, looking out the window. My grandma Pearl did not tell me; no one told me I was going to be adopted that day. But I was playing with my toys when I was little, so I looked out the window by the couch and saw my sister, my dad, and my mom. They were walking to the door. I was so happy that I was being adopted until I saw them, what they looked like, and then I wasn't so happy when I got adopted.

T: Do you think you got scared when you saw them?

K: Yeah.

T: Just think about how you got scared. Do the drumming and think about how you got scared.

K: Think about when I was adopted?

T: Yes, when you saw them for the first time and you didn't want to be adopted and you got scared.

K: (Drums) Okay. They took my mom's car. When I was in the car, I sat in the front of the car. My sister and dad sat in the back, and my mom was driving. So I looked at the knob and I thought it was a button and I pressed it but it was the horn. Then we went to go eat. My mom told me to try the cottage cheese. I don't like cottage cheese and I still don't like it.

T: Think about being adopted and how it scared you and do the drumming until I tell you when to stop.

K: (Drums) So what were we talking about?

T: We were talking about how you were being adopted and how you did not want to be adopted although you did at first.

K: (Drums)

T: Think about your safe place and keep drumming.

These two segments illustrate several aspects of EMDR. One is that even with minimal outward responsiveness on Kip's part, his emotions become activated and reprocessing occurs with his associative chaining. This, in turn, produces a situation where Kip is more cooperative and more verbal in later sessions, and more associative chaining occurs in conjunction with the left-right stimulation. As these segments indicate, even short segments of EMDR can be significant. The segments also suggest the utility of drumming as a method of activating patterned, repetitive stimulation of a left-right nature. Drumming is simultaneously visual, kinesthetic, auditory, left-right, patterned, and repetitive.

## Aren't You Going to Kiss Me Good-bye?

I am aware of other cases of attachment disorders in children or adolescents, where attachment has taken place after treatment with EMDR. For example, Donna Lewandowski, an EMDR-trained therapist in Denver, Colorado, described the following account about her adopted 8-year-old daughter. During a period of time when Donna was in a consultation group with me that was focused on using EMDR with children, she decided to see if EMDR might help her daughter when she was having a tantrum. This adopted daughter had been severely neglected and abused by her birth mother for the first two years of her life. As a result, she accepted no physical contact with Donna during the six years since she had been adopted, although she did accept some contact with males in the family. While her daughter was in the midst of her tantrum, Donna said, "Let's try something. Think about that anger and follow my fingers with your eyes." Her daughter was willing to do so, and seemed to be calmed by the procedure. Later in the day, Donna was about to leave the house, and her daughter said to her, "Aren't you going to kiss me good-bye?" Donna joyfully did, with the girl hugging her and kissing her on the lips. Following that event, her daughter continued to be affectionate and continued to attach to Donna in other ways. Since then, the attachment between mother and daughter has continued to grow, with affection and closeness deepening further. In addition, the growth in attachment has allowed other areas of development to progress more normally. Donna told of this experience in the next consultation group, and not only Donna, but also all of us in the group, had tears in our eyes.

Among other things, this case raises an important and frequently asked question: Should parents who are therapists trained in EMDR use EMDR with their own child? In the above example, it had extremely positive results. Because EMDR is a relatively straightforward procedure, it can be used on an ad hoc basis, but the potential for abuse is present. As EMDR is a form of therapy, all of the guidelines for other forms of therapy apply in general. In particular, dual relationships are to be avoided. In medicine, physicians don't treat members of their own families. In law, lawyers and judges don't represent persons with whom they have conflicts of interest (dual relationships) or members of their own families. However, a physician might remove stitches from a son's lip or treat a daughter's broken arm in an emergency situation. An attorney might discuss legal issues with a family member and make recommendations to pursue litigation or not. Analogously, EMDR might be used on an emergency basis with one's own child, but it would be important to have ongoing treatment carried out by an EMDR therapist other than the parent. Anything more than a short-term or emergency intervention with a member of one's own family could put the child in a difficult position or do damage, and professionally would be considered questionable.

Kathy Goodman, another therapist in the same consultation group, began using EMDR with developmentally-delayed adolescents and young adults in foster care who were diagnosed with an attachment disorder (in addition to other diagnoses). In her practice, she would have the foster parent in the room, embracing the client as the client went through EMDR, targeting the individual's losses that had resulted from losing parents and moving from one foster home to another. Often the client would go through a grief reaction in EMDR and then be able to begin attaching to the foster parent, saying something like, "I don't have that person anymore, but now I have you," and then return the foster parent's embrace.

Through this therapist's insightful work and through my own work with children and adolescents who have attachment disorders, I have learned that attachment usually doesn't take place until after the child has grieved his losses. How could a child attach to a new parent if he hasn't grieved the loss of his earlier attachment? In other areas of psychology we seem to understand this phenomenon, such as when a spouse dies and the surviving partner needs to grieve the loss before attaching to a new partner, or when a child dies and the parents need to grieve the loss before having another child. Somehow, though, we have lost sight of this necessary processing with attachment-disordered children who have had losses.

## They Abandoned Me There

The first adolescent diagnosed with attachment disorder with whom I worked using EMDR arrived with his parents from out of state (this case was briefly referred to in chapter 2). Although Bill (age 14) had been diagnosed as an attachment disordered child by a center in Colorado that specialized in treating attachment disorders, he was somewhat unusual in that he had been raised by his natural parents and had not experienced many disruptions of parenting. As an infant, however, he had been sickly and hyperactive, so much so that he seemed not to attach to his parents. He didn't sleep much and was placed on Ritalin at an early age for his hyperactivity. He was tactile defensive, avoided eye contact, and preferred not to give or receive affection. He was withdrawn and kept mostly to himself. In childhood and early adolescence, he engaged in a good deal of unethical behavior, such as lying and stealing. He seemed angry and resentful in addition to being withdrawn. The treatment center had recommended long-term inpatient attachment therapy for him. His parents had decided against that approach for a number of reasons.

When I initially saw him, he slouched in his seat, his baseball cap pulled down so low over his eyes that I could not see his face. As the family had driven from out of state, I conducted both the interview with his parents and Bill's EMDR on the same day. After obtaining background and history information, I started EMDR with Bill. To my surprise, he quickly went back in memory to an incident that happened when he was 3 years old, when his parents took him to a day care center and the rest of the family went on an outing without him. In EMDR he recalled some new information, however. The session, reconstructed from my notes, went something like this.

After establishing a safe place, we targeted problems in the family. Bill said, "My parents were always working. I hated the day care center they made me go to." I asked what he didn't like and he replied, "The people there; I couldn't stand them." His negative cognition was, "They abandoned me there." His positive cognition was, "They didn't abandon me there." Although these aren't particularly good negative and positive cognitions, I went ahead with them, as he seemed at this point to be marginally cooperative. The VOC of the positive statement was 4. He indicated that he felt anger in thinking about the event, and rated it as 8 on the SUDS. After an initial set of eye movements, Bill stated, "I didn't know people. The kids were jerks. My brother and I were separate. I felt alone." I asked him where he felt that aloneness in his body. He said, "Down the back of my spine." I asked him to pay attention to that as he engaged in another set of eye movements. He then said, "My friend is leaving me. He lived across the street. I was 3 years old. Completely alone." I asked, "Where do you feel that?" and he replied, "In my back and in my spine."

We did another set of eye movements.

"They wouldn't let me go to the farm. I just turned 4. I felt terrible. They didn't believe me that I was old enough."

"Where do you feel that?"

"Right in my stomach."

He engaged in another set of eye movements.

"Falling off a slide that day. I slipped. I hurt my leg. Terrible. Clumsy. The teacher wouldn't help me."

"How did that make you feel?"

"All alone and like I didn't matter."

At this point, I checked SUDS. Bill said the anger was at a 3 and rated the statement, "They didn't abandon me there" at a 6. I went ahead and attempted an early installation to see what would happen. After the installation, Bill stated, "It was partly my choice to go there." At this point, he rated SUDS as 2 and VOC at 6. We closed out the session with his safe place.

After the session, Bill and his family drove back home, but his mother called me a few days later, stating with amazement that Bill had started to attach to them for the first time in his life. She said, "He can't get enough of us. He sits next to us, looks us in the eye, talks to us, and gives us hugs." I was as amazed as she was, as I had no idea that the new information that he had recalled in EMDR would promote such a profound shift.

About a month later, the family returned for a second EMDR session (the time lapse was due to their living out of state), in which we again targeted Bill's anger about problems in the family. Between the second and third sessions, a girl who had grown up as a close neighbor was killed in an automobile accident. We targeted that in EMDR, and following that session, Bill went to the waiting room, threw his arms around his mother, and wept. Later, his mother told me that she had never seen him grieve anything before.

By this time, Bill even looked different. His body posture was more open, he had good eye contact, and he was able to laugh and joke. He was no longer lying and stealing, and after he had related to me how he had told his parents the truth about something he would have lied about in the past, he somewhat ruefully confided that he was not sure that he liked having a conscience. His parents regarded his changes as "unbelievable."

These sessions occurred in 1992. There were a total of six sessions, all of them EMDR. In 1996, when Bill graduated from high school, I contacted his family to see how he was doing. He continued to be attached to his family, the lying and stealing had stopped, his grades had improved so that he could attend college, and he had developed into one of the top athletes in his state in a competitive high school sport. When I asked his mother if there was any area in which he seemed different from other teenagers, she said, "Well yes, there is one thing." When I asked what that was, she said, "He still wants a kiss and a hug before he goes to bed at night." Apparently Bill still had a need to make up for lost time from his childhood.

Bill's case is interesting in several respects. Although he had been diagnosed by experts as a reactive attachment disorder, he was not a typical case of the disorder, as he came from an intact and supportive family. Losses did not seem to be as central in his case as in most cases of reactive attachment disorder, although it could be construed that threatened loss (fear of abandonment) might have been central. His early hyperactivity and sickness may have made his development idiosyncratic, perhaps making him more vulnerable for events that would not ordinarily be traumatic. Many children stay at day care centers, often when they don't want to, and they don't develop attachment disorders. In fact, Bill *chose* to stay at day care, rejecting his family, and perhaps this heightened his fear that they might abandon him. That day, he had a miserable day at the center, hurting himself and fearing that his family wouldn't come back and pick him up. Somehow, his recalling that it was partly his decision to go there made a world of difference to him.

How many other children are traumatized by minor events in ways that we don't recognize? Or ways that we do recognize, but discount, such as being bullied on the playground? Or being deliberately humiliated by a teacher or a parent?

Although Bill may have had an attachment disorder long before being left at the day care center, that event certainly heightened his disorder. However, he reacted to EMDR in a way that is more typical of children subjected to simple traumas, in contrast to complex ones. It was only after treatment that we could surmise that it was a simple trauma. The most accurate conceptualization is likely that Bill developed PTSD after the day care center incident, and the PTSD interfered with further attachment.

## The Need to Say Good-bye

Most cases of reactive attachment disorder involve complex and repeated traumas, and are not likely to resolve quickly. A case in that regard involved Nancy, who was also diagnosed with an attachment disorder.

She was a 13-year-old preadolescent when she started seeing me. She had been in therapy for many of her childhood years for anger, depression, and conflict with her mother. The last therapist who saw her before me considered her as severely depressed, suicidal, attachment disordered, and needing medication. She had been adopted from Korea at age 2, after being abandoned by her mother and then placed in a foster home for a year. Initially she was thought to be 18 months of age, but dental charts indicated that she had to be at least 2 years old. She cried when she was taken away from her foster mother. At first, after being adopted, she would roll around and knock into walls. She engaged in head banging and would have terrible temper tantrums in which she'd cry for three to four hours. Although these behaviors gradually subsided after adoption, the tantrums began again in the fourth grade. At that time, they were so severe that it was hard to find sitters for her.

Beginning in the third or fourth grade, Nancy did poorly in school (previously she had done well). In areas that she was interested in, such as theater, modeling, and art, she would get A+s. However, in other subjects, she would start with Bs and then go downhill. Although she read a great deal, she'd often get Fs in English. Standardized group achievement tests indicated average to above average achievement, except in math.

Her adoptive mother saw her as being highly manipulative. They had an extremely conflicted relationship, with Nancy being "hot and cold" and unpredictable. At times, Nancy would scream at her, "Go ahead and abandon me like my mother did!" At times she would threaten to kill herself with a knife. There was suspicion that she was beginning to use illicit drugs.

As can be seen from this rather turbulent history, a number of diagnoses could be possible for Nancy. However, a great deal of information came out in EMDR, which helped to clarify that her deepest issues were attachment-related. I saw Nancy over a two-and-a-half-year period for a total of 38 sessions. She made great progress in therapy, but because of ongoing conflicts in the family the complex nature of the situation makes the eventual outcome uncertain.

Much of this therapy was EMDR, although there was also family therapy at times. She had to be hospitalized on one occasion following a suicide gesture after a major argument with her mother.

Initially sullen and uncommunicative in therapy, to the point that I internally questioned her intelligence, in EMDR she almost immediately showed a keen intelligence, imagination, and animation. She subsequently became highly self-disclosing and talkative even when we weren't using EMDR. In the first year of therapy, Nancy used therapy and EMDR very well. She expressed much anger and rage toward her adoptive mother for her punitive ways of dealing with Nancy when she was having difficulty. Toward the end of the first year, Nancy had the most intense abreactive session that I had seen with a child or adolescent up to that point. It was not an EMDR session. She screamed and cried as she talked about an uncle who began abusing her sexually during summers when she visited her maternal grandmother on the east coast. Much anger came out toward her mother for not protecting her (but she had not told her mother). In this session, she went in and out of dissociation, sometimes remembering the abuse and sometimes being unaware that she had talked about it, displaying "la belle indifference" of hysteria when she dissociated.

Following that session, I met with her and her parents, and told them about the sexual abuse that had occurred over several summers starting between the third and fourth grades. Nancy's parents were initially skeptical, but did report the abuse to the authorities. In the next session, we used EMDR to deal with the traumatic memories of having a sock jammed in her mouth, being raped, cut with knives, forced to perform fellatio on her uncle, and having objects inserted into her vagina until she bled. At the time of the assaults, in great fear because of physical threats from her uncle, she had told her grandmother that she had started to menstruate, to account for her bleeding. In her third session of EMDR dealing with the sexual abuse, Nancy got to a place where she felt she could forgive her uncle. She could say that she was a stronger person for having gone through the abuse. These were her understandings, not ones that came from me. She also wept for what she had lost. As a child, she had wanted to be brilliant, but ended up feeling like she was merely crazy. In the next EMDR session, she cried a lot as well. She also commented on all the other therapy she had gotten over the years, which merely focused on her "bad" behavior, saying, "They didn't touch my problems. All they did is ask me what goals I was going to set for next week."

But it was the next session that was the most startling. We started by once again working on the sexual abuse by her uncle, but as that seemed to be mostly resolved, some new images started coming up unexpectedly. These images were herself as a baby, being bathed in a basin by a woman who looked much like her. She also saw a man whom she assumed was her father, working with a machine. Then a new image came up, with her seeing this man lying in the gutter, with half of his head missing. Her mother is crying. It is cold out.

Later, Nancy said that she did not know if the images were "real," but we used them so that she could say good-bye to and grieve her birth parents. In the following months, Nancy continued to work on a number of issues. Her relationships with her parents improved, as did her grades in school. As she lived in an area between Colorado Springs and Denver, she was able to transfer to an arts-oriented school in Denver, where she began to do better yet. She began to express a sense of identity that she was difficult, complex, and creative. In her last session with me, she said, "Thanks for saving my life." Because of commuting issues, she began to see a therapist in Denver after school.

I don't know what eventually happened with Nancy, but I do have the sense that she worked out a great deal in the two and a half years of EMDR that she had. When she began seeing another therapist, she still had a number of conflicts with her parents, and would still act out from time to time. She continued to feel threatened by her uncle who continued to live with her grandmother on the east coast. Nothing had happened after she and her parents reported him, so she had little sense of safety and was afraid to visit her grandmother.

What can we learn from this complex case? First, that children with reactive attachment disorder often present in strange and baffling ways, with an almost indecipherable mix of problems. To one person, they may seem manipulative; to another, rebellious; to another, bipolar; to another, learning disabled or attentionally impaired; and to yet another, a spoiled brat. A client like Nancy almost seems like a projective test, and mental health professionals and others read in her what they will. Secondly, it is difficult to get to the underlying attachment issues, and even when they are accessed it is not easy to deal with them. Were these veridical memories from infancy on Nancy's part? In a sense, it doesn't matter. Even if they were figments of her imagination, these imagined representations are what she needed to deal with in therapy, and she needed to grieve the loss of those imagined birth parents. Nancy's progress in therapy would have been more certain, if, after grieving for her lost parents, she had exemplary adoptive parents to whom she could attach. But, alas, she didn't. They, too, were baffled by her mixture of problems and even as the sources of the problems became more clear, they tended to hold back in skepticism and have trouble in dealing with their anger at her, even though they had two older children whom they had apparently raised well. It is clear that EMDR could not be a stand-alone therapy in a case like this. Many other interventions are necessary, from family therapy, partial family therapy, legal interventions, academic interventions, psychiatric hospitalizations, suicide precautions. I have now seen enough other children and adolescents with attachment issues, that I know to look for the early memories and emotions around abandonment issues, and to work to deal with them in EMDR, much as I learned to do with Nancy, Bill, and Kip.

## DIVORCE

Two divorce cases will illustrate well the role that EMDR can play in complex traumas related to divorce.

## A Good Nightmare

Aaron, at 4½ years old, was manifesting high levels of fear and rage following his parents' separation and divorce. Not only did he have a divorce to contend with, but he also had a 6-year-old sister who was microcephalic and functioned at a 3½-year-old developmental level. She would often pinch him and pull his hair, and he would retaliate in kind. She had vision problems, coordination problems, and very little speech, making communication with her difficult, although she was learning sign language. Aaron's maternal grandparents lived in town, and favored Aaron so extremely over his older brother (age 9) and sister that Aaron said that he would rather live with them than with his mom and her new boyfriend. His behavior was more aggressive and demanding after he visited his grandparents. He was also more physically aggressive with his sister after such visits. He reported that if he and she got into a fight at his grandparents', they would blame his sister and put her in a room for long periods of time.

Aaron's dad, who was in the military, tended to be harsh in his discipline and easily angered. Aaron would often return from visitation with his dad having nightmares and wetting the bed. Aaron's maternal grandparents sided with Aaron's father in the divorce, against his mother. Eventually, when a court order was obtained requiring the grandparents to resolve issues between Aaron's mother and themselves in therapy before more visitation with them could occur (based on a report by a custody evaluator), Aaron's dad would occasionally take him to see his grandparents, ignoring the court order. Of course, Aaron's behavior would deteriorate following such a visit.

Aaron was first referred to me after he went on a two-week trip with his father and his siblings, during which he tried to kill (strangle) his sister. He was not strong enough to succeed, but both parents became concerned with the level of his aggression and referred him to therapy. As his mother was seeing an EMDR-trained therapist, that therapist referred Aaron to me, knowing that I would likely employ it with Aaron.

Aaron responded very well to EMDR, even at age 4. Initially, we targeted his nightmares and his aggression toward his sister. The following excerpt is from his first EMDR session. At first, I tried to use eye movements with him, but converted to hand taps, as he was too young to track well with his eyes. Notice how short the channels are, and how quickly he goes from negative to positive in his cognitions. However, I was not able to obtain an initial negative cognition, positive cognition, or VOC, due to his young age.

T: Okay, let's try something different. Here, put your hands on top of my hands. That's good. Now, first hit this hand. Good, now hit this hand. Good, now this one. Now this one. Okay, now keep doing that, now one after the other. Do that one. Do this one, just once. Now do this one. Now do this one. Now do this one. Okay. Good job. Good job. Okay, now think of getting mad at your sister last night and hit my hands. That's good. Good job. Okay, and tell me what you're thinking of now.

A: Getting mad last night at Mary (set of hand taps [HT]).

T: Okay. That's good. Now what are you thinking about?

A: Me being happy to Mary.

T: Okay, think about that. (HT) Okay, now what are you thinking about?

A: Um, being nice to Mary. Being nice and nice and nice and nice and nice.

T: Okay, think about that and tap my hands. (HT) Good job. Good job. Now what are you thinking about?

A: Being kind and kind and kind and kind and kind to my sister.

T: Okay, think about that.

Following this session, Aaron's mom noticed that Aaron was less aggressive toward his sister. She noted that even when Mary provoked him he showed restraint.

In the following therapy segment, we focused on Aaron's nightmares. Again, note the brevity of the channels and how quickly the channel goes from negative to positive. No negative or positive cognitions were elicited.

T: This time we'll be tapping your hands. Okay? One at a time. Just one at a time. Do this one first. Now this one. Now this one. That's good. This one. Okay, now let's try this again. Think of that nightmare where the alien ate the spider and then the spider ate the person. And think about how that made you sad. Did it make you scared too?

A: Uhuh.

T: Hold that. Wait. Have you got that picture in your mind? Hold that picture in your mind. Hit my hand. Hit my hand. Hit my hand. That's it. That's good. That's good. Good Good. Good. Okay, now stop. Now tell me what comes to your mind now.

A: A good dream.

T: Okay.

A: A good nightmare.

T: Tell me about the good dream.

A: The thing killing the alien and the spider.

T: Okay. Think about that. Hold that picture in your mind. Oh, you're doing such a good job. Keep doing it. A little bit more. Good. Good. Good. Good. Good. Good. Okay, stop. And what comes to your mind now?

A: Nothing.

T: Nothing. And where is that sad feeling now?

A: It went away (smiling and holding up his hands).

T: It went away? Great. Now, can you think of another nightmare (theme development)?

This was Aaron's fourth EMDR session. His mother reported great improvement in his behavior: He was less aggressive and no longer had nightmares. However, he then spent time with his father, and the nightmares recurred. This time, I had Aaron draw his nightmares before and after we targeted them with EMDR.

In the first nightmare, shown as figure 7.1, Aaron is a big squid, gobbling up his older brother (at 1). The large circular scribble, Aaron said, was his anger. Then Aaron drew the same thing "under the sea," where he is again devouring his brother (at 2). Finally, he drew his own sad face (at 3) and said, "Doesn't it look sad?" I certainly thought so.

After we targeted that nightmare in EMDR, and Aaron's SUDS went to 0, I had Aaron draw his feelings about the nightmare. This drawing is figure 7.2. At 1 in the figure is Aaron's big, happy face. His sad feeling is at 2, and has diminished to a tiny circle.

In another session, we targeted his anger toward his sister (figure 7.3), in which his sister is depicted pinching him (at 1). He drew his angry feeling as a large circle (at 2), and said it was his "big mad feeling." After using hand taps in EMDR and his SUDS had declined to 0, he drew his mad feeling (at 3), now shown as a pinpoint. These were Aaron's own representations, drawn in response to my questions, but I did not suggest any of the images to him.

In each of these EMDR sessions, we used hand taps and visual images drawn by him, which he looked at as I tapped his hands. Although precocious, he was not capable of negative and positive cognitions, so we used images, feelings, and body sensations in the EMDR.

In the subsequent three years of therapy, Aaron has had many ups and downs, related to the family conflicts that have arisen. When I terminated with him, he was doing well in general. His grandparents had refused to meet with

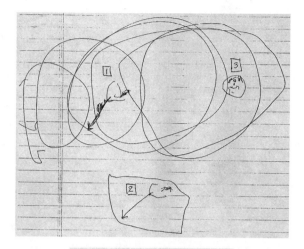

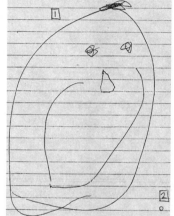

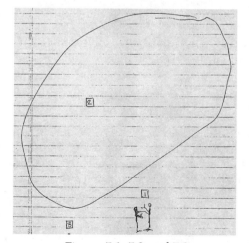

*Figures 7.1, 7.2, and 7.3*

Aaron's mom, with the result that their visitation with Aaron was being held in abeyance until that occurred. Consequently, Aaron's behavior improved greatly, although he missed his grandparents, especially his grandmother. He no longer had nightmares, nor wet the bed, and his conflict with his sister was greatly lessened. Competition between Aaron and his older brother continued, with that conflict causing Aaron a good deal of psychological stress. His grades in school were good, and his relationships with his mother and her boyfriend were good. Visitation with his father now caused fewer problems, as Aaron was more able to handle the differences between his mother's care and his father's care.

## PTSD Hallucinations

The second case involves a family of three boys, who remained in the custody of their father after their parents divorced. All three boys showed psychological disturbance of different kinds, due to the fact that they were abusively treated by their mother and her new husband during their visitation. One of the boys became so fearful that he manifested vivid auditory and visual hallucinations (involving ghosts or spectral presences) over several months. His PTSD symptoms were so severe that they involved such hallucinations, although his thinking processes did not become disordered as would be expected if he were psychotic. It is a good illustration that PTSD symptoms in the *DSM-IV* are not all-inclusive with children. Others have noted PTSD hallucinations in children. For example, Terr (1990) documents that such "ghosts," left untreated, can persist throughout adulthood. Also in another case presented in this book, a child treated with EMDR by Mary Estrada in our children's research not only manifested hallucinations after being traumatized, but actually hallucinated during an EMDR session until the trauma was desensitized. In both of the above divorce situations presented here, EMDR produced dramatic improvements in functioning for the children involved, but full resolution did not occur until the overall situation was improved.

Art, age 8, began having hallucinations and nightmares after he told his father that he and his brothers were being hit by his mother and her new husband (his stepfather) while on visitation with them. Previously, his mother had extracted a promise from him that he wouldn't say anything about what went on at their house. She told him that if he said anything to anyone, his stepfather would go to jail and that she would never be able to see him again. When he violated that promise, he became certain that either his mother or John (the stepfather) would kill him if they got the chance. His telling resulted in a court order to allow no further contact between the stepfather and the three boys (ages 10, 8, and 7), and limited, supervised visitation with his mother.

When I began seeing Art, he was terrified to go to sleep at night or even to bed by himself. The reported violence and abuse had taken several forms. Three years prior to my first seeing Art, his mother and his stepfather had kidnapped the three boys from school and taken them to their home in a nearby town. Although returned to their father after several months, the boys later seemed to sustain minor injuries while visiting with the mother and stepfather (who also had been abusive to a daughter from a prior marriage). The boys would recount being hit or spit at or backed into furniture by an angry parent. In a music class at school, Art told about being hit repeatedly with a hairbrush because he wasn't brushing his teeth fast enough.

In describing his fear about going to bed at night, Art said that he would stay up as late as possible (usually midnight or later) before going to bed. He had nightmares every night, night terrors on occasions, and, worst of all, almost every night would see ghostly figures who were there to kill him. Sometimes his nightmares were of his mother trying to kill him. Sometimes in the dream she would succeed. At times, Art would wake up his father and brothers as he woke up screaming from his nightmares. There were many nights that they all were up most of the night. It got so the only way he could fall asleep was with his hand actually touching his father. He would sleep in his father's bed every night for security, but it only helped him sleep for short periods of time, although that was better than getting no sleep at all.

In the first EMDR session, we targeted the nightmares, and by the end of the session he was somewhat less frightened. In the next session, four days later, we targeted his fear from the apparitions he had seen the night before: a woman and a man. The woman had a knife and was going to kill him. Following that session, Art was more relaxed and had no nightmares. Three days later, however, after a visitation with his mother, the nightmares started again, along with the fear of falling asleep and the ghostly figures. This time he saw his mother coming in the room with a gun. As these symptoms were so directly related to the visitations with his mother, I was able to arrange that Art have no overnights with his mother at all, and to have visitation with her only when he felt ready, although the two other boys continued to have supervised visitation.

Art's father now reported that Art was a "changed person" after each EMDR session. After the visitation stopped and Art had another EMDR session, Art went to sleep quickly that night for the first time in a long time. In addition, he had no nightmares. This is a good example of how each EMDR session produced some symptomatic improvement in terms of greater relaxation, lessened fear, and fewer nightmares, but further improvement was dependent upon changing the overall situation (e.g., limiting visitation).

As Art was now less terrified on a nightly basis, I was able to begin EMDR with his older brother, Ken. Ken felt intense guilt that he could not adequately protect his younger brothers from being hit, pushed, and spat upon. We targeted those thoughts and feelings in his first EMDR session, as documented in the following transcript. Note the importance of the safe place in the session, as Ken spontaneously goes to it several times. Also, when the safe place does come up for him, it's after a set of eye movements, not when he holds up his hand, even though that's what he has been instructed to do. Such an occurrence is not unusual, as the safe place often comes up during a set of eye movements when the child is feeling highly threatened.

Also note that the action in Ken's images is not always realistically feasible. I find that it's best not to intervene when children have unrealistic images, but rather to treat them as indicative of associative visual chaining. Later, if the images have remained unrealistic throughout the EMDR (not very common), that can be discussed after the EMDR has been completed.

T: Can you think of a place where you can go in your mind where you can feel safe, comfortable, happy, relaxed, and calm?

K: Uhuh.

T: Okay, can you get a picture of that in your mind?

K: Uhuh.

T: Describe that picture.

K: Well, it's a house. Do I have to be really descriptive?

T: Can you think of yourself being in a particular place in the house?

K: Uhuh.

T: Describe that: what you see and hear and smell and taste and touch and how you feel emotionally.

K: I'm upstairs in my bedroom, and dad's in there, and I feel happy and safe.

T: Okay, good. As you hold that picture in your mind, being there with your dad and feeling happy and safe, where do you feel those happy and safe feelings in your body physically?

K: I don't know.

T: Well, you might feel them all over, or might feel them in your chest, hands, or feet or head.

K: All over.

T: Okay. Now I'm going to ask you to hold the picture and the good feelings, the happy, safe feelings, and where you feel them all over, and then follow my fingers with your eyes—just for 15 or 20 seconds. We'll do that to install the safe place. Bring up the picture. . . . Got the picture? And the good feelings, notice those. Now follow my fingers. (EM) Now blank it out and take a deep breath. Just relax as you breathe out, just notice the good feelings.

And that's your safe place. We will use that in three ways. One is if during the problem stuff you want to stop, give me a hand signal to stop and we'll have you bring up your safe place. And at the end of the sessions, if your feelings are still upset, we will have you bring up your safe place. And you can use it on your own in between sessions; if you're upset you can go in your mind to the safe place. Can you think of a situation that you want to work on in here?

K: Yeah.

T: What is that situation?

K: Yesterday. Like yesterday, I'm the oldest brother and I'm supposed to be able protect them. But I can't do anything when Mom hits them. Then when I *can* do something, she hits me.

T: Think of that situation when you're with your mom and your brothers are getting hit. You're the oldest and you can't protect them. If you do try to protect them, then you get hit. Can you get a picture of that in your mind?

K: Yeah.

T: What's that picture look like?

K: Well, I'm in my room and I'm with my brother Mike. He got mad at Mom because, well, I don't know why. She's just mad at him, 'cause she just came in, and I went to my room and I saw him crying. Then she came in and she hit him and I told her not to do it and she turned around and said, "Oh, yeah?" and then she hit me and then she walked out.

T: As you hold that picture in your mind, what does it make you think about yourself? What does it make you think about you?

K: That I'm not worth having as a brother, because I can't protect them.

T: What would you rather believe about yourself?

K: That I was bigger and stronger and I could protect them.

T: If you were bigger and stronger and could protect them, what could you say about yourself then?

K: That I would be a better big brother.

T: As you hold that picture in your mind, of your mom hitting Mike, then hitting you, how true do those words seem to you, "That I can be a better big brother," from 1 to 7, where 1 feels not true at all, and 7 feels completely true? Where would you rate that, as you hold that picture in your mind?

K: I don't get it.

T: Hold the picture in your mind. . . . Got the picture? . . . As you hold that in your mind, how true do those words feel to you, "I can be a good big brother," from 1, where they feel not true at all, to 7 where they feel completely true?

K: Six.

T: So it seems mostly true?

K: But not if I have to live with my mom for the rest of my life.

T: If you had to live with your mom for the rest of your life, how true does it feel, from 1 to 7?

K: Zero.

T: As you hold that picture in your mind, and that negative thought of not worth having as a big brother, what kind of feelings does that make you have right now?

K: Sad.

T: Any other feelings?

K: Mad at Mom for making me feel this way.

T: Holding that picture in mind, how strong are those feelings of sadness and madness, from 0 to 10? Zero is not there at all, and 10 is as strong as those feelings could possibly be—how strong are they now?

K: Ten.

T: Where do you feel those emotions in your body physically?

K: In my stomach and brain.

T: Now, what I'm going to ask you to do is to hold the picture along with those negative thoughts and feelings, that "I'm not worth as having as a big brother," and the angry, mad, and sad feelings that you get and where you feel them in your stomach and brain; hold all of that together in your mind and follow my fingers. The main thing is just to let whatever comes to mind, come to mind. You don't have to make anything come to mind or keep anything from coming to mind; just let whatever comes up, come up. Okay, bring up the picture. . . . Got the picture? . . . and the thoughts and feelings, "I'm not worth having as a big brother," and the sad and mad feelings? Follow my fingers. (EM) Let it go, take a deep breath. Relax as you breathe out. Good. What do you think of now?

K: My happy place. (It came up spontaneously.)

T: Hold the happy place in mind. Just think about that and follow my fingers. (EM) Let it go, take a deep breath. What do you get now?

K: Nothing.

T: Let's go back to the picture of your mom. (When "nothing" comes up, go back to target.) Bring that picture up again and tell me what it looks like now.

K: I'm scared.

T: Hold that picture with your mom and the thoughts and the feelings that go with it, "I'm not worth having as a big brother because I can't protect them," and the sad and mad and scared feelings. Hold that, follow my fingers. (EM) Let it go, take a deep breath. What do you get now?

K: Dad comes in and takes me and Scott and Mike in the car and we go home, and we never have to see Mom again or John.

T: Hold that; follow my fingers. (EM) Let it go, take a deep breath. What do you get now?

K: When we went home. Mike and Scott are with me and dad in the happy place. (Again the safe place came up without his raising his hand. Properly installed, the safe place allows for this extra measure of security, if needed.)

T: You're doing good. Think of that and follow my fingers. (EM) Okay, blank it out. What do you get now?

K: I don't get anything. (Again, the first thing to do is go back to the target to restart the processing.)

T: Let's go back to the image that we started with. Bring up that memory again and tell me what you get now.

K: It never happened because I was able to protect Mike, because I grabbed her hand and pushed her out the door, and a lock appeared on the door and I shut it and locked it. (As alluded to before, an intervention is not necessary here, as he is bringing up fantasy images.)

T: Think about that; follow my fingers. (EM) Let it fade. What do you get now?

K: I'm in my happy place. (With high levels of fear, it is not unusual that a child returns to his safe place repeatedly. Rather, it is positive that he can use it so adaptively.)

T: Stay with that and follow my fingers. (EM) Blank it out, take a deep breath. . . . Let's get a check on those feelings, those feelings of being sad and mad. How strong are those right now, from 0 to 10? Zero is not there at all; 10 is the most upsetting they could be. (It would have been better if I had him bring up the target first, and then check the SUDS.)

K: Three.

T: Now I want you to hold two things in mind: one is the thought that we are working toward, that "I can be a good or better big brother." Hold that thought and the original memory that we started with your mom. Got both? . . . Hold both. (EM) Let it go, take a deep breath. What do you get now ("therapeutic choice," as we are close to the end of the session)?

K: That I'm a better big brother.

T: How true does that feel, from 1 to 7; where 1 feels not true at all and 7 feels completely true?

K: Five.

T: Before you rated it as a 6 that it was true. Five means that it's less true. Does it feel less true or does it feel more true?

K: All the way true: 7.

We completed the session using regular closing procedures. In the next session, three days later (because of the intensity of the emotional issues, I was seeing Ken and Art as frequently as possible), Ken's dad stated that Ken was doing very well since the last session. He said that Ken was more lighthearted and playful. Ken said that he felt much better, that he really *was* okay as a big brother, and his SUDS was now down to 0. While the overall situation has not changed, there has been symptomatic improvement on both Ken's and Art's part.

Over the next year and a half, the three boys' symptoms waxed and waned, depending on their relationships with their parents. When their symptoms worsened, EMDR was consistently helpful in reducing their severity. With limited visitation, and a stable home life with a supportive and nurturing father, their mother began to make amends with her boys. They continued to have no contact with their stepfather. Increasingly, EMDR was not a part of therapy, but rather family therapy approaches were helpful and relevant. The boys' mother was increasingly integrated into the family sessions with the result that the relationships were repaired, both parents supported the boys' relationships with the other parent, and all three boys reattached to the mother they had once hated and feared during a time of intense emotional turbulence.

## Clarity of Results with Complex Traumas

One additional case shows quite clearly how EMDR can provide improvement, and how environmental events can interfere with that improvement. Libby, 5 years old, moved to Colorado from another state with her mother and 8-year-old brother after her dad (divorced from her mother) tried to drown her. There was also the possibility that Libby's father (diagnosed with bipolar disorder) had sexually molested her. Libby's prior therapist had strong suspicions in that direction, causing her mother to confront her dad, who didn't deny the allegation, but said that any man who has a daughter thinks that way about "his girl." Following that, the mother fled the state with her two children. After the attempted drowning, Libby started having nightmares about big snakes eating her up. When her mother told her that it would be a long time before she saw her dad again, she was again able to sleep in her own bed. At Christmas, before I began seeing her in therapy, Libby's dad called three times, causing her to again start having nightmares and sleep on the floor in her mother's bedroom. She also began wetting her bed every night.

In the first session with Libby, we targeted the nightmares. The EMDR appeared to have good resolution, and Libby set a goal of sleeping in her own bed that night. In the next two weeks she had only one more nightmare, although she had been having them nightly before the EMDR session. She had also slept all but four nights in her own bed, and went four nights without wetting the bed, although we had not targeted the bed-wetting at all. Again, we used EMDR, focusing on the nightmares. As a target for the nightmares, she drew an ugly, scary man (figure 7.4). Following that session, Libby slept in her own bed every night and had no further nightmares. However, she continued to wet the bed. In two more sessions, we targeted the bed-wetting, and Libby did not wet for an entire month.

However, her father was able to obtain their phone number and called three times, making Libby feel unsafe again. She returned to wetting the bed on a nightly basis, as she no longer felt safe. On the other hand, the nightmares have not recurred. As Libby is currently continuing therapy, outcomes remain in doubt. Of potentially great significance, though, is that her mother sent her father a powerful and articulate letter, detailing the negative effects of his phone calls on Libby, and he has agreed to make no further contact. This information may be useful in the future in helping her feel safe.

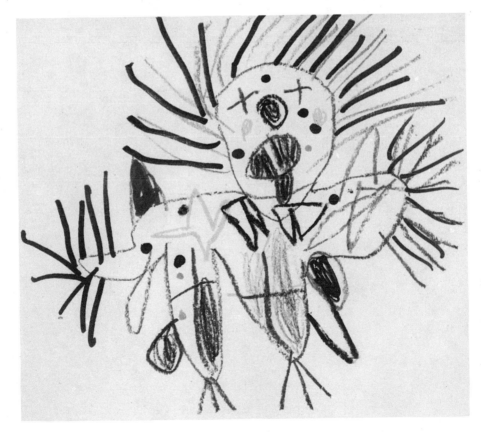

*Figure 7.4*

Most striking about Libby's case is the way cause-and-effect relationships are laid bare. EMDR reduced her symptoms, but they recurred when she felt threatened. Such is the nature of complex traumas and EMDR. Not all cases of complex trauma will be this clear, but the principles underlying the results of EMDR remain constant.

In the next chapter, before considering the remaining chapters on symptoms and diagnoses, we will look at troubleshooting; that is, what to do when EMDR is not working well.

_eight_

# Troubleshooting

"I can sing a song to you."
—STAN, AGE 7

NOW THAT WE HAVE EXAMINED how EMDR can be used with both simple and complex traumas, we can take a look at troubleshooting, or what to do if EMDR doesn't seem to be working. We'll look at what to do if the child doesn't cooperate with EMDR; if the child starts EMDR, but doesn't want to continue; if the processing doesn't move toward resolution within a session; if processing seems to go well within a session, but changes don't occur afterward; and what to do if the processing itself isn't productive. We'll also address specific questions about EMDR.

## NONCOOPERATION WITH EMDR

This kind of situation usually plays out like this: You've conducted an initial session with the parents, obtaining a thorough developmental history and a clear statement of the presenting problem, and from that you've developed a good idea of several potential targets for the child. In your initial session with just the child, she indicates that she will not engage in EMDR, won't cooperate with setting up a safe place, and won't agree to talk about potential targets. She may indicate that the trauma is too overwhelming for her to deal with—not by words necessarily, but certainly through behaviors or emotions. What do you do now?

First, consider that you may need to do more to establish a working relationship. If you don't have a working relationship with the child, nothing else will happen, whether you're using EMDR, hypnosis, talking about the problem, using structured or unstructured play therapy, or even just drawing pictures.

Perhaps the best way to think about establishing a working relationship with a child is to think of it as simply getting to know the child and her world. Thus, you end up talking about everything she likes to do from sunrise to sunset, and all the things she hates to do. You find out about who is in her family, including all the family pets, or her own personal pets. Does she have relationships with grandparents, aunts, uncles, adult friends who think she's special? Who are her friends, her boyfriends? Does she have favorite jokes? Does she like to play games? If she does, play a game with her. Make sure she wins. See how she deals with rules, structure in games. Later, how does she deal with losing? Her reactions to losing are often particularly diagnostic, because here is where the problem behaviors often emerge.

Overall, there are probably as many ways to establish a working relationship with a child as there are children. It takes tact, knowledge, interest, a liking for children, an ability to communicate that liking, and an ability to relate on the child's level, no matter what it is. Ideally, the child gets the impression that "This is a person who has an interest in me, likes me, and wants to get to know me." So, if the child initially refuses EMDR, the beginning task of therapy then becomes not conducting EMDR, but establishing a relationship so that EMDR can be conducted later.

A second approach can be to change the target that was originally selected. If the child doesn't agree to the first target, or can't get started on the first target, select another. We found in our research with children that a good way to get at what was troubling a child the most was to ask what feelings he most wanted to get rid of or donate to the study. Most children had a very good idea of that, and then follow-up questions could be asked about what situations were associated with those bad feelings.

If all problem-related targets are rejected, pick self-esteem-enhancing targets; if those targets don't work, pick prior happy times; if those targets don't work, pick an idealized happy time. If that doesn't work, go back to the safe place, do sets of eye movements there until the child feels comfortable. Then play a game, draw a picture, use free play, work on an improved relationship.

Another possibility for a course of action when a child does not want to start with EMDR is to bring in the child's parent or caregiver. This can allow for a number of other approaches to occur. If the child is older (9–12 years old), there can be an additional discussion about the purpose of the sessions, and possible targets can be mutually discussed. If the child is younger, and apprehensive about being alone with the therapist, the parent can be involved in the treatment in various ways described in earlier chapters.

# IF THE CHILD STARTS BUT DOESN'T
# WANT TO CONTINUE EMDR

This problem occurs most frequently when the child becomes frightened by the emotions that are coming up. If it occurs during the session, have the child bring up the safe place and then conduct sets of eye movements until the child is able to continue with the original target. If the child demurs from continuing with the original target, then the same sequence can be followed as detailed above: Pick a different target, or a more positive one, and continue. If the child refuses all EMDR, engage in other activities or work at establishing, reestablishing, or improving the relationship.

It may also happen that the child refuses to continue EMDR in a second session, after the first EMDR session has been completed. Here, it is likely that the child has been frightened by the emotions that have been aroused in the previous session, and which may have continued to be frightening during the week. If gentle encouragement doesn't work to re-engage the child in EMDR, and changed or lesser targets are not acceptable to the child, then engage the child in other activities, other forms of therapy, and work on rebuilding trust in the relationship, so that EMDR can be tried again later.

The most difficult children I have ever worked with in EMDR are children who have been so severely abused early in life that they have not repressed the bad memories; they have repressed the good memories. One 10-year-old boy with whom I worked initially liked EMDR. He had been adopted at age 5 from a family in which he and his siblings had been subjected to severe physical and emotional abuse. When we began reprocessing some of his early negative memories, the results seemed to conflict with deeply-held beliefs that not only was he was a very bad person, but also that other people were never to be trusted. He then refused to engage further in EMDR. However, he thought hypnosis would be pretty neat (as most 10-year-old boys do). He was able to enter a deep trance, but what he recalled in those trances were happy memories, although there were only a few. They included such things as having a good birthday party or someone being kind to him. When he came out of these trances, he had no recall for what had transpired in the trance. He had repressed the good memories because they threatened his early and intense beliefs that the world is a predatory place.

We began using EMDR while he was in a trance state, but as changes began to occur, he began to reject hypnosis. Eventually, treatment was unsuccessful. This boy definitely had problems attaching to his adoptive parents, and underlying that was a self-conception that he was a bad, perhaps evil, person. He also had hopes of being reunited with his abusive birth family. I have seen a limited number of others like him, but none so steadfast in a negative certainty about himself and the nature of the world. He also is an example of a child who has not relinquished his emotional attachment to his birth family, and therefore cannot attach to his adoptive family.

Several aspects of this case are significant in terms of the use of EMDR. One is that EMDR was producing threatening changes in the world view that he held, and likely would have produced more, but he began acting out against those changes, to the extent that his adoptive parents had him placed in another setting, thus terminating treatment. This reaction is similar to that of adults who enter a period of instability during EMDR change; for example, alcoholics who begin to drink more heavily as upsetting memories from the past come up with such intensity that a protected setting is sometimes required for external control. Such a protected setting may be similarly required for those children who are severely damaged early in life.

This case raises another important issue: Conventional wisdom tends to interpret what is going on with a child like this as having abnormal aspects of brain functioning, perhaps for hereditary reasons. This interpretation cannot be proven wrong, and may even be partially or totally true, but the EMDR treatment laid bare the boy's beliefs that made his behavior understandable and appropriate, given his early experiences. Psychology often relies on "deficit" explanations of abnormal behavior; that is, a child acts in a certain way because he has deficits of some sort. While this kind of explanation is sometimes true, it can be so seductively plausible that it distracts us from more accurate understanding and explanation. Nowhere is this more true than with children who manifest deficits in an academic setting because they have been traumatized. We design programs with measurable, behavioral goals to increase their spelling and math skills in a discrete number of days, when they can't really pay attention because of emotional interference from prior events in their lives. Or we medicate them because they can't pay attention well enough, not realizing that the attention "deficit" is related to prior events in their lives. At times, therefore, it is we as adults who have the "deficit" in our (lack of) attention to traumatizing causes.

This is not to excuse his behavior. That is a separate issue. The two issues of understanding and responsibility are often confused in our culture. Understanding this youth's behavior does not excuse it, but in our culture, attempts are usually made to use the understanding to mitigate responsibility of the individual involved. For example, if this boy assaulted another person (which he had done on occasion), understanding of his background might be used to excuse his behavior. However, there is no necessary reason to connect the two issues, and to do so does not clarify, but rather confuses. Thus, a defense attorney will attempt to bring up issues that aid in understanding his client, with the implicit or explicit purpose of convincing the judge or the jury to assign a lesser level of responsibility to his client. On the other hand, the prosecuting attorney will attempt to prevent such information from being discussed, again so that a greater level of culpability can be assigned. While I am describing this in terms of a courtroom drama, we all tend to mix the issues of understanding and responsibility in our minds. Greater clarity is achieved if the two issues are considered separately.

Going back to the issue of understanding, the essential issue becomes whether the understanding achieved leads to behavioral and emotional change. EMDR was beginning to do so, but treatment was interrupted. On the other hand, invoking biochemical or hereditary explanations often leads to a spurious sense of understanding and certainly different interventions.

Another important aspect of this case is that it illustrates that, with difficult cases, EMDR can be combined with hypnosis. Using EMDR while the client is in a trance can produce results that would, perhaps, be unattainable in other ways.

Finally, the issue of intentionality becomes important here. If a person doesn't want EMDR to work, it won't. This boy did not want EMDR or the combination of EMDR and hypnosis to work. When he perceived that it was having an effect, he acted out against the effects that were being produced. Had he continued in treatment, the issue of his intentions would have to be dealt with before continuing EMDR, just as a Vietnam veteran's fear of losing benefits would have to be dealt with, before EMDR could be helpful. Thus, sometimes when EMDR is not producing the results that might otherwise be expected, it becomes important to look at the intentionality of the individual.

## WHEN PROCESSING DOESN'T MOVE TOWARD RESOLUTION WITHIN THE SESSION

Let's say you have begun EMDR with a child and within the session the processing isn't moving toward resolution, but seems stuck in some way. Here, a large number of interventions are possible, ranging from less intrusive to more intrusive.

Less intrusive interventions include: changing the direction of the eye movements, using longer or shorter sets of eye movements, returning to the target memory more frequently, returning to the safe place for additional sets of eye movements, or using hand taps. If these are not successful in getting the process restarted, other, more distinctive shifts can be considered, such as the use of drumming, which provides visual, kinesthetic, and auditory stimulation, and thus is probably more effective than just auditory input. Also, in some cases it can be ethnically relevant.

If processing still does not move forward, consider changing the target. A minor change would be go select another aspect of the same target. For example, when Judy (in chapter 6) could no longer get the image of pushing at her mother, who had died, I asked her to image her aunt coming into the room; when she could no longer access that image, she was able to return to the image of her mother. A major way to change the target would be to select an entirely different target. The new target could be problem-oriented, or if targets of that nature are rejected, try more positive targets.

Somewhat akin to changing the target in minor ways would be to employ theme development, for example, "Think of another part of that event." Then, when that part of the event goes from negative to positive (in the channel), the child can be encouraged to "think of another part of the same event." As mentioned before, theme development can focus on the event itself, feelings, behaviors, or thoughts.

Another way to approach the problem of stalled processing is to encourage associative chaining directly. Ask the child to stay with the form of patterned stimulation that is being employed (eye movements, hand taps, drumming, using puppets, toys, etc.) until she gets something "new." This could be a new thought, feeling, physical sensation, or image. This sets up a paradoxical situation: The patterned stimulation continues until something else comes up. There can be positive effects from the stimulation itself, and staying with the original feeling, thought or image, and there can be positive effects from the new association.

Another way to deal with stalled processing is through the use of interweaves. In EMDR training, only one kind of interweave is discussed or labeled—the cognitive interweave. With children, cognitive interweaves often may be too cerebral or too intrusive and therefore must be used sparingly. However, when the process is stuck, other kinds of interventions can be considered interweaves, such as asking, "Where do you feel that in your body?" or "What feeling comes up when you hold that picture in mind?" or "As you think about that now, what picture comes up?" If the processing is stalled, those statements can be considered kinesthetic, emotional, or visual interweaves, respectively.

Overall, the two most basic rules in EMDR that I can think of, are: (1) if the process is flowing, keep the child in the process; interventions are not necessary, and (2) if the process gets stuck, intervene in some fashion to get it moving again. Use mild interventions at first, increasing the strength of the intervention only as needed. With children, consider cognitive interweaves a last resort. Almost always, other interventions will be superior to cognitive interweaves, because with the cognitive interweaves you are often asking the child to think like an adult, which is a dubious proposition.

It may help at times to stop and provide some additional instructions to the child. Sometimes what appears to be noncooperation can be rooted in some misunderstandings about the process. Table 8.1 lists interventions that can be used when the processing becomes stalled within an EMDR session.

## WHEN PROCESSING OCCURS WITHIN THE SESSION BUT THERE IS NO PROGRESS BETWEEN SESSIONS

When EMDR seems to go well within the session, but overall no progress seems to be made, the first thing to check is whether the situation is a complex trauma and one that you were initially conceiving as simple. An example here would be a child who was bed-wetting, who, in the EMDR sessions would get great res-

---

### TABLE 8.1
#### Interventions for Stalled EMDR Processing within a Session

Change the direction of the eye movements

Use longer sets of eye movements

Use shorter sets of eye movements

Return to target more frequently

Return to the safe place

Use hand taps

Use drumming

Use other auditory input (L-R)

Modify target

Focus on target elements

Focus on positive targets

Focus on self-esteem–enhancing targets

Employ theme development

Employ associative chaining instructions

Provide additional instructions

Consult with parent

Use child's drawings as targets

Use visual interweaves

Use emotional interweaves

Use kinesthetic interweaves

Use cognitive interweaves

Use resource installation

olution each time, with the channels going from negative to positive, the SUDS declining to 0 and the VOC increasing to 7, but who did not stop wetting the bed. This, then, is potentially the kind of case that would make a therapist who is new to EMDR quit using it, thinking that the method was not helpful.

However, there are alternatives to abandoning EMDR. The first would be to complete a more detailed analysis of what is going on in the family. One way to approach this is to say something to the parents to the effect of, "Billy has done really well in the EMDR sessions each time, but his bed-wetting hasn't gotten better. I wonder if there is anything going on in the family that might be interfering?" Probes can, of course, be much more specific: "What's coming up in the EMDR is that he feels really distressed by his older brother picking on him" or "He feels completely unable to please his dad" or "He just hates going to school, and that's where his most intense feelings come up. Is that similar to what he says to you?"

It is also possible to check for blocking beliefs (I'm not worthy; I'm not good enough; I'm not big enough or strong enough or smart enough) or earlier sources of trauma, which might have to be resolved before the original target can be resolved. The main thing to know here is that if the EMDR is processing well within the session, then something not being dealt with in the session itself, something outside the session, is blocking the results. The hard work is finding the blocking elements.

There may be physiological impairment that is blocking improvement. For example, a child who has ADHD might become traumatized on the playground. Dealing with the playground trauma might help to some degree, but the child still has ADHD. On occasion, I have had some very good parents bring in a child who has documented physiological impairments with the hope that EMDR will provide additional benefits. To the extent that the parents have provided an enriched environment, the child has not been traumatized, and has had his needs met emotionally and physically, then EMDR may not provide any additional improvement. That is, there is not a strong emotional component to the limited functioning, so there is little or nothing for EMDR to treat.

Limiting conditions that may not benefit from EMDR interventions include brain damage, developmental delays, obsessive-compulsive disorder (biologically based; not a result of trauma), biologically based depression, ADHD, and psychosis. However, many times it is not possible to tell ahead of time whether a given condition will respond to EMDR, and it is often advantageous to try EMDR with a wait-and-see attitude, rather than to assume that it won't be helpful. Some of the most exciting and astonishing sessions have occurred when the clinician attempts EMDR in cases where he doesn't think it will work. EMDR's advantage over conventional therapies is that its efficacy can be determined in a few sessions.

Recently I had two youths referred to me with obsessive-compulsive symptoms. One was a 12-year-old who had a severe case of trichotillomania; he had pulled out all of his eyebrows and eyelashes, and had five or six bald spots on his head. He was negative and obsessional in his thought patterns and was diagnosed with ADHD as well. Both of his parents, who were relatively successful, had family histories of learning problems, ADHD, and obsessional characteristics. While he was on several medications to alleviate depression and increase attentional focusing, he was not on clomipramine, which would be expected to help with the obsessional thinking and the trichotillomania. I consulted with the physician, who then began prescribing Anafranil (clomipramine). At the same time, I began using EMDR with the boy, whom I'll call Roger. Although Roger seemed to gain some alleviation of anxiety with EMDR, it was my distinct impression that he began doing much better in reducing his hair pulling after the medication reached a therapeutic level. His hair grew back, his eyebrows grew back, and he stopped combing his hair over his eyebrows to conceal his lack of them. He also began to go hatless at times, whereas before he had always covered his head as much as possible. However, he continued to pull out his eyelashes. We continued to work on this with EMDR with no success, and after five or six additional sessions of it, mutually agreed that the cost-benefit ratio didn't justify additional sessions. (This case is detailed in chapter 9.)

Ten-year-old Richard was referred to me about the same time, for obsessions and compulsions (see chapter 9 for a detailed description of this case). He was extremely fearful of any foreign substance. For example, although one of his hobbies was putting together plastic models of cars and planes and painting them, he worried about the paint or the glue poisoning him. He was bright and liked chemistry, but had a similar problem there, fearing to touch the toxic chemicals. When, at a sporting event practice, another boy was shining a red laser pointer at people, Richard obsessed for weeks afterward that permanent damage might have been done to his eyes. Compulsions were of a hand-washing nature, and Richard was very afraid of germs and touching doorknobs. Richard had concerned and supportive parents who were distressed by their son's difficulties. They were surprised and delighted when Richard responded well to EMDR in three sessions, and lost all his obsessions and compulsions. He began to sleep better and was generally less anxious during the day. No traumatic events could be identified, which might have been causative in his obsessive-compulsive disorder (unlike Julie, for example, who had developed her obsessive and compulsive symptoms after two auto accidents).

I am at a loss to explain why Roger did not respond to EMDR and Richard did. Roger did seem to have a stronger family history for depressive and obsessive symptoms, but my initial hunch was that neither one would respond to EMDR, and that both might need evaluation for medication. However, these

two cases illustrate how EMDR can be used diagnostically as an initial procedure that is relatively inexpensive and has relatively clear-cut results.

## WHEN THE PROCESSING ITSELF ISN'T PRODUCTIVE

One way the processing can seem unproductive is if it goes from one topic to
another, and another, so that the chain of associations gets farther and farther
away from the target event. When this happens, you can provide some control in
the session by going back to the target more frequently: "Let's go back to where
we started. Bring up that memory again. What do you get now?" Therapists have
different standards for divergence of associations from the target situation, with
some therapists keeping a tight focus and others allowing more latitude with the
chain of associations. How tightly to control the chain of associations depends on
the characteristics of the client. A relatively healthy child with good self-esteem
can be allowed a good deal of latitude with little concern of the part of the therapist, but a child with poor self-esteem, attentional difficulties, and multiple traumas is likely to need a lot of help to keep on track and not get emotionally
overwhelmed or tangential in EMDR. Also, a younger child (ages 3–5) is likely
to do better with closer control on her associations.

A child can also manifest an overly-rigid focus in EMDR, not able to go from
one channel to another. Here, a general prompt might be helpful, "What does
that remind you of?" Such a prompt can often trigger a chain of associations on
a different channel. Also, theme development is useful here, as well as the
instructions for prompting associative chaining, "Hold that in mind and follow
my fingers with your eyes until you think of something new. It could be a new
picture, a new thought, a new feeling, or feeling something in a different part of
your body."

When looping occurs, any of the methods listed in table 8.1 can be used,
starting with the least interventive. Looping is when the child goes over and
over the same material, with no change, over several sets of eye movements.

## WHAT ABOUT MEDICATION?

Medication, properly used, can assist in the process of EMDR. A boy with
ADHD features, for example, might have trouble maintaining his attention during EMDR, but when placed on medication, could sustain his attention for
longer periods of time. Or, a severely depressed child could respond to antidepressants and, in a less depressed state, have an improved response to EMDR.
After effective EMDR, the child's medication could be reduced or discontinued.
Matt, aged 10, was referred for suicidal ideation, depression, irritability, and
general fearfulness. He was a good student and was sensitive to others. His

father was highly intelligent, depressed, and self-critical; he also was in therapy and on medication for his depression. Matt was on an antidepressant, which was helpful to some degree, but his parents were concerned about his being on psychoactive medication at such a young age, and were hopeful that successful EMDR treatment might allow him to be taken off medication. Matt was seen on a weekly basis for six months, with the majority of his sessions being EMDR. He improved a great deal, but when he was taken off his medication, he became angry, irritable, depressed, and self-blaming, although to a lesser extent than formerly. He was placed back on the medication, and continued in therapy for another three months. This time when medication was discontinued, he maintained the progress he had made. At this point, he is doing well in school and at home. He is not depressed and not on medication. (Additional detail on Matt's case is provided in chapter 9.)

In Matt's case it would be easy to assume that there were hereditary and biological bases for his depression, and that he would have to be on medication for the rest of his life (many of my clients—both adults and children—have been told words to that effect by other mental health practitioners). Matt's case illustrates that medication can be helpful in conjunction with EMDR, and that EMDR can be helpful in assisting people to get off medication. It also suggests that it pays to be persistent in working toward goals of eliminating medication.

Davy (see chapters 2 and 4), who was traumatized by surgery at age 14 months and subsequently had night terrors, was taking Dexedrine to reduce his hyperactivity and hyperarousal prior to EMDR. Following EMDR, and the elimination of his night terrors, it was possible to reduce his medication for hyperactivity. Again, this is a good example of EMDR and medication working well together.

## SPECIFIC QUESTIONS

*What if the child has epilepsy?* Check with the child's physician as to whether eye movements are likely to cause a seizure. If the answer is affirmative, or if the issue is in question, use hand taps. I know of no child who has triggered a seizure by playing pattycake. Also consider using drumming.

*What if the child is involved in legal proceedings?* If the child is involved in legal proceedings, either as a victim or as a perpetrator, check with the attorneys involved. If the child is a victim and will have to testify in court, the attorney is likely to be able to indicate whether any therapy with the child will be deleterious to the child's case. If therapy in general will not cause a problem, then EMDR can be asked about specifically. If the attorney is concerned that EMDR will impair the case, it is probably best to wait. However, some trials are so long in coming to court, that it can mean that the child will not be treated with

EMDR for a year or more. In these cases, you can be a source of education for the attorney. Provide him with information about EMDR. Indicate that in the state of Washington, there is a legal precedent that EMDR is not the same as hypnosis. This ruling is important because a witness who has been hypnotized can be disqualified as a witness. Thus, a child treated with EMDR in the state of Washington is still qualified to testify. The attorney for the child, once educated, can negotiate with the opposing attorney about getting the child into effective therapy for the trauma on humanitarian grounds. Very often an agreement can be reached.

If the child is a perpetrator, the child is also likely to have been a victim previously, and, either way, needs treatment. Again, talk to the child's attorney. Generally, treatment issues can be worked out through such discussion.

*When should I not use EMDR?*

1. When the child is involved in legal proceedings, unless you have cleared the use of EMDR with the child's attorney.
2. When the child's parents are involved in divorce or custody disputes. Again, in this situation, any use of therapy or EMDR would have to be agreed upon in advance by both parents and their attorneys.
3. When there is such instability in the child's life that those instability factors require attention first. For example, if matters of food, clothing, shelter, and personal safety need to be attended to, see that those are attended to first. An oversimplified way of putting this, is that if a child is being beaten, the beatings have to be stopped before starting EMDR. If the beatings continue, EMDR cannot be expected to do any good.
4. When there are serious issues with secondary gain. Let's say a child who has great difficulty in school is injured in an auto accident. Following the accident, the child has PTSD symptoms of nightmares, bed-wetting, and flashbacks. He becomes afraid to fall asleep, but also becomes aware that the PTSD symptoms get him out of going to school. EMDR is not likely to help with the PTSD symptoms until the secondary gain issues are resolved. Deal with those first.
5. When the child has medical difficulties that might make EMDR dangerous. The issue of epilepsy has already been mentioned. Check things out medically first. In medicine, the standard of the Hippocratic Oath is "Do no harm." That should also be a goal in psychotherapy. Of primary importance is "Do no harm to the client." Of secondary importance is "Do no harm to yourself." Practice EMDR so that you don't jeopardize yourself. I'm reminded of an incident that occurred when we conducted our adult research in EMDR. We excluded women who were pregnant to ensure that EMDR would not have an injurious effect on the fetus. It wasn't that we

knew that EMDR would injure the fetus (e.g., the mother might abreact intensely, which could affect the fetus), but the only way we could be sure that EMDR would do no harm was to exclude pregnant women. One woman initially was a participant in the study and had completed the pretesting, but then found that she was pregnant. She was excluded from the study, and later miscarried. Had she remained in the study, we would not have been certain that EMDR had not caused the miscarriage, and we would have been vulnerable to legal action by the bereaved parents. So, first, protect the child, and, second, protect yourself by practicing in a way that honors the integrity of the client and yourself.

*Can I use EMDR with children with developmental delays?* Yes, absolutely. Simply modify the protocol to fit the developmental age of the child rather than the chronological age.

*Why do children yawn in EMDR?* Children yawn *so* frequently in EMDR that this question often comes up. I have come to take it as a sign of processing, as it occurs most intensely when the child is very deeply involved in EMDR. Adults in EMDR yawn too, but for reasons of etiquette suppress it more. It's a sure sign of active involvement in EMDR when it occurs. Someday we'll have a good neurophysiological explanation of why the yawning accompanies EMDR processing, but in the meantime take heart when you see it occurring.

*Can EMDR be conducted in groups with children?* EMDR has been tried in this way, but no systematic data on its effectiveness has been collected. My understanding of the format was that first the children drew and painted pictures about the natural disaster they had been subjected to, followed by alternate left-right tactile stimulation in a group setting, viewing their own pictures as targets. The tactile stimulation consisted of each child crossing his arms across his chest and tapping on the left shoulder with the right hand and the right shoulder with the left hand in an alternating fashion, while looking at and thinking about the previously drawn picture. This tapping was referred to as "butterfly hugs." Children who showed distress were then worked with separately by adults trained in EMDR. Following this procedure, the children then drew another set of pictures. This creatively designed group format could easily be researched using several different types of control groups after a natural disaster, a large-scale accident or shooting, or armed conflict after hostilities have died down. Also drumming and/or singing could be investigated in much the same group format. Before-and-after pictures could be analyzed for emotional changes that the different procedures produced.

*Could singing be a part of EMDR with children?* Children love to sing, drum, and draw pictures, as these are very engaging activities at preschool and elementary school levels. I think these activities will increasingly be integrated into

EMDR protocols for children. Singing especially has been underused as an approach. I have been experimenting with having a child sing as she drums, and we make up songs about resolving the problem areas as we drum.

The troubleshooting suggestions in this chapter are not exhaustive. Much of what goes on in clinical practice involves coming to an impasse and then problem-solving to resolve it. A clinician recently asked, "When things aren't going well, I just have longer discussions between sets of eye movements—is that okay?" Of course it is, if it resolves the impasse. Many times it could be expected to, as it becomes a part of that problem-solving process. If nothing in the above list of suggestions fits the problem situation you have, improvise. It's what we all do.

The next chapter focuses on applying EMDR to diagnostic categories. Although there are difficulties with childhood diagnoses (discussed previously), it can be useful for the practicing clinician to access information about EMDR in its application to commonly occurring childhood diagnosis. Such an approach can also be useful in elucidating where EMDR has been applied, and where it hasn't, which in turn may further stimulate the exploration of EMDR boundaries.

# nine

# Diagnostic Categories

"There are other things to be thought."
—JOHN, AGE 13

A CENTRAL PREMISE OF THE present book is that in using EMDR with children, it is possible to estimate the length and outcome of treatment by paying close attention to the characteristics of the trauma(s) that the child has endured. This assumes that EMDR is being applied to children who have been traumatized. In some cases, however, children are brought to treatment because they are manifesting problems, but no trauma has been identified. In some of these cases a carefully obtained history will bring to light possible traumatic causes of the disturbed behavior, emotions, or thoughts; these traumas then can be used as starting targets for EMDR. In cases where still no trauma is ascertained, one course of action is to target emotional stuck points (ESPs) in EMDR. However, a diagnostic formulation may be helpful to the clinician in order to assist in treatment planning in those cases that seem to have no clear-cut traumas or ESPs.

A second reason to look at diagnosis is to arrange the present book to be optimally useful to the practicing therapist. Thus, the therapist who asks, "Can I use EMDR with ADHD children?" can find an answer in the present chapter. Or the therapist who inquires, "How can I use EMDR with an anxiety-disordered child?" or, "What can I expect with a child with obsessive-compulsive symptoms?" can turn to the appropriate heading here. Because the primary focus of this chapter is on the application of EMDR, the criteria for the diagnosis will be discussed only briefly, but enough so that a clinician can be reminded of the diagnostic features and can see the fit between the diagnosis and the case examples being presented. In addition, traditional or empirically supported methods of treatment will be mentioned where pertinent.

Whatever the diagnosis, however, clinicians are encouraged to conduct a thorough trauma history to minimize the chances of overlooking a traumatic origin for symptoms with a particular child. For example, in a recent study, Meuser and others (1998) found that in adults, PTSD was underdiagnosed in a sample of 275 patients with severe mental illness (e.g., schizophrenia, bipolar disorder, borderline disorder). Lifetime exposure to traumatic events was extremely high, with 98% of the sample reporting exposure to at least one traumatic event. On average, exposure to 3.5 different *types* of traumatic events was reported in their sample. While the rate of comorbid PTSD was 43%, only 3 of 119 patients with PTSD (2%) had this diagnosis in their charts. Meuser and colleagues found that the rate of PTSD was highest in patients with depression (58%) and borderline personality disorder (54%), followed by "other diagnosis" (47%), bipolar disorder (40%) and all other personality disorders (40%), and lowest in schizoaffective disorder (37%) and schizophrenia (28%). Women were more likely to have experienced sexual abuse as a child (52% in women, 35% in men) and as an adult (64% in women, 26% in men), whereas men were more likely to have been attacked with a weapon (49% in men, 24% in women) and to have witnessed a killing or serious injury to another (43% in men, 24% in women) as an adult. Over a lifetime, having a close friend or relative killed by a drunk driver was the only trauma related to PTSD for men, while for women PTSD was related to sexual assault, physical assault without a weapon, and witnessing a killing or serious injury. Meuser and colleagues note that although many studies have documented the high rate of interpersonal trauma in the lives of patients with severe mental illness (e.g., Briere et al., 1997; Carmen et al., 1984; Greenfield et al., 1994), relatively few studies have explored the relationship of trauma and diagnosis with PTSD. They conclude, "Failure to diagnose PTSD as a comorbid disorder in severely mentally ill patients could have important implications for assessment and management of their illnesses [and that] attention will need to be directed toward developing and evaluating interventions for PTSD in this population (p. 498)." Perhaps EMDR could be one of those interventions.

But what about children? Bruce Perry (1998) has pointed out that PTSD is very likely underdiagnosed in children. For example, he notes that between 1982 and 1992, 10 million children (out of 60 million children in the total United States population) were abused. Despite this, the current "official" estimate of PTSD in children is 0.25–0.50%, which would indicate that only 1.5 million to 3 million children would be diagnosed as having PTSD from *any* cause. However, if only 25% of the 10 million abused children developed PTSD, there would be 2.5 million children with PTSD from child maltreatment alone (not even counting other sources of PTSD, such as motor vehicle accidents, assaults, and natural disasters). In addition, in evaluating approximately 1500 maltreated (neglected and abused) children in the medical setting in which he works, Perry (1998) noted that initially only 2% of these children came in with PTSD diagnoses, but when a careful trauma history was taken, 82% were found to have PTSD. Compared to Meuser and colleagues' (1998) findings, it suggests that PSTD could be underdiagnosed in children to an even greater extent than in adults.

Certainly, more formalized research needs to be completed. It would be very interesting to see if the results for children would be similar to those found for adults, that is, seriously mentally disturbed children have high comorbidity for PTSD, sexual abuse is highly associated with PTSD, certain diagnoses are more related to PTSD than others, boys are more likely than girls to develop PTSD for different kinds of traumas, and PTSD is underdiagnosed and undertreated in children. If such findings are confirmed, it would imply that many children who could be treated for PTSD are not, with profound effects affecting their subsequent psychological, social, interpersonal, and intellectual development. Perhaps we would find that the longer the PTSD remains untreated, the more profound the effects are over a lifetime.

## *DSM-IV* DIAGNOSES

Vagaries of PTSD diagnosis aside, we will now look at the different childhood diagnoses found in the *DSM-IV* and how EMDR can be applied to them. We will examine in most detail the diagnoses for which EMDR has been found clinically to have a positive effect, such as PTSD, other anxiety disorders, mood disorders, disruptive behavior disorders, ADHD, and reactive attachment disorder. Although elimination disorders are listed as separate diagnoses in the *DSM-IV*, in the present text they will be considered as symptoms and be discussed in the following chapter.

Diagnoses where the application of EMDR with children has been limited, nonexistent, or not likely to be of benefit, such as schizophrenia or pervasive developmental disorders, are not considered in the present chapter. However, if a child with a pervasive developmental disorder, such as autism, for example, becomes traumatized, a clinician familiar with working with autistic children and EMDR might consider working with one of the modified EMDR protocols for use with children. I recently talked with a clinician who has used EMDR with a few children with autism (high functioning) who made dramatic progress after EMDR sessions. As children with autism often have good right-hemisphere abilities (such as music, art, visual-spatial skills), but are impaired in their left-hemisphere abilities (such as language), it makes some sense that EMDR could be beneficial to them, if we postulate that EMDR facilitates the transfer of information between the two hemispheres.

Diagnoses with which I have not had direct experience but with which EMDR could be applicable and of benefit, such as eating disorders in children (although with adolescents and adults, I have seen EMDR to be of great benefit) will not be dealt with extensively. Those disorders include somatoform disorders, learning, motor skills, and communication disorders, and miscellaneous other diagnoses, such as tic disorders, selective mutism, and gender identity disorders.

In all, there are great opportunities to explore the application of EMDR in areas outside of PTSD, mood and anxiety disorders, ADHD, and disruptive behavior disorders. For example, there may be clinicians unknown to me who have applied EMDR to those diagnoses. Certainly, the theoretical rationale is not difficult to guess: Find the traumas or emotional stuck points and use those as targets for EMDR.

## LEARNING DISORDERS

It has been hypothesized that emotional trauma interferes with learning. As EMDR reduces or eliminates the psychological aftereffects of the trauma, if it is applied to a child with learning difficulties, and the emotional interference from the trauma cleared, the child would then be able to learn. Diagnosing learning difficulties is an inexact science. Often, all that is known is that for some reason the child is not learning in school as would be expected (based on behavioral observations and intelligence and achievement testing). Sometimes, the difficulty can be traced to ADHD, hereditary aspects of brain functioning, such as dyslexia (Pennington, 1991), or sociocultural or socioeconomic aspects of the child's environment, but many times the reason(s) are simply not known. Some of these learning difficulties may be due to recognized or unrecognized traumas, and thus might improve with the application of EMDR.

Robbie Dunton (personal communication, March 22, 1992), an educational consultant, pioneered the use of EMDR with children with learning difficulties, focusing directly on unlearned material and using eye movements to install the newly learned material after she taught it in small segments. She also used it as a secondary approach, with traumas or stressors as initial targets; when the initial targets were desensitized, the next focus was upon the unlearned material as secondary targets.

## SOMATOFORM DISORDERS

EMDR can also be useful in the treatment of somatoform disorders (where children complain of aches, pains, and various other physical symptoms that cannot be definitely linked to a physical condition). Functional somatic complaints occur in about 20% of children who are brought to pediatric clinics with physical symptoms (Robinson, Greene, & Walker, 1988; Walker, McLaughlin, & Greene, 1988). When no physical cause can be found, stressors in the child's life are then looked for. Most of these complaints resolve spontaneously, but those that persist and are pervasive are considered to be "somatoform disorders." It's a short cognitive leap to consider using identified stressors in the child's life as targets in EMDR, whether those stressors are past traumas or current difficulties.

# EATING DISORDERS

Although I have treated older adolescents and adults who have eating disorders (such as anorexia nervosa and bulimia nervosa), I have not treated children with such disorders. This is not too surprising, as onset tends to be during middle to late adolescence (Agras, 1987; Bruch, Czyzewski, & Suhr, 1988; Kronenberger & Meyer, 1996). Thus, I do not consider eating disorders to be true disorders of childhood, but rather of adolescence and adulthood. I regard EMDR to be an excellent approach with anorexia and bulimia, as the approach resolves the underlying dynamics better than anything else I have used.

The *DSM-IV* lists three other eating disorders: pica, rumination disorder, and feeding disorder of infancy or early childhood (which is a new diagnosis in *DSM-IV*, but resembles the medical diagnosis of nonorganic failure to thrive). Although discussion of these is outside the scope of this book, it does not preclude the possibility that clinicians working in specialty areas might find EMDR useful in treating those disorders. The same goes for other disorders that present less frequently in general clinical practice, such as tic disorders, selective mutism, and gender identity disorders. Hopefully, clinicians with an interest in those diagnoses will use EMDR in creative ways to impact those problem areas and report their clinical experiences at conferences and in journals.

Here is a brief example of treatment with EMDR of a young woman (a college student) who was severely bulimic. The bulimia remitted after she dealt with her mother's emotional fragility and the emotional and sexual abuse from her father. In childhood, she felt she had to parent her mother, who was depressed and unable to protect her from her father. As a young adult, she experienced a "gaping hole of emptiness," which she then tried to fill with food, but then would expel the food in self-disgust. This young woman had tried many different approaches to therapy prior to EMDR, and was seriously suicidal when she entered treatment and during much of treatment. With EMDR she resolved her early experiences (the emotions connected to them faded in intensity), and she lost the empty feeling and the need to binge and purge to fill it.

A very important point is raised by this particular case. When a child who is being severely abused (or tortured) perceives the adults in her life as not protecting her or caring enough to notice the abuse, the rejection implied by this neglect is experienced as worse than the trauma itself. The resulting fears of annihilation and worthlessness are so intense that they persist into adulthood and become the most difficult and deepest targets to resolve in EMDR. The way this manifests clinically is that the client, even after desensitizing all of the targets related to trauma, still feels miserable. Only when the fears of annihilation and the profound sense of worthlessness are targeted and satisfactorily reprocessed can the client experience improved emotionality. This understanding, in turn, has informed my work with children and EMDR. Even if I can't access this fear directly with children who have been left unprotected, I can assume that it is there, and promote targets related to the conjectured fears of annihilation whenever it seems pertinent (i.e., when other targets have been desensitized but the child does not improve). For example, I might ask the unprotected child, "Did that make you feel that you were going to die? Think about that and follow my fingers" or, "Did that make you feel worthless?" Note then, when a child does not improve, despite having desensitized targets related to the trauma, there are now several possible reasons: There are other traumas that haven't been reprocessed; there are ongoing problems in the family that block improvement; or the child has felt so unprotected that fears of annihilation and feelings of worthlessness need to be targeted. In adults, these underlying fears and feelings are referred to as blocking beliefs and are somewhat verbally accessible, but in children they are not likely to be elicited through direct inquiry. Thus, the therapist's sensitivity to the possibility of these underlying beliefs becomes important for full resolution of problems with multiply traumatized children.

This fear of annihilation as the most profound fear of adults who were severely maltreated as children has also affected my ideas of the basic needs of children. Next to needs of food, clothing, and shelter, I regard the deepest need of young children to be the need for positive, protective attention. If the child is not getting this attention, it arouses fears of death, even in infants, and causes a profound sense of worthlessness. We often hear that children need love, and I agree. But children will survive without love if they recognize protective attention is being provided. Not experiencing such attention, however, can cause great deviations in brain development (Perry, 1998), nonorganic failure to thrive (now called feeding disorder of infancy and early childhood), and arrested development and bonding, which we see in children who have been warehoused in substandard orphanages and foundling homes. So while love is better, I regard the need for protective attention as the more basic need. When this need has not been attended to, it can become the most important underlying issue to be resolved in therapy with both children and adults.

We will now consider diagnoses where EMDR is more commonly applied and is likely to have positive outcomes. The general format will be to describe the diagnosis and what is known about treatment, and to provide some case examples to illustrate how EMDR can be applied to the disorder.

# ANXIETY DISORDERS

## Posttraumatic Stress Disorder

A number of PTSD cases have already been described: Davy, who had night terrors after surgery to repair a cleft palate (see chapters 2, 4); Brent, who was struck by lightning (chapter 5); Julie, who had been in two car accidents (chapters 2, 5); Stan, who was hit by a car when he was walking with his dad (chapter 5); Mike, who was in an auto accident (chapter 5); and Judy, whose mother died unexpectedly of cancer (chapter 6). In addition, the cases of a few other children presented earlier in the present book qualify for the PTSD diagnosis. One additional case will serve to further flesh out the major characteristics of the diagnosis and treatment approaches using EMDR. First, a brief review of the diagnostic criteria for PTSD is in order. Please remember that the *DSM-IV* is a quasipolitical, quasiscientific document, and as such is subject to periodic review and revision.

Posttraumatic stress disorder refers to the development of intrusive, avoidant, and hyperarousal symptoms after exposure to a "traumatic event," which is defined as an event involving a threat to the physical integrity of self or others, and which involves intense fear, terror, helplessness, and disorganized or agitated behavior (with the last criteria applying to children only). Intrusive symptoms include memories of the event, which children may express through repetitive play or reenactment, dreams or nightmares related to the event, reliving all or part of the experience, and psychological or physiological upset in response to the cues related to the event. Avoidance symptoms include avoidance of thoughts or activities related to the event, amnesia for part of the trauma, reduced interest in activities, feeling of detachment, flat or constricted affect, and sense of a shortened future. Hyperarousal symptoms include difficulty sleeping, irritability, diminished concentration, hypervigilance, and exaggerated startle response. According to the *DSM-IV*, the symptoms are similar for both children and adults, although children may have fewer cognitive symptoms and more behavioral symptoms. Previously, I have suggested that the overwhelming terror in children may sometimes manifest as hallucinations and while this has been noted in the PTSD literature on children, it has not made its way into the official diagnosis as a symptom. The reason for mentioning it here is to reduce the chances that hallucinations will be mistaken for psychosis in a terror-stricken child who in actuality has PTSD. Also as mentioned previously, I think Criterion A (the event must be life-threatening) should be dropped from the *DSM-IV* diagnostic criteria. If the child (or adult) is evidencing the requisite number of intrusive, avoidant, and hyperarousal symptoms, he should qualify for the diagnosis, regardless of whether the clinician thinks the event was life-threatening. This would also make the PTSD diagnosis more compatible with other *DSM-IV* diagnoses, which are not defined in terms of the event, but only in terms of the symptoms manifested.

With respect to incidence rates for PTSD, Fletcher (1996) cites an unpublished meta-analysis (Fletcher, 1994), which examines the incidence of PTSD in children. Based on 2,697 children from 34 samples, he found that 36% of children exposed to traumatic events developed PTSD, compared to 24% of traumatized adults (based on 3,495 adults from five samples). Similar results were found in an unusual study of the reactions of both children and adults to the same event—a school shooting: Schwarz & Kowalski (1991a, 1991b) found that 27% of the children (5 to 14 years old), versus 19% of the adults, were diagnosed with PTSD (not a significant difference). Comparing these data with recent estimates of how many children are exposed to violence each year (3 million, according to Schwarz and Perry, 1994), we again come up with an estimate that about 1 million children in the United States each year likely develop PTSD. How many of these children are being identified and treated? How many aren't? What are the societal costs of not identifying and treating these children? How many lives are wasted?

With respect to treatment of childhood PTSD, there is no controlled research that demonstrates the effectiveness of any method of therapy or any medication. There is an assumption that methods and medications used with adults could be used with children. Thus, cognitive-behavioral approaches such as systematic desensitization, exposure, or prolonged exposure might be used. The trouble is, these approaches are very stressful for traumatized adults and could be seen as abusive for children (e.g., to what do you expose a sexually or physically abused child?). Play therapy might also be considered as an avenue of treatment, especially as traumatized children frequently act out the trauma elements in play. However, there is a lack of controlled, comparative research with play therapy (as there is with EMDR; hopefully that will change).

## Case Example

John was a preadolescent, 13-year-old boy who shot and killed his 8-year-old cousin with a shotgun. John's aunt (his cousin's mother) decided not to prosecute, as there were elements to the situation that indicated it was an accident. John had taken his grandfather's shotgun (which his grandfather used at turkey shoots) and loaded it, but then said he was unloading it when he dropped it, causing it to fire as it hit the floor. John had rather severe PTSD symptoms of intrusion (nightmares and flashbacks), avoidance (dissociation, emotional numbing, lack of interest in school and other activities), and hyperarousal (difficulty sleeping, irritability, diminished concentration). He also began to stuff himself with food when he ate. When John was 9 or 10 years old, his stepfather sexually abused him several times per week at night when John's mother was at work. The abuse had continued for about 3 years.

John had been in therapy for about four months before his therapist referred him for EMDR. After setting up a safe place, we began with an image related to the shooting. "He's laying on the floor. Blood everywhere." John stated his feelings were sad and frustrated as he held the image in mind, with a SUDS rating of 9. His negative cognition was that he was a "bad person." When we started the eye movements, his initial images were of his calling 911, the police coming, having to wait 30 minutes for them to get there, having to jump over his dead cousin's body to let in the police. As eye movements continued, he recalled being taken to his grandmother's, but not being able to sleep that night due to the nightmares of his cousin coming to get him. He remembered getting to see his mother the next day, and getting to play with his cat. He then cycled back to images of the shooting and visualized having to sit by the body as he waited for the police; he remembered being taken to the police station, and how very, very frightened he felt at that time. By this time, his SUDS had declined from 9 to 3, and his positive cognition of wanting to be a good person had risen from 3 to 6. It was an incomplete session. I was very unsure how much had been accomplished, as John tended to dissociate easily, and I had had to work to keep him present in the session. In fact, at the beginning of the session, he had become highly preoccupied with a splinter in his finger, which allowed him to block out other feelings. Being a completely equipped therapist, I took out my Swiss Army knife and helped him extract the splinter. I was pretty sure that if the splinter remained, he would find it too easy to be distracted from the EMDR that was about to occur.

In the next session, we reinstalled his safe place (a creek where he could hear the birds, feel the water around his feet, swing on a rope out over the water, and then let himself go). We started with the same image as before, as the first session had been incomplete. In bringing up the image, John stated, "He's lying on the floor; blood everywhere." This time the feelings were "scary," with a SUDS of 4. Within a few sets of eye movements, he reported that the image became blurry and then faded, saying, "I don't see anything." At this point, the SUDS had declined to 0, and the VOC of being "a good person" had increased to 6. Checking suggested that John had nothing more to process on his cousin's death.

Since it had not come up spontaneously, I decided to target the years of sexual abuse at the hands of his stepfather (if I had it to do over, I'd stop sooner and target the abuse in a later session). John agreed to work on the sexual abuse.

His feeling was one of embarrassment and his negative cognition was "I'm sick." External indicators of processing were minimal over the next half hour, but then John shuddered (visible on the videotape of the session) and indicated that the negative feelings had lifted.

Nonetheless, despite the possible overloading of therapeutic work, very positive changes accrued from these sessions. In the next session, John reported that he had had no nightmares for two weeks. He had stopped gorging himself when he ate. He was now going to sleep at 9:30 P.M., and waking up at 6:30 A.M., instead of not being able to fall asleep until 11:00 P.M. Further, he was no longer waking up at 2–3:00 A.M., unable to go back to sleep. He said that after the shooting he had felt continually depressed and was angry a lot, but now he felt happier. When asked to bring up the memory of the shooting, he no longer felt intense emotions. He stated, "I learned to deal with it. Life goes on. I can't always think of one thing. There are other things to be thought." When I checked on the sexual abuse, John reported very low distress levels.

Following this session, John continued in family and individual therapy, as there was a great deal to work on in those areas, as one might expect. When I checked on his functioning a month later, his mother indicated that treatment gains had been maintained: He had had no nightmares, he was sleeping well, his eating patterns were back to normal, and he was doing better in school and wanted to maintain that.

But an interesting question can be posed here. Did I help John become sociopathic, or more sociopathic, by conducting these EMDR sessions with him? If I had the task of providing EMDR to murderers, pedophiles, rapists, would I do so? I would answer yes, knowing that EMDR would reach some persons and not others. But each clinician has to make his own choice, based on his moral convictions and the qualities of the person he is being asked to treat. Did EMDR "cure" John? Most decidedly not. What EMDR did was to help him resolve some initial distress (florid PTSD symptoms) so that he could begin working on other issues—or continue with these same issues on a deeper level.

This was very similar to our work in Oklahoma City after the bombing of the Federal Building, where we helped first responders (firefighters and police) get over their nightmares, flashbacks, and other PTSD symptoms, so that they could go on with their lives. After EMDR, they no longer had bombing scenes "tattooed" to the inside of their eyelids, as one person had put it, but rather were able to deal more appropriately with other issues and problems.

## Specific Phobia

The primary feature of specific phobia is an irrational fear of an object or situation that almost invariably produces an immediate anxiety response. It differs from normal fears in that the fear is extreme, out of proportion to the actual danger posed by the object, has a significant impact on daily functioning, and is resistant to attempts to extinguish it. A specific phobia is diagnosed when these features are severe and occur together.

In discussing specific phobias, Francine Shapiro (1995) discriminates between simple phobias (defined as a fear of an object that is circumscribed and independent of the client's actions, such as a snake or spider phobia) and process phobias (defined as fear of a situation in which the client must actively participate, such as a phobia of flying or of public speaking). In applying EMDR to simple phobias, Shapiro (1995) has developed a protocol for adults, which includes the following steps:

1. Teach self-control procedures to handle the fear of fear (such as the use of safe place, audiotaped visualizations, and the light stream technique).
2. Target and reprocess the following:
   a. any ancillary events that contribute to the phobia
   b. the first time the fear was experienced
   c. the most disturbing experiences
   d. the most recent time it was experienced
   e. any associated present stimuli
   f. the physical sensations or other manifestations of fear, including hyper ventilation
3. Incorporate a positive template for fear-free future action.

With respect to process phobias, Shapiro (1995) adds three additional steps to the simple-phobia protocol:

4. Arrange contract for action.
5. Run mental videotape of full sequence and reprocess disturbance.
6. Complete reprocessing of targets revealed between sessions.

Other than EMDR, treatment of specific phobias has involved behavioral interventions (such as systematic desensitization, in vivo desensitization, and modeling), psychotherapy (cognitive-behavioral interventions such as self-monitoring, self-talk, and role playing), and family therapy. The most recent research on the treatment of specific phobias in children comes from Muris and colleagues (1998), discussed below and in chapter 6.

### Case Examples

Three cases of successful EMDR treatment have already been presented where the child developed phobias as part of PTSD: Julie, who had been in two automobile accidents and developed a phobia about tornadoes (chapters 2, 3, 5); Mike, who became phobic of garbage trucks and of being in cars after being in a motor vehicle accident (chapter 5); and Brent, who had been struck by lightning and was phobic of clouds afterward (chapter 5). An additional two cases, in chapter 6, illustrated successful EMDR treatment of animal phobias (primarily dogs): Kerry, who was afraid of all animals, but especially dogs, and Jay, who was specifically afraid of dogs. In both cases, the fear was extreme and significantly interfered with all family activities that involved leaving the family home.

The results from these cases (with the exception of Jay) are discrepant from the one study reported in the literature, by Muris and others (1998), which found that in vivo exposure was effective with spider phobias in children, but that EMDR was not (although SUDS declined in children who were provided EMDR), as measured by actual approach to a spider. Besides the possible reasons I suggested in chapter 6 for the discrepancy between that research and my clinical experience, an additional possibility is that EMDR works better with more severe phobias or phobias that are related to a PTSD diagnosis. Muris and colleagues' (1988) sample might have been a subclinical sample, as participants were recruited via newspaper ads for "free" treatment of a spider phobia and consisted exclusively of White, middle-class girls with an average age of 12 years. Those with comorbid diagnoses (e.g., PTSD) were excluded. The children I worked with were younger, boys as well as girls, with phobias severe enough to warrant direct referral, either for the phobia or the PTSD. While it appears that Muris and colleagues followed a portion of the EMDR protocol as outlined above, they did not teach self-control procedures or install a future template. They also did not target the physical manifestations of the fear response or desensitize any associated stimuli. Further, they conducted a single EMDR session with each girl, as opposed to the several conducted with my clients. Thus, among other things, it may be that more a complete treatment protocol is required to obtain good phobia outcomes with EMDR.

If and when further research is conducted on phobias with children, I would suggest that it focus on children who become phobic and/or develop PTSD after being bitten by a dog. The national Centers for Disease Control and Prevention rate dog bites as the number one public health problem of children. Over half of all children under 12 have been bitten by a dog. Such a research focus would also help to avoid recruiting a subclinical sample of children with phobias of a trivial nature. Parents rarely refer their children to a mental health professional treat a spider phobia.

Other productive areas for research with children's phobias would be for medical and dental phobias, and phobias following road accidents, as they too are more clinically relevant than spider phobias. Perhaps the present discrepancy between observed clinical resultas and laboratory results will lead to additional and clarifying research.

In the meantime, EMDR clinicians would do well to follow complete protocols in working with childhood phobias, and to keep track of their effectiveness. Also, I have found Shapiro's distinction between simple and process phobias less important for children than for adults. With children, it appears to be important to include protocol steps 4–6 (action contract, mental videotape, reprocessing of targets arising between sessions) in simple phobias as well as in process phobias.

## Obsessive Compulsive Disorder

In children, the symptoms of obsessive-compulsive disorder (OCD) are quite similar to those of adults. Common features of OCD in children are persistent, automatic, and intrusive thoughts, images, or impulses; repetitive behaviors; cleaning, repeating, checking; and hiding the disorder as long as possible. Occasional features are such things as difficulty concentrating, lack of productive or purposeful activity, and sudden onset.

The most frequent compulsions seen in children and adolescents with OCD are washing, hoarding, checking, touching, counting, arranging, repeating, and scrupulosity (Leonard, Swedo, & Rapoport, 1991). Common obsessions are doubts, danger, disorder, contamination, aggressive thoughts, sexual thoughts, and guilt for imagined negligence. Symptoms commonly change over time; for example cleaning rituals may be replaced by repeating or checking (Leonard et al., 1991).

With respect to etiology, theories have tended to cluster around biological, psychoanalytic, and behavioral explanations. The biological theories focus on genetics and neurotransmitters as primary causes for OCD. Psychoanalytic explanations focus on the use of OCD symptoms to inhibit anxiety and the conscious awareness of it, and stress the importance of uncovering the underlying (unconscious) conflict and resolving it. Behavioral theories explain obsessions and compulsions as maneuvers that provide anxiety relief. Preventing a compulsion from occurring causes an increase in anxiety, which is relieved by engaging in the compulsive act. Thus, the compulsion is reinforced by the anxiety relief. A strict behavioral theory does not explain the emergence of the OCD symptoms, but in conjunction with the biological theories can explain both the emergence and maintenance of OCD symptoms. That is, a child could be predisposed to high anxiety for genetic or biological reasons, and then develop OCD symptoms for dealing with the distressing levels of anxiety.

Treatment options for OCD consist of behavioral interventions, including in vivo desensitization, exposure therapies, systematic desensitization, flooding/implosive therapy, satiation, and response prevention, although only a few of these can be used with children; family therapy; inpatient hospitalization; cognitive-behavioral interventions; and medication. Exposure and response prevention seem to have the best chance of success of the psychological interventions (for adults), as documented by several researchers (Emmelkamp, Kloek, & Blaauw, 1992; McCarthy & Foa, 1988). However, specific medications appear to be effective with OCD, such as clomipramine (Husain & Kashani, 1992; Leonard et al., 1991). Abel (1993), in a review of OCD treatments, concluded that the most effective treatment for OCD is a combination of medication, exposure therapy, and response prevention.

## Case Examples

In the above reviews of treatment of childhood OCD, EMDR has not been considered as a treatment modality. Also, at the present time, there exists no study of the effectiveness of EMDR in treating childhood OCD. Therefore, the case examples and the conceptual frameworks I present should be taken as working hypotheses, to be expanded upon and altered by other clinicians.

The most important thing I have noticed in using EMDR with children with OCD is that some respond very well to EMDR and their OCD is quickly resolved without medication or other interventions, while others respond minimally to EMDR but very well to medication. What's more, I can't tell the difference ahead of time, even through careful history-taking. I'll give an example of each.

Richard, 10 years old, was referred to me because of his excessive fears of contamination (obsessions), which led to compulsive washing of his hands or any part of his body that might have been contaminated. He was preoccupied with fears that chemical warfare might break out in the world and he would become contaminated. He had the same concerns about nuclear warfare. He was fearful that he could contract a bone-eating disease, and was afraid to touch doorknobs and other things that might be contaminated. Although he liked putting plastic models together, he agonized about getting chemicals on himself from the glue and paint. His activities were gradually becoming more and more circumscribed due to his obsessions about becoming contaminated. Although his compulsions were not yet severe, he was compulsively avoiding more and more situations, and attempting compulsively to decontaminate himself when he was exposed. While these preoccupations were time-consuming (more than an hour per day), the greatest concern came from how much distress they were causing Richard.

Although his developmental history was unremarkable, his father characterized himself as a procrastinator and a paternal uncle had been diagnosed as having an obsessive-compulsive disorder. Further, his mother had been anorexic for 15 years, which can be seen as a form of, or related to, an obsessive-compulsive disorder (the anorexic is obsessive about weight loss and engages in compulsive activity to manage anxiety about weight). It may be that anorexia is one current expression of an obsessive-compulsive disorder facilitated by our cultural obsessions, just as cleanliness may have had much cultural support in turn-of-the century German culture.

I saw Richard for a total of three sessions of EMDR after an initial session with his parents for detailing the presenting problem and obtaining developmental and family histories. In the first session, Richard indicated that he got "kinda paranoid" about being exposed to toxic substances. Contamination could be from something he ate that might be spoiled, toxic, or contaminated in some way. If he suspected that, he would compulsively rinse out his mouth repeatedly. Contamination could also be from animals, such as squirrels, that might be carrying fatal diseases, or chemicals, such as airplane glue or his sister's nail polish. He also worried about airborne diseases. Speaking of his obsessions, he said, "I can't get it out of my mind." In terms of strengths, he was an "A" student in his elementary school and particularly liked science. He also liked sports, especially hockey.

In this first session, we set up a safe place and then selected an initial target of when a bottle of acetone fell and broke in front of him. His negative cognition was "I'm stupid" and his positive cognition was "I can deal with it," which he rated with a VOC of 3. The emotions he reported were feeling "weird" and "scared," with a SUDS of 4. After a few sets of eye movements, he felt "better" and "peaceful." His VOC had increased to 6, and his SUDS had declined to 1.5.

In Richard's next session, two weeks later, our initial check on the EMDR of the previous session showed that his SUDS had declined to 0.5 on the original target and image, and his VOC had increased to 7. Richard reported that in the intervening two weeks, he had attempted to be less obsessive and to take more risks. His mom noted that he could let go of his obsessions and fears more easily. This time we targeted an incident where another boy at hockey practice was playing with a laser pointer and shined it into Richard's eyes. Richard's negative cognition was "I'm going to go blind," with his positive cognition being "I'll be okay." His VOC was 4 and his emotion of being "worried" was rated with a SUDS of 4. After an initial set of eye movements, he stated, "If I go blind, I go blind. At least it's not as bad as dying." After additional sets of eye movements, he indicated that his SUDS had declined to .0001 (his language) and his VOC had increased to 7, and we were able to do an installation. In the next session, three weeks later, Richard stated that he had been happier, was obsessing less, and was worried less. His mother confirmed that she had noticed the changes, as had the other hockey mothers.

In Richard's final session, he reported that he had helped out at the local soup kitchen and had not obsessed about becoming contaminated by persons there.

Also, he had gotten burned two times in the kitchen and had not obsessed about getting the burns contaminated and did not go through compulsive behavior to cleanse the possible infection. He also had watched the movie *Titanic*, which previously would have set off a new series of obsessions and compulsions, but did not do so, which pleased him. In this session, after checking to see that the previous targets remained desensitized, we targeted his fears of spiders. He couldn't remember the first time he had become afraid of spiders, but he could readily remember the worst time: when there was a huge red spider on his head and he had had to knock it off. His negative cognition was that he could get hurt and his positive cognition was that he would be okay. His starting VOC was 5 and his initial SUDS was 3. After several sets of eye movements, his SUDS had declined to .00001 and his VOC had risen to 7. We then completed future projections and ran a movie, stopping to use eye movements each time he felt anxious. Follow-up information from a month later indicated no rebound effects in any area that we had worked on, and no residual fears, obsessions, or compulsions about spiders.

The next case involves Roger, a 12-year-old boy with trichotillomania, which the *DSM-IV* classifies as a separate disorder. Although the *DSM-IV* indicates that it is a separate diagnosis, the only distinction made between the two diagnoses is that trichotillomania does not arise out of specific obsessions, but is mostly a compulsion. However, with Roger, he began eyebrow plucking after a classmate criticized his eyebrows as being "too bushy" when he was about 11, so it's possible that an obsession (i.e., "too bushy") underlay his compulsive behavior. Further, it would seem that two disorders, so much alike, would be classified together, unless there is evidence that they are not the same thing (e.g., the genetics and age of onset are different; they respond to different medications). This is not the case with obsessive-compulsive disorder and trichotillomania; the only discriminating feature is that trichotillomania is less connected to obsessions. So, for the purposes of the present chapter, trichotillomania will be considered as a form of obsessive-compulsive disorder.

In fact, Roger had been previously diagnosed as having an obsessive-compulsive disorder by a neuropsychologist who had evaluated him several months prior to his being referred to me. His parents reported obsessive-compulsive symptoms other than trichotillomania in the past two years. They noted that he would line up his clothes in perfect order and would organize his room until it was perfect. Since his eyebrow plucking started, his grades began declining, and he seemed to spend increasing time in obsessive ruminations, which he was secretive about. At the very least, Roger appeared to be comorbid with respect to obsessive-compulsive disorder and trichotillomania. Information gained from family histories indicated that the mother's nephew had trichotillomania for several years, and that OCD, ADHD, and Tourette's syndrome ran in her side of the family. OCD and ADHD also ran in the father's side of the family.

By the time Roger was referred to me, he had plucked out all of his eyebrows, all of his upper and lower eyelashes, and had five or six bald spots on his head, the largest being on the crown of his head (about the size of a 50-cent piece). Roger combed his bangs forward over his face, so that his lack of eyebrows wouldn't show, and continually wore a baseball cap to cover his bald spots. His parents had obtained special permission for him to wear the hat during school to minimize teasing. He avoided eye contact and seemed depressed, despite having been placed on several medications for depression and ADHD. After 10 sessions of EMDR with cognitive-behavioral techniques added in the last five sessions had shown no improvement, I arranged for Roger to be placed on clomipramine. Within two weeks of being placed on that medication, which has been shown to be particularly effective with OCD, Roger began to show improvement in hair and eyebrow growth. The log he kept of hair-picking episodes showed a steady decline over the next month. Roger's eyebrows grew back completely, as did the bald spots on his head. More recently, he has gotten a haircut that is a buzz cut, and his only remaining problem is that he contin-ues to pull out his upper eyelashes. We made that a focus of treatment for an additional five sessions, but made no progress, and mutually agreed on termi-nation. As of this writing, Roger has maintained the progress he has made, has become more outgoing, and now has a girlfriend. His grades have improved to As and Bs. He still pulls out his upper eyelashes, and has difficulty giving eye contact, perhaps because of self-consciousness about his missing eyelashes.

Why did EMDR prove quickly helpful in one case and not in the other? In both cases there was a family history that was positive for OCD and related dis-orders; both boys were bright, but also had some learning difficulties; both had supportive parents. Initially, I could find nothing that would cause me to think that EMDR would be helpful in one case and not the other (in retrospect, there was greater evidence of comorbidity with Roger). When I have talked to other EMDR therapists, they have reported much the same thing to me: EMDR is greatly helpful in some cases and not in others. In addition, I have found the same thing with adults who have OCD: Some improve dramatically with EMDR, as Richard did, and some do not improve at all. Those who do not improve with EMDR are likely to improve with clomipramine or similar medication. It appears that there may be two disorders here with the same presenting symp-toms. Certainly, that would be an interesting and researchable topic.

In terms of seat-of-the-pants clinical management with children who have OCD, it makes sense to start with EMDR and, if that is not effective, to refer for a medication evaluation while continuing therapy with cognitive-behavioral approaches and EMDR, which would help to maximize the effectiveness of the prescribed medication. I hope that in the future, someone will be intrigued enough to investigate systematically the differences between those who respond to EMDR and those who don't.

# ATTENTION-DEFICIT/HYPERACTIVITY DISORDER

Attention-deficit/hyperactivity disorder (ADHD) is characterized by inattention, restlessness, impulsivity, and hyperactivity. It is one of the most frequently occurring childhood disorders, affecting 3–5% of children; it occurs more often in boys than in girls, with ratios of 2:1 to 10:1 (American Psychiatric Association, 1994).

According to the *DSM-IV* there are three types of ADHD: inattentive, hyperactive-impulsive, and combined. Children must meet either six of the inattentive symptoms or six of the hyperactive-impulsive symptoms to qualify for the diagnosis and exhibit them in at least two different situations over a six-month period. Onset of the symptoms must occur before age 7, although actual diagnosis can occur later.

ADHD frequently is comorbid with a number of other disorders, chiefly conduct disorder (CD) or oppositional defiant disorder (ODD), with as many as 50% children with ADHD qualifying for one or the other of these two diagnoses (Barkley, 1991). In 30% of children with ADHD, the disorder is also frequently comorbid with depressive symptoms and anxiety disorders (Barkley, 1991). These data suggest that children with ADHD should be evaluated for these associated disorders, and that treatment should encompass the additional symptoms if they are present.

It is extremely interesting that there is almost no information available about the comorbidity of PTSD with ADHD, especially since the two disorders have overlapping symptomatology. The *DSM-IV* does not even mention making a differential diagnosis between ADHD and PTSD. However, a child who has been traumatized and has symptoms of intrusion, avoidance, and hyperarousal could easily be misdiagnosed as ADHD, with the PTSD symptoms being interpreted as the hyperactivity/impulsiveness and inattentiveness of ADHD.

For example, in some cases the child could have been traumatized as a toddler or as a preschooler, so that astute parents might notice a change in behavior before and after a car accident or a divorce and connect the emotional and behavioral changes with the event. In other cases, however, the traumatization might have occurred so early in life that no before-and-after comparison could be made. A child born into a chaotic and conflicted family might be traumatized from day one by the noise and aggressiveness; a child born into an environment that is immediately abusive or neglectful would be traumatized in the same way. Since the known biological causes of ADHD account for only a small percentage of ADHD cases, it is quite possible that early traumatization is an unrecognized factor in many children diagnosed with ADHD. I have already pointed out that PTSD is underdiagnosed in both children and adults; perhaps it is also underdiagnosed in children who have ADHD. Additionally, Perry (1998) found that 65% of his sample of 1500 maltreated children had initial diagnoses of ADHD, but after reevaluation only 49% were still diagnosed ADHD. These preliminary figures suggest that PTSD is highly comorbid with ADHD, at least in his sample, and that ADHD is being somewhat overdiagnosed, with PTSD being greatly underdiagnosed. One would wonder if the same would be found in other samples of maltreated children.

The preceding information suggests that ADHD presents in exceedingly complex ways, and the volume of research and books written about the disorder attests to the complexity. Probably the best single source of information about ADHD is Russell Barkley's (1995) *Taking Charge of ADHD: The Complete, Authoritative Guide for Parents*. Not only is the book an excellent guide for parents, but it also contains enough up-to-date and technical information about ADHD to be extremely useful for the mental health professional. As good as this book is, however, it contains not a single reference to PTSD or trauma, or any indication that the two conditions might have any comorbidity.

In terms of treatment, medication for ADHD is the most frequently employed alternative, due to improvement rates as high as 70–80% with methylphenidate (Anastopoulos, DuPaul, & Barkley, 1991; Barkley, 1995). The most frequently used medications are Ritalin (methylphenidate), Dexedrine (dextroamphetamine), and Cylert (pemoline), with Ritalin being the most widely prescribed. If the child has depressive symptoms, a tricyclic antidepressant, such as Norpramin (desipramine) or Tofranil (imipramine) might be prescribed instead of or in addition to the psychostimulants. For example, desipramine has been shown to produce a 68% improvement rate for children with ADHD (Greenhill, 1992). More recently, the SSRI (specific serotonin reuptake inhibitor) antidepressants are also being employed.

Because medications have side effects, and because large numbers of children are being diagnosed with ADHD and medicated, this area is not without controversy. Zealots appear on both sides of the issue. A story that I've heard concerning the extreme positions taken on medication goes something like this: A boy was having difficulty in school. After being evaluated many times, it was discovered that he had poor eyesight and could not read well from the board at the front of the classroom. Eyeglasses were prescribed, and the boy's vision was much improved. However, administrators at the school discouraged the use of the glasses for the boy, saying, "Prescription eyeglasses don't fit into our curriculum here. We regard them as a crutch, and prefer that children learn to compensate and find other ways to deal with their poor vision." On the other hand, the doctor prescribing the eyeglasses told the boy and his parents, "Now we have found the problem! It's poor vision. With these eyeglasses, you can learn all you need to on your own. Don't bother going back to school." We can see how ridiculous both of these positions are in the area of myopia, yet such extreme positions are often taken in the debate over medication.

Medication is often helpful in treating ADHD, but it is not sufficient. Other treatment approaches involving schools, parents, and the child are important for optimal results (Barkley, 1995). These approaches involve educating the parents and the schools about ADHD, so that environmental and reinforcement modifications can be made, and helping the child cope with the disorder through such areas as self-control and relaxation techniques, tutoring and interactional skills.

A great deal of research has been directed toward discovering the causes of ADHD. Biologically-based research is garnering the most attention; research on genetics indicates that some genetic disorders, such as Fragile X, cause attention deficits and hyperactivity. However, the majority of ADHD children do not have genetic disorders. A second line of genetic research shows that relatives of children with ADHD have higher rates of ADHD, depression, alcoholism, conduct disorders, and antisocial disorders. However, the increased incidence of ADHD and other disorders among family members may be due to environmental factors that remain stable from generation to generation (e.g., low socioeconomic status, poor patterns of parenting). Another biological line of inquiry focuses on brain injury, caused by such factors as poor prenatal care, anoxia at birth, or closed head injury. However, only a small minority of ADHD children have a documented history of brain injury. A final area of biological interest has to do with the neurophysiology of ADHD, where the interest focuses on the neurotransmitters, such as the catecholamines. While it is true that the medications that increase the catecholamines in the brain, such as Ritalin, Dexedrine, and Cylert, have a positive effect on inattention, hyperactivity, and impulsivity, there is no clear evidence that children with ADHD have a catecholamine deficit (Kronenberger & Meyer, 1996), as research findings are conflicting.

Although biological factors are important in ADHD, psychological and environmental factors also play a role in the expression of the disorder, including its severity and particular characteristics with any given child. Trauma and environmental stress can exacerbate the underlying disorder. Children with ADHD are repeatedly stressed or traumatized on a daily basis by their parents, other adults, peers, siblings, and the school system. "They often say things indiscreetly without regard for the feelings of others or the social consequences to themselves. Blurting out answers to questions prematurely and interrupting the conversations of others are commonplace. The layperson's impression of them, therefore, is often one of irresponsibility, immaturity or childishness, laziness, and outright rudeness. Little wonder that they experience more punishment, criticism, censure, and ostracism by adults and their peers than do normal children" (Barkley, 1990, p. 42). This is where EMDR fits in. While EMDR does not rid a child of ADHD, it can lessen the effects of daily stresses.

Three case studies will illustrate the effects of EMDR with ADHD or possible ADHD. The first case is a child with ADHD with hyperactive-impulsive features coupled with an oppositional defiant disorder; the second case features a child with ADHD with inattentive features; and the third is a child who appeared to have ADHD, but who improved so much with EMDR that it seemed the ADHD diagnosis was not warranted. I am including the third case because EMDR therapists occasionally see this kind of improvement in children who have been diagnosed with ADHD. It may be tempting to think that one has "cured" ADHD, but it is more likely that the child has been misdiagnosed.

### Case Example: Attention-Deficit/Hyperactivity Disorder, Predominantly Hyperactive-Impulsive Type, with Oppositional Defiant Disorder

I began seeing Ed when he was 10 years old, and continued to see him and his parents in a combination of individual, family, and marital therapy over the next three years. In all, there were 71 sessions. He was referred by his pediatrician, with a diagnosis of ADHD and oppositional defiant disorder, which I agreed with, after conducting my own evaluations (psychoeducational and familial).

Ed's parents separated when he was 2 and divorced when he was 3. They remained in conflict with each other over such things as child support, summer visitation, and whether Ed should be on medication (Ed was taking Ritalin, 20 mg, sustained release, plus an additional 10 mg in the morning). Ed's mother had remarried within a few years. The whole family was under a great deal of stress: The maternal grandparents lived with them (not without tension!); Ed's parents had adopted a boy with fetal alcohol effect who was seven years younger than Ed and who had significant developmental delays and problem behaviors; and Ed's mother's health was poor.

Ed's parents described him as very bright, but very distractible. In school he had difficulty getting along with his teachers. For several years, daily reports from school were required to help keep Ed's behavior under control. He had become increasingly aggressive over the past six months. Recently, he had smeared a peanut butter sandwich into the face of another student, choked a peer who wouldn't give up his place in tetherball, and was increasingly engaging in name-calling. He had begun hanging around with another boy in his neighborhood with behavioral problems, and together they had broken into a neighbor's house to steal baseball cards. Also, he had stolen rewards from a reward system at school, but refused to admit it, even though the principal knew he had done it, and was offering him the opportunity to make it right. On the positive side, Ed was a good athlete, and could be loving and helpful, and was capable of doing well in school for short periods of time. Ed's parents noted that his behavior became much worse when he was not on the medication. He was more distractible, hyperactive, and aggressive. Developmental-history taking and family histories turned up nothing remarkable.

Therapy is likely to be long-term in such a complex situation, involving chronic individual problems (Ed's ADHD), family problems, and extended family problems. EMDR is not likely to produce miracles. However, it often helps a very angry, defensive child to open up and become more amenable to change and therapy. When this happens, the child very often becomes less hyperactive, aggressive, oppositional, and emotionally volatile, and requires less medication. A good example of this is the case of Davy (chapter 4), who had night terrors after cleft palate surgery. Although Davy was developmentally delayed and hyperactive due to fetal alcohol effect prior to his surgery, after EMDR Davy was less hyperactive and his medication was reduced. EMDR did not eliminate his hyperactivity, but reduced the symptoms caused by his PTSD.

The following excerpts illustrate how EMDR can reduce ADHD symptoms. The first excerpt is from Ed's eighth EMDR session (his 43rd session overall). Ed had never been this self-revealing in therapy before. The session also demonstrates using clinically relevant material as it comes up as a starting point for EMDR. The second segment indicates that as therapy progressed, Ed began to set goals and show appreciation for others—abilities or qualities that had not been apparent previously.

The segment begins with Ed talking about how he and his family had gone out to dinner, but had come back home to find the basement flooded as a result of something that Ed had inadvertently done earlier that day. Swinging a golf club outside, he had broken off pieces of a plastic pipe protruding above ground and the pieces had fallen into the pipe itself, causing the water heater to flood the basement.

E: It made me mad. I ruined everything again. We had a really nice night. Everything was going great. Something had to happen that spoiled our whole evening.
T: Can you picture that in your mind: what happened that night when you got back from the restaurant and found the basement was flooded?
E: Sure can.
T: As you hold that picture in your mind, what's it make you think about yourself?
E: That I can't do anything right.
T: If you can't do anything right, what's that mean about you? (I'm probing for a better negative cognition.)
E: That I'm a pretty stupid person.

T: Ed, what would you rather believe about yourself than "I'm a pretty stupid person"?

E: That I can clean this stuff up. That I can be on my good behavior again.

T: Would it be something like "I can do well"?

E: Yes.

T: As you picture that scene in you mind, how true does that statement seem to you, where 1 is not true at all and 7 is completely true? How true does that feel to you?

E: Six.

T: So it seems real true to you as you picture that, or not true?

E: Maybe a 5.

T: Okay. It seems mostly true to you that you can do well.

E: Yeah.

T: As you hold that scene in your mind again, what kind of feelings go with that scene?

E: I just want to run away from home. I've felt that probably a hundred times.

T: When you want to run away from home, what does that feel like emotionally to you? Does that feel mad or sad or . . . ?

E: Mad.

T: How mad? From 0 to 10, where 0 is neutral and ten is the strongest the feeling could be?

E: About 8.

T: About 8. Where do you feel that mad feeling right now as you think about it?

E: My fists.

T: Now, Ed, I'm going to ask you to follow my fingers with your eyes as you hold in mind that image and the negative thoughts, and negative feelings that go with that. Can you get that image?

E: Yeah.

T: Do you remember the negative thoughts that go with that, "I'm a pretty stupid person"?

E: Well, I hate my parents, I hate myself. I wish God never gave birth to me. I wish my mother never gave birth to me. All I've caused is trouble to them.

T: That's a real, real strong feeling, huh?

E: I might as well just live my own life alone.

T: That must feel pretty awful, to feel "I wish I'd never been born."

E: Have you ever felt like that?

T: Uhuh. How much have you felt that way? (I'm not in the mood for self-disclosure; back to you, Ed.)

E: It all goes on and off. Every time I get busted I wish I could get away from it.

T: Okay. Let me ask you to hold that image of what happened that night and the feelings that go with it and thoughts. Okay. Follow my fingers. (EM) What do you get now?

E: You know those things in the bakery that roll and crush the dough?

T: Uhuh.

E: I feel like I'm in one of them.

T: Think about that. (EM) What do you get now?

E: Nothing.

T: Let's go back to the original scene that we started with. Can you still get that picture in your mind? Has that changed at all?

E: Hold on. Let me try to get it back in my mind. . . . What was it?

T: It was when you came back from the restaurant.

E: Oh yeah, yeah. Want me to tell you?

T: Yeah.

E: When I got home. Well this is a different thing. I feel that when we got home, instead of it just leaking it felt like it blew up.

T: How do you mean? What blew up?

E: The whole water heater exploded and trashed the house. I don't even know where I got that from.

T: So it just kind of felt that way?

E: I felt like it should have been that; I got in so much trouble.

T: Uhuh. What kind of feelings do you get right now as you think about it?

E: I'm getting blown away and sucked down there to h-e-l-l. My mom said something like that to me. She probably didn't mean to say it, but it came out. She said, like, "You better stop this right now or you're going to be going, dare I say, down there. H-e-l-l." And what I felt like saying then, is, "Someday, someday I'll prove you wrong and maybe you'll go down there. If you don't have enough trust in me then you shouldn't trust yourself."

T: Okay, hold those thoughts and feelings in mind. (EM) What do you get now?

E: That I was born without any arms or legs. Then maybe I would be a better person because I can't do anything. So that's sometimes how I feel.

T: Think about that. (EM) What do you get now?

E: My mother went to the circus with me. And this is on a repeat of a long time ago. It's why I'm afraid of Halloween masks—putting them on and off and on. There was one time I was in a mall where I was about 3 or 4. It was Halloween Day or something. There was this clown who kept on following us around. Meemaw (Ed's grandmother) told him to get away, get away. They're not supposed to go in stores. So he followed us in a card store and Meemaw was running from him and carrying me. She told another man and they kicked him out and he lost his job. The police came and arrested him.

T: Stay with that. (EM) What do you get now?

E: I don't care what my parents do to me as long as they protect me. (The issue of protection comes up spontaneously.)

T: Do you think they will protect you?

E: Yeah. Dad said that if any clown started to (inaudible), he'd knock him out.

Excerpt from therapy six months later.

E: I think I have an A+ in English, A in Reading, A+ in Math, I'm not sure about science. I think I might have a . . . I don't know. I'd better do good on this test. I got one C on a report thingamabob. This one kid was talking to me so I got a C instead of a B. I didn't like that at all.

Five minutes later

T: As you hold that picture in your mind of breaking into that house, what's that make you think about yourself?

E: Well, it makes me feel, like, terrible. I mean, like, the . . . say if I did it again, I mean, I'd feel so bad. Well, I wouldn't do it again, so . . .

T: And that terrible feeling is a feeling, but what does it make you think or believe about you?

E: I'm really lousy. Why would I break into a house just to steal cards or something? It's a stupid reason to get into trouble.

T: What would you rather believe about yourself?

E: I'm not that stupid. I'm smart. Let anybody break in. I don't care if anybody breaks in his house, it just better not be me.

T: Okay, holding that picture in your mind, follow my fingers. (EM)

E: I'm attending school at Yale University and I'm doing really good there. I get out of the senior year with straight A's and one B; A and B average. I get out of there and like this law firm calls me up and I go to law school and do really good there. Then I become this rich, rich lawyer and I probably dedicate that to my dad because he made me see the importance of school. Remember when I first came in here? I don't know, would you have anything from my first day?

The preceding segments from EMDR sessions with Ed are noteworthy for several reasons. In the first one, for the first time Ed is able to talk about all the trouble he gets into and his sense of failure. With most children with ADHD, this is a very difficult area to access, but I have seen such openness occur more often with EMDR than with any other approach I have used. This emotional openness then sets the stage for other changes to occur inside and outside of therapy. It is interesting that Ed goes on to talk for the first time about an event that sounds like it was traumatic for him (the clown in the mall). Although it sounds minor in some respects (certainly not life-threatening), it produced last-ing effects for Ed in terms of his fears of clowns and masks. This, too, had never been mentioned in therapy before, and is a good example of how traumatic memories often come up unbidden in EMDR.

The second segment with Ed occurred six months later and illustrates the amount of progress he has made. His grades, as well as his behavior in school, have improved dramatically. At the end of the previous school year, his disrup-tiveness in class had reduced his teacher to tears of frustration on several occa-sions. He made frequent trips to the principal's office and had been banned from riding on the school bus. His peers shunned him because of his hostile, aggres-sive, and impulsive behavior. This second excerpt illustrates that he is now proud of his accomplishments, able to think about long-range goals, show appreciation for what another person has done for him (his father), and con-scious of the changes he has made, noting how he thinks differently about breaking into someone's house and inquiring about what he was like when he started therapy.

This is not to construe that therapy was over for Ed. I continued therapy with Ed and his family for another two years, as family stresses continued to be high, and Ed's ADHD continued, as did his struggle with the problems associated with that. He also continued on the same level of medication, which provided a def-inite benefit for him. As Ed got older, he had stronger desires to live with his birth father, who lived in another state. Because of the ongoing nature of these issues it is hard to know what long-term outcomes for Ed might be, but the three years of EMDR-oriented therapy turned his behavior, thoughts, and feel-ings in a much more positive direction.

### Case Example: Attention-Deficit/Hyperactivity Disorder, Predominantly Inattentive Type

Danny was 11 years old when I began seeing him. He was doing poorly in school and was still wetting the bed. Although he was toilet trained at age 3, he regressed at age 4, when his younger brother was born, and continued wetting the bed after that. On the intake form, his parents described him as follows: "Though bright, Danny doesn't achieve his potential. He needs incentive con-tracts to participate actively and is easily distracted. He is socially immature and displays odd behavior for his age." School reports confirmed this information and added that Danny would often retreat into fantasy life. He was seen as being unable to form relationships, having limited social skills, drifting in and out, being uninvolved and unfocused in discussions, and engaging in bizarre behav-ior such as feeling textures on walls and making erasing motions in the air.

Danny's developmental history indicated that he was slow in developing speech and fine motor skills. He did not do well athletically, and although he seemed to be bright, did not do well in school, getting mainly C's. Danny's mother indicated that she was dyslexic as a child. School evaluations found anxiety, difficulty maintaining attentional focus, and some intellectual deficits (on the WISC III he scored a Verbal IQ of 121, a Performance IQ of 90, and a Full Scale IQ of 106—a pattern often associated with problems in social perception and decision making). In additional testing, I found that Danny scored below average in both sequential and simultaneous processing. Overall, Danny appeared to be a boy with mild to moderate processing handicaps.

Including an initial session with Danny's parents to obtain developmental and family histories, and several sessions for psychological testing, I had a total of 18 sessions with Danny. In a feedback session with Danny and his parents, I recommended enrichment programs for Danny, tutoring in a few subjects, a medication evaluation with a physician to help with attentional focus, and EMDR for his anxieties. Most of the remaining 12 sessions were with Danny, and were EMDR sessions.

In Danny's first EMDR session, we started with a positive target, as ADHD children have often had so many negative experiences that it is very hard for them to begin with focusing on a failure or a problem situation. Their own sense of failure is just too strong from repeated daily failures and humiliations. The following excerpt from that first session illustrates how starting with good experiences will often shift into more negative experiences, when it would not have been possible to start with the negative experiences. Like the excerpts from Ed's sessions, it also shows how EMDR promotes a greater level of openness and less defensiveness. This was the first time Danny had shown such a lack of defensiveness with me.

T: Take a deep breath. . . . Real good. . . . What comes to mind now?
D: When we first got a computer. (I had asked him to recall times that were good for him, and he had mentioned several at this point.)
T: Okay, that's good. Let me have you hold a picture of that in your mind: when you first got the computer. (EM) What do you get now?
D: When I acted really weird in fourth grade and I got teased about that because I acted weird.
T: What happened?
D: What do you mean, "What happened?"
T: How did you act weird? What did you do?
D: Well, how it first happened was that I used to like to play with these people who I liked and it came up then and we always changed what we'd do every week or something. And then one week we, one week we came up with chasing girls. I would do that and then what happened is I, instead of just normal chasing girls, I'd say, "Raaaaaa" when I'd chase them. Then I'd go around

saying that to annoy them but then people would think I'm stupid because I acted that way. I heard that people might beat me up when I'd get into maybe the sixth grade or something, if I acted weird then and they try to stop me.

In the next session, a week later, Danny said that the above incident wasn't "stuck in his head anymore." We continued to use EMDR to focus on positive events and memories. In the following session Danny again indicated positive results and said, "It makes me not worry as much about things that I used to worry about." In the next session, we targeted Danny's bed-wetting; he showed almost immediate improvement, and only had one incident over the next 17 days. With this kind of success, and the use of future projections, Danny decided that he wanted to go to scout camp. At scout camp, though, he wet several times and got teased about it. However, he wanted to continue working on staying dry and set a goal of staying dry over the next two weeks. During those two weeks he had one accident, but then had none over the following two weeks.

With school beginning, Danny started taking Ritalin. That year, he had excellent teachers who were able to make accommodations in the classroom that were helpful to him. As he continued to do well in school, to socialize more, and to stay dry at night, we terminated with the understanding that if further problems came up, Danny would return for more EMDR. He did not return, and at Christmas I got a card from his parents, which read:

Dear Dr. Tinker,
   I want to thank you for your help for my son Danny this past year. I know when we first started therapy with you, my wife and I just didn't know what to do to help Danny.
   Since undergoing therapy with you, and with the continued help of Ritalin, Danny had made a remarkable transformation. Danny is getting A's and B's in school. Danny has two very supportive teachers in middle school. Although still shy, Danny had also managed to establish a few new friendships. Late this year Danny decided to switch Boy Scout troops, and is now in a troop with some friends from school.
   In short, things are going a lot better than they were last year. I believe your efforts had much to do with this pleasant turn of events. I wanted to share our good news with you and to thank you once again for your skill in turning a sad situation into a success story.
   Best wishes.

Danny's case indicates well that medication can be very useful with ADHD, including the inattentive type, and it supports the use of EMDR to establish greater emotional openness and the reworking of prior stressful events. We tend to call these everyday humiliations and embarrassments "little t" traumas as opposed to the "big T" traumas of disasters, accidents, and assaults, but who among us doesn't have a few "little t" traumas that we remember like they happened yesterday? Think how much more often they happen with the ADHD child. Danny's bed-wetting was eliminated prior to the administration of Ritalin, so his treatment also demonstrates the effectiveness of EMDR with bed-wetting, something that will also be considered in the chapter on symptoms.

### Case Example: Apparent ADHD, But Symptoms Remitted

Six-year-old Trent manifested many ADHD symptoms early in life. He was colicky in infancy, and showed excessive restlessness in his first six months, with diminished sleep because of restlessness and easy arousal. His mother characterized him as constantly into everything, having an excessive number of accidents, compared to other children. As a toddler, he had had his stomach pumped once (for eating a mothball), had emergency bronchial surgery twice (each time for getting part of a hot dog caught in his trachea), and had required emergency medical attention for spraying his eyes with paint from a paint compressor. In kindergarten, he sometimes had trouble focusing and settling down to an activity. His mother also described him as impulsive, hyperactive, acting like he was driven by a motor, heedless to danger, being more active than his siblings, and having a poor attention span and frequent temper outbursts. He also interrupted often and did not listen when spoken to. By age 5, Trent had already had six months of neurofeedback (EEG biofeedback training to treat hyperactivity and attentional difficulties, designed to increase beta-wave activity and decrease theta-wave activity), with not much progress being noted. At intake, Trent's mother wrote, "Because Trent has been an active child and sometimes difficult to get along with, I have frequently lost my temper with him. I have worried that I may have hurt his self-esteem. Now that his father and I have separated and will probably eventually divorce, I worry that this may further impact on him negatively." In fact, Trent's behavior and emotional volatility had considerably worsened with his parents' separation and impending divorce.

However, Trent made such good progress in EMDR that I only saw him a total of seven times over eight months. In his first EMDR session, he focused on the sadness he felt in his heart when he feared he wouldn't see his dad anymore because of the divorce. His associative chaining rapidly went from negative to positive, ending with images of feeling happy. After that session, he showed "dramatic" improvement, according to his mother: He was much more calm and relaxed and was willing to listen and not argue so much. Breakfast time was reported to go much better (Trent had been especially oppositional then). He himself was excited about the session. In the second EMDR session, we again focused on changes occurring because of the divorce. Trent started with an image of his dad not being in his parents' bedroom, "but he's supposed to be."

His negative cognition was, "I did something bad." Again, Trent's associations rapidly went from negative to positive.

Following this session, Trent's behavior reverted to his previous negative and hyperactive patterns, but his mother admitted to having a very emotionally difficult week, being overcome with depression and guilt. She seemed so overwhelmed that I arranged with her therapist for her to have EMDR in addition to her regular ongoing therapy. She had several intense EMDR sessions, which included reprocessing a childhood rape.

Trent's behavior again improved, to the point that his mother realized he did not have ADHD; the hyperactivity was emotional and connected to the divorce. Trent went on to reprocess four events that were traumatic for him: eating a mothball, spraying his eyes with paint, and choking on a hot dog (on two separate occasions). We also focused on a nightmare he had, in which he fell out of a car that his mother was driving; he got left behind because his mother didn't notice, and felt "very, very, very bad." He drew a picture of the nightmare, showing his mother driving the vehicle and Trent lying on the ground beside it (figure 9.1). We used this picture as a target and quickly resolved the bad dream. As we continued to use EMDR, Trent would reprocess events like the nightmare and be willing to discuss the events with his mother, which promoted additional resolution. We began to space out his appointments to monthly visits. While Trent continued to have some emotional ups and downs around divorce issues (as might be expected), his difficult behavior could now be seen as related to events and was manageable with discussion between his mother and himself.

It is possible that Trent was comorbid for ADHD and PTSD, but when his emotional disturbance about his parents' divorce was diminished through EMDR treatment, his behavior became manageable. That is, it was manageable by his mother after she was able to work out her emotional issues through EMDR. If she had not obtained or responded to EMDR, would Trent have been diagnosed ADHD and placed on medication? Possibly. What does this say about diagnosis of ADHD?

Perhaps the major point to be made from this case is that when there is an effective treatment for certain childhood disorders, results from that treatment may begin to change our conceptualizations about a variety of diagnoses. And this may be true whether the treatment is medication or EMDR.

## DEPRESSIVE DISORDERS

The *DSM-IV* indicates that the major symptom for depressive disorders is depressed mood, which meets diagnostic criteria for dysthymic disorder in children if it exists for at least a year, for most of the day, for most days (with adults it needs to be two years). In children and adolescents, the mood can be irritable

*Figure 9.1*

(with duration of one year). If the diagnosis is major depressive episode, (five or more) symptoms must be present for at least two weeks: depressed mood most of the day, most days; diminished interest or pleasure in most activities; significant weight loss or gain; insomnia or hypersomnia; psychomotor retardation or agitation; fatigue; feelings of worthlessness or excessive guilt; diminished ability to think or concentrate; recurrent thoughts or suicidal ideation.

There has been a good deal of debate in this century as to whether children can become depressed. Currently it is pretty well accepted that even very young children can be depressed, although the symptoms manifest differently at different ages. Shafii and Shafii (1992) propose the following demarcations:

1. *Birth to age 2.* Syndromes of anaclitic depression, hospitalism, and toddler depression appear between birth and age 2. Anaclitic depression has symptoms of withdrawal, slowed or stunted growth, dazed facial expression, and intellectual and social deficits. Hospitalism is a more extreme form of anaclitic depression, with slowed motor response, expressionless face, bizarre and self-stimulating behaviors, and extreme intellectual

decline. Toddler depression is characterized by irritable mood, nightmares and night terrors, self-stimulating behaviors, oppositional behaviors, fears, decrease in play, and delay in meeting developmental milestones.

2. *Ages 3–5.* At these ages the most common symptoms are sadness, apathy, irritability, withdrawal, weight loss, motor retardation, and suicidal ideation.

3. *Ages 6–12.* At these ages, depression more clearly resembles that of adults, with more clear depressive mood and cognitions.

There are two major theories of the etiology of depression: the genetic-biological and the cognitive-behavioral. Generally, there is a good deal of support for a genetic causation, although exactly how much it contributes to depression is open to debate. It is generally accepted that genetics provides a mild predisposition for depression, but that other (e.g., environmental) factors contribute to its full development. Cognitive-behavioral theories emphasize various beliefs and attitudes that are maladaptive and promote depression. Primary among these theories are Beck's model of cognitive errors (1976) and Seligman's learned helplessness theory (Seligman & Peterson, 1986). Stress and coping theories postulate that children (and adults) may become overwhelmed by stress and subsequently develop depressive symptoms. Supporting this thesis is research that indicates that depressed people have experienced more stressful life events than controls and that stressful events frequently precede the development of depression (Kazdin, 1989). Also, Meuser and colleagues (1998) found the highest rate of comorbidity between depression and PTSD in their adult sample, which emphasizes the importance of stressful events in both disorders. EMDR can be seen to fit in well with this theory, as it can be used to target the stressful events. If the person becomes less depressed after an EMDR focus on the stressful events, the stressful events can then be construed as related to the depression.

However, a third model of depression can be derived from the results of EMDR with children and adults. In the EMDR model, stressful and traumatic events give rise to a negative emotional constellation, which exerts a depressive influence on the individual and the individual's cognitions and behavior. In other words, it is not the negative, irrational, and overgeneralized thoughts that give rise to the depression, but rather the stressful events and their impact on the emotions. When the EMDR process causes the negative emotional constellation to "wash out" or become neutralized, the negative cognitions can then realign more positively. This model predicts that the emotions have a stronger influence on higher-level cognition than the other way around. Thus, while it is possible for cognitions to drag emotions in a positive direction in some therapies, it is relatively inefficient compared to having the emotions shift in a positive direction, with the changed emotions then dragging the cognitions into a more positive, realistic, and rational arena.

Treatment of depressive disorders in children has consisted of psychotherapy (play therapy, group therapy, family therapy, and cognitive-behavioral interventions) and medications (specific serotonin reuptake inhibitors and tricyclic antidepressants). Empirical support for these approaches is rather sparse (Kronenberger & Meyer, 1996).

## Case Example

Ten-year-old Matt was referred to me by a psychologist who was treating Matt's father for depression. When I met with Matt's parents in an initial interview, they described him as bright and a good student, but depressed. Pregnancy, birth, and early developmental milestones were described as being within normal limits. They described how Matt's father had been placed on Prozac and how it had made a day-and-night difference for him. Because Matt appeared to have very similar problems (depression, anger, poor frustration tolerance), they went to Matt's pediatrician, who was willing to put him on 5 mg of Prozac. Matt responded favorably to the Prozac, becoming noticeably less depressed, more outgoing and relaxed, and not so hard on himself. However, his parents were concerned about having such a young child on medication, and having heard about EMDR from the father's psychologist, decided to see if EMDR might be helpful for Matt. They hoped it might produce enough benefit so that Matt would be able to discontinue the medication eventually. That seemed to be a formidable task because, prior to being on medication, despite having supportive and loving parents, Matt would often say, "I have a terrible life; nothing is good." His parents had to restrict him from playing videogames because he would get upset and cry in anger and frustration when he would lose and be extremely self-critical. He worried about his parents or sister getting hurt or dying. He had become extremely upset when his dog, Sam, was killed by a car. Matt blamed himself for Sam's death: "He ran. I couldn't hold him. I thought it was my fault when Sam got run over." However, as upsetting as that incident was for Matt, it had not seemed to cause Matt's depressive mood, which preexisted Sam's death. Matt enjoyed karate, but would avoid going when he was to be tested to earn a higher belt. He thought he wouldn't do well enough.

I saw Matt a total of 31 times over a year (for the first 6 months, I saw him weekly). We started EMDR in his first session with me. I was surprised that his safe place was in a cage, so that he wouldn't get hurt by other people. The cage had no door and was surrounded by a fence so that no one could get to him. He said, "No one can hurt me. I can't hurt myself."

After setting up the safe place, we decided to target Sam's death. The image was that of being at the front door. Matt's mother opened the door to get the newspaper and Sam ran out the door, despite Matt's attempts to hold him back. His negative cognition was "It's my fault; I couldn't hold the dog." His positive cognition was "It was a mistake, it didn't mean to happen, I did the best I could," which we shortened to "I did the best I could." His emotions were bad, sad, and scared, which he rated at a SUDS of 5. Within a few sets of eye movements, Matt was able to say, "It's like it didn't happen; it wasn't my fault," and rate the VOC at 7 and the SUDS at 0. Next, we targeted a nightmare, where his new dog fell off their back deck and broke her front feet. Again, after a few sets of eye movements Matt was able to say, "It seems like it didn't happen," with his feelings now faded and a positive cognition strongly endorsed. Because these targets had desensitized so quickly, we now targeted an incident where Matt had accomplished something he was proud of (a self-efficacy target to enhance self-esteem). That also went well. From this initial session, I could see that Matt would respond well to EMDR.

In three subsequent sessions, we targeted peer relationship problems (negative cognition: "I'm not any good") and his not wanting to participate in the baseball league he had signed up for during the summer (negative cognition: "No one likes me"). Behavioral changes began to be apparent. His mother reported that he was looking forward to summer activities, and participating happily, rather than resisting and wanting to withdraw (these were activities that Matt had chosen and initially had wanted to participate in). She also noticed that he seemed more positive, which could be heard in the tone of his voice.

In EMDR, we continued to target self-efficacy issues for several sessions, until Matt said that he wanted to work on his nightmares, which still occurred five times a week and were upsetting enough that he stayed up as late as he could before going to bed. Within a few sessions, the nightmares were no longer occurring on a regular basis, and overall improvement in Matt's mood seemed excellent. He no longer seemed to be caught in a mixture of depression, anxiety, and anger. Matt had now been in EMDR for three months and had had 12 sessions. After consultation with his parents and his pediatrician, Matt stopped taking Prozac. Unfortunately, Matt gradually became more depressed, anxious, and easily frustrated—not to the extent that he had been before beginning therapy, but noticeably so. He was placed back on Prozac; the depression, anxiety, and anger improved as before. In EMDR, we continued targeting events and feelings as they emerged, and after twelve more sessions, Matt seemed to be doing well enough to again withdraw him from the Prozac. This time he did not spiral downward into depression, anxiety, and anger. After spacing out his visits to once a month, and seeing him maintain his gains, we eventually terminated, a year after he had begun therapy.

Matt's case illustrates how EMDR can work well with depression in conjunction with medication. The Prozac assisted in the therapy process, taking off enough of an edge of the negative feelings so that Matt could use the sessions well. In turn, the EMDR was eventually effective enough that the medication could be eliminated. With childhood depression, EMDR is not likely to be a short-term proposition. Rather, there are likely to be many targets and much self-efficacy work to be completed. While Matt's parents were supportive and nurturing, Matt's dad had lifelong problems with depression. He and Matt were very similar. Is this a hereditary trait or a learned behavior that starts so early in life that it just looks innate? Although Matt made excellent gains in EMDR, I would not be surprised if additional therapy is required in the future. For example, if Matt's father did not continue in therapy, or on medication, his behavior might revert to greater depression with the result that he would be more critical with himself and Matt. Matt might then require additional EMDR to deal with that. If the situation continued, family therapy might also be required. Because the future is so open ended, one cannot assume that no additional EMDR will be beneficial later on. However, Matt's case illustrates once again that EMDR can be effective in a relatively short period of time, with additional interventions possible in the future, if the situation warrants.

## DISRUPTIVE BEHAVIOR DISORDERS

There are two forms of disruptive behavior disorders: oppositional defiant disorder (ODD) and conduct disorder (CD). Oppositional defiant disorder is defined as a pattern of negativistic, hostile, and defiant behavior lasting at least six months, during which four or more of the following are present: often loses temper, argues with adults, actively defies or refuses to comply with adults' requests or rules, deliberately annoys people, blames others for her mistakes or misbehavior, is touchy or easily annoyed by others, angry and resentful, spiteful or vindictive. Further, these behaviors must occur more frequently than normal and cause significant impairment in social, academic, or occupational functioning.

On the other hand, the essential feature of conduct disorder is a repetitive and persistent pattern of behavior in which the basic rights of others or major age-appropriate societal norms or rules are violated. Three or more characteristic behaviors must have been present during the last 12 months: aggressive conduct that causes or threatens physical harm to other people or animals, nonaggressive conduct that causes property loss or damage, deceitfulness or theft, and serious violations of rules.

The *DSM-IV* points out that estimates from twin and adoption studies show that conduct disorder has both genetic and environmental components. The risk for this disorder is increased in children with a biological or adoptive parent with antisocial personality disorder or a sibling with CD. The risk is also increased in children of biological parents with alcohol dependence, mood disorders, schizophrenia, or prior ADHD or CD. Similarly, in oppositional defiant disorder, the risk is higher for children from families in which one parent has a history of a mood disorder, ODD, CD, ADHD, antisocial personality disorder, or a substance-related disorder. ODD is also more common in families in which there is serious marital discord.

Kronenberger and Meyer (1996) point out that although research supports ODD and CD as separate syndromes (with ODD occurring earlier developmentally and being easier to treat because of its lesser severity), the same treatment approaches are used with both. They go on to state that behavioral and cognitive-behavioral treatments have the best record of success, with medication sometimes being used as an adjunct in the most severe cases. Cognitive-behavioral treatment includes such approaches as modifying coercive family interactions, teaching the child problem-solving skills, and strengthening social relationships.

## Case Example

Allen was a 6-year-old who met all the criteria for ODD. In fact, he met all eight of the criteria listed above. At intake, his mother wrote, "Allen is having trouble following directions and is disruptive in his first grade class. He expresses a lot of anger, rebellious attitude, and insecurity (at times—nightmares) at home." Pregnancy and birth information was unremarkable. However, his mother said things had been a fight ever since his birth. Because of his angry and oppositional behavior, when Allen was 4 years old he saw a child psychologist for six months without much improvement. Allen was considered "strong willed" at that time, as well as very angry. He insisted on sleeping in his parents' bed every night, so the psychologist suggested that Allen's parents simply be firm with him and continue putting him back in his own bed until he went back to sleep. Allen stayed up all night, continuing to get back in his parents' bed each time he was replaced in his own.

In first grade, Allen was highly aggressive, sometimes strangling other children. He wrote the word "fuck" three times across the top of a math paper. At recess, in the week before he was referred to me, he kicked a girl in the face. His parents, who were now separated, had an acrimonious relationship, frequently arguing with each other both before and after they separated. Allen, in his 6-year-old wisdom said, "Dad likes to argue. He argues about everything. I'm copying Daddy." However, his anger was out of control. When placed in a time-out "thinking chair," he got so enraged that he banged his head against the wall until he was made to stop. At other times he would beat his fists on the table while enraged. During the month before he was referred to me, he had had a full month of nightmares, right after Christmas.

After an initial three sessions, Allen's behavior had not improved. His mother was continuing to get calls from school and notes about Allen's anger and aggressiveness on a daily basis. On the way to his fourth appointment, in a rage, he was hitting his mother in the car, because he hadn't wanted to leave his bike locked at school. That morning before he went to school, he had gotten angry and told his mother that if people made fun of him in school, it would be all her fault. He had gotten so angry at a playmate recently that he felt sick to his stomach and dizzy. He said that it was all his playmate's fault. His friend had fallen and accidentally broken part of a toy. After a session where his mother had come with her boyfriend, Allen threw a three-hour tantrum, because he didn't approve.

In all, Allen had a total of nine sessions, after my initial session with his parents. Out of those nine sessions, five were EMDR. In the first EMDR session we targeted his anger at his mother because she wouldn't let him take his bike from school. His chain of associations quickly went from negative to neutral.

First, I asked Allen if he could get a picture in his mind of when he was mad. He responded with, "I'm crying and I don't feel good. I don't want it to happen again." He gave an outstanding negative cognition for a 6-year-old: "I'm out of control and too mad." His positive cognition was "I'd rather feel good." I had him complete a set of eye movements with the image, feelings, and negative cognition in mind. Allen responded that his emotions then felt "good" and said, "It didn't happen," when asked what came up. We did another set of eye movements and he said, "We just ride bikes and nothing happens." After another set of eye movements, "It doesn't happen," and after a final set, "Nothing happens."

While Allen's verbalizations could be taken as denial, his subsequent behavior suggests that it was not. In the next session, his mother reported that he had been loving to her after the session and the rest of the day, and less angry during the week. His mother was very encouraged. In the next session, we again targeted Allen's anger.

After that session, Allen's behavior turned angry and aggressive, apparently because he and his mother were going to move to a city 75 miles away. We targeted that concern in EMDR in the next session. I asked Allen if he could get a picture in his mind about his moving. Allen answered by saying, "I'm not happy. We're packing boxes." I asked him how he'd rather feel and he said that he'd rather feel "okay about moving," but right then he was "sad and unhappy." I asked him to show me on a piece of paper how sad and unhappy he felt, by marking on a horizontal line between a sad face on the left and a smiley face on the right. He put an X closer to the sad face (see p. 244, at 1). We did a set of eye movements, after which Allen stated, "Away from friends. I don't like moving. You have to do all the stuff and it's unhappy." I asked him to think about that and go through another set of eye movements. He responded, "The problem doesn't happen. The bad feelings." We did another set of eye movements. Allen stated that he got nothing. After another set, he said, "I just feel happy." I then asked him to show me on the diagram how happy he felt, and he marked an X at 2 on the diagram below.

Following that session, Allen's mother indicated that Allen would still lose control but that his anger no longer lasted all day; he would get over it sooner. In the next session, we targeted an incident when Allen became enraged and threw a tantrum because they had to stop for gas and he didn't want to do that.

I asked Allen to start by getting a picture in his mind of being mad. He respond-ed, "I'm pouting. I'm not happy. I'm stamping my feet, crying. I don't want to go to the gas station. I feel the mad in my head." His negative cognition was "I'm stupid" and his positive cognition was "I'm smart." We did a set of eye movements and Allen said, "I'm pouting. I turn it around." After another set of eye movements, Allen reported a "happy feeling." We did another set, with Allen responding, "Still super happy feeling." After another set he exclaimed, "Superduper happy feeling!"

Allen had three more sessions after that one, in which we continued to tar-get his anger. In his fifth EMDR session I asked him to think of a recent time when he was mad. Allen replied, "At day care. It didn't make sense." I asked him what feelings he had and he indicated that he felt angry and upset, experienc-ing those feelings in his head and chest. His SUDS level was at 10. We did a set of eye movements and the level dropped to 9. After another set Allen stated, "It doesn't happen." His SUDS level was now at 0. For theme development, I asked him to think of another time he got angry. Allen indicated that a friend hurt his feelings at lunchtime. We used a similar diagram as before to have him mark the intensity of his feelings on the paper as follows:

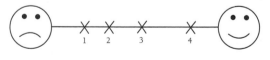

*1. Anger intensity at lunchtime*
*2. Anger prior to EM*
*3. Anger after onset of EM*
*4. Anger at end of EMDR on that incident*

We then targeted his being nervous about his report card. We also targeted an incident where he didn't want to go to a restaurant for breakfast—he wanted his mother to make him breakfast. He refused to get out of the car, had no breakfast, and stayed angry for three hours.

When we terminated, his anger was under much better control. Allen said that when he got angry, he could now "turn it around," meaning he could let go of the anger. A few months after termination, his mother wrote the following note:

> I was in town on business and I wanted to say hi and let you know how Allen has been doing. You worked wonders with him. He has been better than *ever* in his entire life. He is behaving at school, getting good grades. He was elected to student council. He controls his behavior at home and he shows more affection. I thought you should know.

EMDR therapists often require special training in how to be self-deprecating and learn to memorize statements like, "It's not me, it's the EMDR." The thing is, experienced EMDR therapists really do know it's not the therapist primarily, but rather the approach. We are reminded of this every time we attend an EMDR conference, workshop, or study group, swapping clinical vignettes and hearing about other therapists who have even more exciting stories than our own. EMDR is a very democratic therapy. It is one of the few approaches where the originator is not the most outstanding practitioner or does not develop an entourage of practitioners who mimic the leader; rather, each clinician produces as many or more "miracles" as the founder, thus ultimately becoming the "expert" as he or she gains experience.

Nonetheless, all children with ODD cannot be expected to respond to EMDR in the same way Allen did. Often children with ODD or CD are enmeshed in ongoing situations that require interventions at multiple levels, including family, marital, academic, and legal, as well as individual. In Allen's case there were definite family difficulties and stresses, including separation, divorce, a father and mother who argued angrily before and after the separation and divorce, a father who was quite punitive in his discipline, a move, and a new boyfriend. While these difficulties were noted in Allen's case, they required minimal intervention because Allen's behavior improved without attention to them. In other cases, those problem areas might require a great deal of attention.

# REACTIVE ATTACHMENT DISORDER

Reactive attachment disorder (RAD) is characterized by disturbed and developmentally inappropriate social relatedness in most contexts, beginning before age 5. The inhibited type is diagnosed when the child fails to initiate or respond in a developmentally appropriate fashion to most social interactions, as shown by excessively inhibited, hypervigilant, or highly ambivalent and contradictory responses. The disinhibited type is marked by diffuse attachments as shown by indiscriminate sociability with an inability to exhibit appropriate selective attachments, such as excessive familiarity with strangers. RAD often co-occurs with feeding disorder of infancy or early childhood, but the *DSM-IV* makes it clear that RAD can be separately diagnosed from that disorder.

Cases presented in chapter 7 indicate that EMDR can be effective with RAD. Donna Lewandowski's adopted daughter, who refused to attach to her for six years, responded to a single EMDR intervention; Bill, who was 14, but who had never attached after being left at a day care facility when 4 years old; and Nancy, who had been adopted from Korea, but then was subsequently sexually abused by an uncle, are all examples of RAD. It might be noted that in each case improvement was possible with EMDR because the child was in a family situation that was nurturing and supportive of psychological growth. It is doubtful that EMDR would have been effective if the child had remained in a situation where the parenting or caretaking was highly deficient and had led to the attachment disorder in the first place.

At this point, we have covered the major diagnoses of childhood and seen where and how EMDR can be applied. The rules are fairly simple: Seek out traumas, upsetting events, emotional stuck points, and apply EMDR regardless of the diagnosis. Become knowledgeable about the diagnostic area before applying EMDR. Be aware that the characteristics of the trauma(s) will help to predict treatment outcomes. Know that there are many areas where much more can be learned about EMDR and diagnosis. The future looks very exciting as we apply this paradigm to new areas with children. EMDR has been soundly criticized by experts in psychotherapy as being touted as a panacea for all diagnoses. But isn't this true of psychotherapy itself? Hasn't it been promoted as a remedy for everything from addictions to marital distress and existential anxiety? We need to continue to find out where EMDR is most effective and least effective. Perhaps this chapter is a step in that direction.

In the next chapter, we will look at how symptoms can be targeted with EMDR. Using symptoms as starting points is one of the most simple and powerful ways to approach therapy with EMDR. We will consider such commonly occurring childhood symptoms as anxiety, fear, nightmares, guilt, anger, depression, among others.

*ten*

# Symptoms as Targets for EMDR

(And where is that sad feeling now?)
"It went away!"

—AARON, AGE 4

THE BEAUTY OF BEING ABLE to target symptoms with EMDR is that most symptoms respond directly to such a focus. This allows the clinician to deal immediately with the presenting symptoms about which the parents or referring parties are most concerned. Thus, if the initial diagnosis is obscure or uncertain or if traumas are nonexistent or unknown, symptoms can be clear-cut starting points. Even when traumas are clearly identified and diagnoses have been formulated, symptoms can still be starting points for EMDR. If the symptoms immediately improve, that can be seen as diagnostic in itself, and if they don't improve, that too has diagnostic implications. For example, if a 7-year-old child is referred with symptoms of bed-wetting and nightmares, and no possible causes can be ascertained, the clinician could simply focus on the nightmares and bed-wetting. If they quickly improve (which often happens), the clinician could conclude that the overall situation was probably not complex. On the other hand, if the bed-wetting and nightmares do not improve within the initial three EMDR sessions, the clinician could surmise that the situation was complex, and make additional efforts to find underlying causes or blocking beliefs. The underlying assumption here is that disturbed behavior is a meaningful expression of situational factors and the child's preexisting characteristics—certainly an assumption that most therapies hold in common.

In this chapter, we cover the most common symptoms for which children are referred, such as anxiety, anger, depression, guilt, and conduct problems. In each case, the age of the child and the complexity of the situation will determine whether the symptom can be targeted directly and how it might be targeted. Case examples clearly illustrate how to apply EMDR in particular instances.

## ANXIETY AND FEAR

Children frequently present with symptoms of anxiety, and it is often productive to target the anxiety directly. Megan was 11 years old when she was referred for severe anxiety. She had a supportive family, did well in school, and other than her anxiety, seemed to have no major problems. She had a younger brother who also had difficulties with anxiety, and a mother who was an excellent mother, but who also was overly anxious about issues in her own life and who had been highly anxious as a child. However, Megan's mother did not seem to transfer a lot of her anxiety onto an excessive preoccupation with Megan's problems, as many overly anxious mothers are wont to do. Rather, she was primarily supportive and loving with her daughter, whom she characterized as very serious and very sensitive. Megan's father worked for a computer company and did not have any apparent problems with excessive anxiety. Further, he did not come from a family with evidence of those difficulties. Megan was an "A" student and tended to be highly conscientious in academics as well as at home. As Megan was growing up, her parents learned that she couldn't handle watching horror movies, as she would often become frightened and have nightmares or not be able to sleep for a night or two afterward. They learned to help her restrict her movie viewing so that she would not become unduly frightened.

However, about three months before I saw Megan, she went to a friend's house for a slumber party where the girls stayed up late and watched scary movies. When Megan returned home, she was not able to go to sleep at night. Over several weeks, her parents tried all the things that most parents do to help her sleep, as well as all the things that had helped before, to no avail. Finally they took her to see a psychologist who was skilled in the application of cognitive-behavioral approaches, hypnosis, and relaxation techniques. Nothing worked. The psychologist knew that I specialized in EMDR, and referred her to me, informing Megan and her parents that EMDR was a short-term therapy that might be helpful.

At this point, no one in Megan's family was getting much sleep. In the evenings, Megan's anxiety would escalate, and she would run from room to room in order to stay out of the dark. In spite of her anxiety, she would go to bed at her regular bedtime, but then lie awake in a frightened state for several hours. She would then climb into bed with her 6-year-old brother for comfort, with the only result being that neither one of them would sleep much. About two or three A.M., Megan would show up in her parents' bedroom, and they would let her attempt to sleep with them. That didn't work either, and Megan's parents were becoming exhausted as well.

In the first session with Megan, she indicated to me that she was too anxious and scared to sleep. The feelings had not gone away since the slumber party. On several occasions she had become so frightened that she had vomited. She was noticeably tense in the session with me. One reason for that tension was that the night before coming in for her first appointment with me, Megan had had a nightmare in which her new psychologist (me) told her he would kill her if she didn't get better in two sessions. Rapport did not come easily with this young woman, if at all.

In fact, in the second session, Megan was just as tense as in the first one, but we began EMDR anyway, with Megan huddled in the corner of my couch. She did not relax outwardly throughout the entire session. Inwardly, she might have become less tense, as she reported some emotional changes from EMDR. The target image she selected was seeing herself in her own bed, not being able to fall asleep, with the thought that the boy in the movie was going to kill her. Her negative cognition was "I'm helpless and a scaredy-cat"; her positive cognition was "I'm brave and I can go to sleep without any problem." Her VOC was 3 and her SUDS was 5, with Megan experiencing the scared feeling in her stomach "like butterflies."

Megan's processing in this session followed the format of a performance anxiety desensitization, in that she visualized herself going to bed each night during the week and dealing with each anxiety as it came up. For example, she visualized going to bed, but having to look under the bed to see if anything was under there. Finding nothing, she could go to bed and sleep. Then she visualized the next night; this time not having to look under the bed. These visualizations were self-directed; only the starting image had been mutually determined. Her SUDS declined to 0 and her VOC ("I am brave") increased to 7, but she still looked tense at the end of the session. I was pleased that these changes had occurred, but was troubled that she had not relaxed outwardly. The next day, Megan's mother reported that Megan had seemed more relaxed and to have more self-confidence and generally felt better, but still had ended up in her parents' bed. However, Megan had agreed to stay one or two nights in her own bed; something she had not been able to agree to before.

In the next session, she targeted scenes from the horror movie itself that she had found so scary. In the week following that session, Megan slept for three nights in her own bed. At this point, she no longer ran from room to room at night; was now able to go in the basement or upstairs at night by herself. She set a goal in her next session to sleep every night in her own bed. In the EMDR session, she targeted the anxieties that still came up at night when she went to bed, such as hearing a car go by or hearing little noises in the house. She was able to visualize herself in bed saying to herself, "I am brave and I can do it," and then being able to fall asleep.

Over the next two weeks, Megan slept every night in her own bed. She had had three EMDR sessions over a three-week period, with improvements accruing over each week. While I still saw her as a serious, diligent, overanxious child, EMDR had greatly helped her manage her anxieties. Due to her anxious nature, however, I half expected to see her back in my office at some later point, anxious and fearful about some other event. And in fact this happened. Three years later, Megan asked to come back for more EMDR. She had begun reading books with frightening themes, and was beginning to have difficulties falling asleep. She did not want it to escalate to the point it had before. This time we had a single session and she began sleeping well again.

Megan provides a good example of a young woman who is overly anxious, but who had a supportive and nurturing family. If her family had been less supportive I suspect she would have had more problems with anxiety as she grew up. However, her problems with anxiety have seemed to lessen as she has gotten older. Between family support and EMDR, her self-confidence and ability to cope with anxiety has grown.

In another case that demonstrates the utility of focusing directly on symptoms of anxiety, Curt, who was 7 years old, developed intensified fears of vomiting after his father was transferred to a foreign country because of his job. The anxiety about vomiting had started about nine months before he learned his father was being transferred. Curt missed his father greatly and his anxiety about vomiting worsened even though he knew that he and the rest of the family were going to join his father overseas. He was somewhat aware that missing his father made his stomach feel funny, which in turn made him fear vomiting. In addition, he developed anxieties about having an aneurysm after a boy he knew died of one. Curt would begin to think about getting an aneurysm, which would cause him to get a headache, which in turn would convince him that he had an aneurysm.

Curt had a total of three sessions, two of them EMDR sessions. His safe place was his bedroom. In EMDR, he recalled that when he was 2 years old, he ate a poisonous mushroom that made him sick to his stomach. Following that, he recalled other times he had gotten sick to his stomach: In preschool, when he had heat stroke he felt like throwing up; another time in preschool he actually did vomit on the floor and then stepped in it; he vomited at school a year later, and his mother had to be called to come get him. He worried about getting sick on Chinese food. After recalling and reprocessing in EMDR the incidents about being sick to his stomach, his SUDS declined to 0 (I was unable to elicit negative and positive cognitions because of his age).

In the next session, Curt and his mother indicated that he had not thought at all about getting an aneurysm over the past week and he had been much less anxious about vomiting. We again targeted the vomiting anxieties and this time we were able to establish negative and positive cognitions ("I'm sick"; "I'm healthy"). The VOC started at 1 and rose to 7 during the course of EMDR, and the anxiety diminished from 6 to 0.

No further sessions were conducted as the family moved overseas for a year. At one-year follow-up, after the family had returned to the United States, Curt had been free of anxieties about vomiting and having an aneurysm for the full year. He had, however, developed an anxiety about nosebleeds, but we treated that in one session, and he has had no recurrences.

These cases suggest that EMDR can not only be useful with the fears and anxieties that are secondary to PTSD, but also that EMDR can be used to ameliorate anxiety symptoms not associated with PTSD. The above cases are good examples of simple traumas or upsetting events (i.e., a frightening movie; the father being transferred to another country) and the effectiveness of EMDR with those singular events where there are minimal complicating factors in the present environment.

In chapter 7, an example was given of the effectiveness of EMDR with anxiety related to PTSD. In that case, a 10-year-old girl was retraumatized when her older brother who had molested her was allowed to move back home. He was angry and threatening to her in his behavior, with the result that she developed a variety of anxiety-related symptoms. She was described by her parents as whining, crying, sad, having low energy, and complaining of somatic problems (headache, nausea). On a rating scale, her mother rated her as impulsive/overreactive, socially withdrawn, agitated/restless, accident prone, having multiple somatic complaints, sleep disturbances, nightmares, and much clinging behavior, and being preoccupied with fearful stimuli. She met enough of the *DSM-IV* criteria of intrusions, avoidance, and hyperarousal to qualify for the diagnosis of PTSD. After her family made sure she felt protected from the older brother who had molested her, EMDR was effective in eliminating her anxiety symptoms. She stopped having nightmares and night terrors, and her other anxiety-related behavior ceased being a problem. These changes occurred within five EMDR sessions.

In this case, we again see the importance of the child feeling protected and nurtured. If her parents had not protected her, it would be likely that fears of annihilation would have emerged ("No one will protect me and I can't protect myself") and the attendant feelings of worthlessness ("I must be worthless; no one will protect me"). As noted earlier, these thoughts and feelings can persist into adulthood, becoming the worst trauma of all. This case also indicates that when a child is being traumatized, the trauma has to be stopped before EMDR can be effective. Even after EMDR was initiated, her nightmares progressed into night terrors until the traumatization stopped.

Clinging to a parent is a frequent behavior in younger children (ages 1–7) who have been traumatized and then are afraid to leave their parent's side. It can also be referred to as separation anxiety or a separation anxiety disorder. Research that has been conducted on "secure" versus "insecure" attachments may be missing the boat in assuming that insecure attachments are due to a poor parent-child relationship; in many cases the "insecure attachment" may be due to unrecognized traumatization of the child. An excellent example of separation anxiety after trauma is seen in Julie (chapters 2 and 5), who became clingy and dependent, afraid to leave her mother's side after two motor vehicle accidents. Also, Linda (chapter 3) was afraid of separation from her parents after the Oklahoma City bombing, even though she was an older child (10 years old). Mike (chapter 5) slept on the floor outside his parents' bedroom after being traumatized in a motor vehicle accident. It really is not surprising that frightened and traumatized children would turn to their parents for protection and alleviation of their fears (assuming their parents are not the perpetrators). To assume that this clinginess is the result of relationship difficulties, as the secure-insecure attachment research implies, is especially misguiding to clinicians, who may then be encouraged to make the same assumptions as underlie the research.

At the present time, a cognitive-behavioral approach, developed by Philip Kendall at Temple University, has shown promise in treating anxiety disorders in children. A series of research articles supporting the approach, which consists of 16 sessions (the first eight of which are psychoeducational in nature; the second eight are graduated exposure experiences) have been effective enough that the approach has been placed on the American Psychological Association's list of "probably efficacious" empirically supported therapies. The treatment has been applied to children aged 9–12 who have an anxiety disorder (generalized anxiety disorder, separation anxiety disorder, and social phobia, but not PTSD, specific phobia, or OCD) (Kendall, 1994; Kendall et al., 1997). In one sample 66% of the children no longer met diagnostic criteria after treatment; in the other, 50%. Long-term follow-up of the two samples indicated that the treatment gains were maintained for one year and more than three years (Kendall et al., 1997; Kendall & Southam-Gerow, 1996).

This research is likely the standard against which EMDR results with children with anxiety disorders will eventually have to be compared. In the meantime, Kendall and his associates are to be commended for conducting research that indicates that anxiety disorders in children are treatable, which is highly pertinent to the practicing clinician. As their treatment is manualized, controlled comparisons between manualized EMDR and his cognitive-behavioral approach become quite feasible.

## NIGHTMARES AND NIGHT TERRORS

One area where EMDR is distinctly more effective than other therapies with children is the area of nightmares and night terrors. I know of no other therapy that has such a direct and immediate effect on these symptoms. It supports the argument that EMDR has consistent effects on children that go beyond what other therapies provide. It raises the possibility that EMDR produces subcortical as well as cortical effects (the effectiveness of EMDR with phantom limb pain is suggestive of the same interpretation).

In children, nightmares can be associated with PTSD, as in the case of Julie, who had nightmares after being in two automobile accidents (presented in chapters 2 and 5); in the case of Mike, who also had PTSD symptoms after being in a car accident (chapter 5); and in the case of John, who shot and killed his younger cousin (chapter 9). Night terrors can also be a symptom associated with PTSD, and quickly remit when treated with EMDR, as shown by Davy's case (chapter 4), in which Davy had night terrors over a 18-month period of time (more than half of his young life of 2 years, 9 months) after having had cleft palate surgery at 14 months of age. The night terrors stopped after less than 10 minutes of EMDR. With Mike, John, and Davy, the nightmares or terrors were not targeted directly, but rather the traumatic events were. Yet, the nightmares and night terrors were quickly eliminated. In Julie's case, both the traumatic events and the nightmares were targeted directly, with good results. Thus, in PTSD, it appears that there is room for therapeutic choice in choosing to target nightmares or the traumatic event or both. With night terrors, however, the event itself has to be targeted, as the child will always have amnesia (by definition) for the night terrors.

When nightmares occur, and they are not associated with PTSD, as with Matt (chapter 9), who was depressed and having nightmares, the nightmares can be targeted directly with good results. Libby (chapter 7), whose father tried to drown her and who may have sexually molested her, developed nightmares and bed-wetting when she felt unsafe (i.e., when he called). Again, it was effective to target the nightmares directly.

## ENURESIS

Another area where EMDR has outstanding results with children is with enuresis, if medical problems are not involved. Five-year-old Amanda was toilet-trained for bowel and bladder at 3 years of age. However, when her parents separated and divorced, she became very clingy and dependent with both of her parents, and she began wetting the bed on a nightly basis. After obtaining a detailed history from her parents, in the first session with Amanda, in EMDR I had her focus on her anger, sadness, and staying dry at night. She missed her next session because her father had car trouble, but when she returned two weeks later, her father reported that she had been dry at night the entire two weeks. Amanda was very proud of herself, and her pleasure made it easier for her to continue therapy.

Danny, age 11, who had a bed-wetting problem in addition to being diagnosed with ADHD (chapter 9), stopped wetting after less than five EMDR sessions focused on that problem. Libby (chapter 7), stopped bed-wetting after two EMDR sessions, but then began wetting again after her abusive father made phone contact with her family; she no longer felt safe.

Enuresis cannot be diagnosed before age 5, per *DSM-IV*, and must occur at least two times a week for at least three months. Developmental age can be used instead of chronological age if the child is developmentally delayed. Medical reasons must be ruled out before the diagnosis can be made. Although we are treating enuresis as a symptom here, it is necessary to keep the above criteria in mind. Further, enuresis can be divided into primary enuresis (bladder control has never been achieved) and secondary enuresis (bladder control has been accomplished but lost); and nocturnal and diurnal types. Most enuresis is of the primary type (Scharf, Pravada, Jennings, Kauffman, & Ringel, 1987), and in these cases medical consultation is essential.

For secondary enuresis, the oldest, most successful, and most widely used method is the urine alarm system that awakens the child when wetting occurs at night. It is effective in stopping bed-wetting 75% of the time, but has a 41% relapse rate, which can be reduced to perhaps 10–20% if the alarm is programmed to sound 70% of the time when wetting occurs (Doleys, 1977). There has been a good deal of behavioral research for the treatment of enuresis, generally combining the use of the urine alarm with other behavioral learning methods. Success rates for these more complex interventions are in the same range as the urine alarm system, although relapse rates may be somewhat lower (Kronenberger & Meyer, 1996).

Medication has also been used to treat enuresis, but the medication with the longest history of use (imipramine) has success rates of only 20–40%, with relapse rates of 40–60%, likely because no new learning is involved (Kronenberger & Meyer, 1996). Newer medications may be more effective initially, but they would also have high relapse rates unless combined with behavioral treatments.

Treatment of secondary enuresis with EMDR seems much more simple and straightforward, as children often stop wetting after one or two sessions and have low relapse rates, as indicated above in the case examples. However, controlled research with a series of cases will be necessary to obtain overall response rates in comparison to other treatments. A couple of additional case examples will further illustrate the effectiveness of EMDR with enuresis.

Everett was a 10-year-old who wet the bed and set fires. He had been caught setting a fire in a laundromat. He had been seen at the sites of several other fires, but did not admit to setting those. However, he showed a fascination with fires which suggested that he was not being truthful. His mother had a single sexual

encounter one night when she drank heavily at an office party, and got pregnant with Everett. His biological father did not know about the pregnancy or birth. Everett had many questions about his father, but his mother had told him very little. While he and his mother were close, they had a very argumentative relationship, which contributed to Everett's lack of self-esteem and high level of stress. He did get good grades at a private religious school.

After an initial five sessions in which we focused on relationship and compliance issues, Everett set a series of fires in his home while his mother was away. In the next session, we used EMDR for the first time. Rather than focus initially on the fire-setting, which was a relatively low-frequency behavior, I decided to focus on Everett's bed-wetting (secondary enuresis), as it had been occurring four or five times per week over the last six months. I had Everett target the uncomfortable sensations he felt when he woke up in the wet bed. This was done in as much detail as Everett could stand. Although Everett was uncomfortable in doing so, he was able to recall the feel of the wet sheets, their temperature, their smell, and his emotions. He obtained positive changes in the session. When Everett came back a month later (I had been out of town), he proudly told me he had not wet the bed for an entire month. As we continued sessions over the next year, Everett never wet the bed again. We also repeatedly targeted the fire-setting, with the result that Everett's preoccupation with fire gradually diminished. To his mother's knowledge, he never set another fire, although she remained apprehensive (with good reason) for a considerable length of time. As she saw his fascination with fire diminish, she was gradually able to relax. Everett is a teenager now, and fire-setting and enuresis are no longer a concern.

Five-year-old Spence was sexually abused by his maternal grandmother when he was 3 years, 6 months old. After coming back from a 10-day visit with her (when the abuse occurred), he had nightmares, wet the bed, and rubbed his nose until it was raw. At age 5, he continued to have nightmares and wet the bed. After two EMDR sessions, he stopped having nightmares and wetting the bed. This was one of the first children I treated for bed-wetting using EMDR. In more than 20 years of working with children (and adults), I had developed internal norms about how long it took to treat various disorders and how much effort was involved. With EMDR, I was finding that those internal norms were no longer fitting. Spence was a child whose changes were instrumental in causing that shift.

## ENCOPRESIS

In order for encopresis to be diagnosed, the *DSM-IV* indicates that the child must be over 4 years of age, and there must be one or more encopretic events

per month for at least three months. While encopresis is discussed as a symptom in this chapter, and not a diagnosis, we will follow the *DSM-IV* definition. Encopresis can also be categorized as primary (bowel control has never been achieved) or secondary (bowel control was achieved, but then lost), involuntary or intentional, and retentive (where the stool becomes impacted because of retention, eventually causing overflow around the impaction) or nonretentive. Involuntary, retentive encopresis appears to be more common than the intentional, nonretentive subtype (Wald & Handen, 1987). Stressful events have been found to be present in a large percentage (70%) of children with secondary encopresis (Bellman, 1966). If primary encopresis is involved, a medical evaluation would be necessary prior to beginning psychological treatment.

Treatment for encopresis typically involves both medical and psychological aspects. Since most cases of secondary encopresis are associated with constipation, enemas, suppositories, and stool softeners are used to counteract the constipation. Dietary approaches that increase fiber in the child's diet are also used to support natural bowel function. Medical management by itself produces success in about a third of the cases (Stark, Spirito, Lewis, & Hart, 1990), but when medical approaches are combined with behavioral interventions the success rate goes up to 60–70% (Wald & Handen, 1987). These behavioral approaches generally involve the use of reinforcement, negative reinforcement, or punishments to shape toileting behavior.

When encopresis is of traumatic origin, it can often be quickly resolved in EMDR. A case in point is that of Sean, 11 years old, who was initially referred by his mother for anger and behavior problems, but who was also soiling on a nightly basis (see chapter 4). However, when I interviewed Sean and his mother, they revealed that Sean and his brother were being beaten by their stepfather, their mother's present husband. The abuse was immediately reported to the Department of Social Services, and I continued to see Sean in individual therapy. In that first session, Sean's mother indicated that Sean was encopretic on a daily basis, usually at night. She stated that the behavior had started a few years ago after Sean had been molested by some older boys. Following that incident, Sean began inserting his finger in his rectum, which would induce soiling. He was referred to a counselor, and the encopresis improved, but was not eliminated during the year he was in therapy. It worsened after therapy was terminated. Sean initially stated that he didn't remember the molestation, but said that he would like to stop soiling himself. He wasn't very confident about his ability to do so, as he had worked on it before in therapy. Also, he said, "Sometimes I don't know I'm doing it till I wake up."

In the next session, Sean stated that he remembered the molestation, which was multiple events that took place over a one-month period when he was 6 years old. He indicated that the boys who did it also molested other children in

the neighborhood. He was very relieved when his family moved away. Sean agreed to use EMDR to work on the encopresis. After we set up a safe place, the session went as follows:

T: Okay. Bring up that picture of the safe place, lying on the couch in the living room, watching your favorite TV show. Notice the relaxed feelings that go with that, the safe feelings that go with that, and where you feel those physically in your body and in your head, and hold all of that and follow my fingers. (EM) That's good. . . . Okay, blank out your mind, take a deep breath, and just relax as you breathe out and notice the good feelings. Real good. Again, we'll use that safe place if you want to stop during any part of this; just hold up your hand. At the end of the session we'll use it to make sure that you feel good. Now, can you get a picture in your mind of this incident that happened dealing with these older boys?

S: (Nods)

T: Describe that picture.

S: Under a picnic table with a blanket over it.

T: And what's happening?

S: They're on top of me.

T: And what are they doing?

S: Sticking their penis up my butt.

T: As you picture that in your mind, what's it make you think or believe about yourself?

S: That I'm weird.

T: What would you rather believe about yourself?

S: That I'm normal.

T: In holding that picture in your mind, how true does that statement feel to you, that "I'm normal," from 1, which feels not true at all, to 7, which feels completely true. As you hold that picture, how true does that feel?

S: Two.

T: Still holding that picture along with the negative thought, that "I'm weird," what kind of feelings does that make you have right now?

S: I just want to get out of there. (Note that this is not a feeling being expressed, but rather an intention, so I inquire further.)

T: Okay, and that tells me what you want to do, but there's probably a feeling associated with that. It might be that you're scared or it might be that you're hurt or it might be that you're angry. What kind of feelings would go with that?

S: Scared.

T: Okay, and how strong is that scared feeling right now, where 0 is not there at all and 10 is the most upsetting that the scared feeling could be?

S: Nine.

T: Now what I'm going to ask you to do is hold the picture in your mind along with the negative thoughts and feelings: "I'm weird" and the scared feeling. Where do you feel that scared feeling in your body?

S: All over.

T: All over. Okay. I want you to hold all that in mind, especially the picture. Follow my fingers. And the main thing is that you just let whatever comes to mind, come to mind. You don't have to make anything come to mind or keep anything from coming to mind. Just let whatever comes up, come up (this instruction is deliberately paradoxical). Okay? Got the picture? And the thought "I'm weird" and the feelings of being scared and where you feel those? Follow my fingers. (EM) That's good. . . . Okay, blank out your mind, take a deep breath, relax as you breathe out. What comes to mind now?

S: My safe place. (Once again, this shows the importance of having previously installed the safe place and how frequently it gets used.)

T: Hold that image of your safe place and follow my fingers. (EM) Okay, let it go, take a deep breath. And what do you get now?

S: Nothing.

T: Okay, let's do a check. That feeling of being scared. How strong is that feeling right now, from 0 to 10, where 0 is not at all, 10 is the worst it could possibly be? (We're at the end of the hour, and I want to check SUDS before closing out the session.)

S: Two.

T: (I decide to attempt an installation) Now, I want you to hold two things in mind. One is the statement "I'm normal" and the other is the original memory that we started with. Got both? Follow my fingers. (EM) Okay, let it go, take a deep breath, relax as you breathe out. And what do you get now?

S: Nothing.

T: Doing a check on that statement "I'm normal," how true does that statement feel right now from 1 to 7 where 1 feels not true at all, 7 feels completely true?

S: About a 7.

T: Wow, what a change. One more check on the feeling. How strong is that scared feeling, from 0 to 10; 0 is not there at all, 10 is the worst it could be?

S: Zero.

T: Okay. Sean, let's talk about this for a minute. What's it seem like to you? What was it like for you to go through this kind of strange procedure where you move your eyes back and forth and your feelings and your thoughts change?

S: Relaxing.

T: Uhuh. Are you surprised at how the feeling went away?

S: (Nods)

T: And what does that statement seem like to you, that "I'm normal"?

S: Two.

T: Sean, what we've done here is gone through a procedure that has really start-ed a process that is likely to continue after you leave here, that you may have more thoughts, more feelings, and more images about this. Everybody's dif-ferent and continues on the process differently. I just want you to notice what it's like for you and then when you come in next time we'll talk about what kind of thoughts and images and feelings come up for you. Some people afterward feel really, really good and other people feel kind of off-kilter emo-tionally, and sometimes it affects people's dreams. Just notice what it's like for you. We'll talk about it next time. What I'd like to do now is have you bring up your image of the safe place again and tell me when you can picture that clearly and notice the good feelings that go with that; the relaxed feelings, the safe feelings. Follow my fingers. (EM) Okay, and let it go. Take a deep breath and again notice the good feelings that go with that. And those good feelings can stay with you—a few minutes, a few hours, even the rest of the day. And again, let's just talk about this for a minute. How do you feel now?

S: Relaxed.

T: Do you feel like anything's changed?

S: Uhuh.

T: What's changed?

S: The way that I feel. Before I felt all upset and stuff and now I feel relaxed and happy.

T: Good. That's what this is supposed to do. And we can take other problem sit-uations and work on them like this.

When Sean came in the next week, he and his mother reported that he soiled one time, the night after the session, but had not soiled since then. We did another EMDR session and this time the image changed for Sean. He saw him-self yelling at the molesters and chasing them away. His mother also noted that Sean seemed less angry and more "at peace." No further encopresis occurred over the next month, during which we had one more session. Sean stopped coming in for appointments after that, probably because his stepfather objected to the therapy because of the child abuse report that had been filed. Four months later, another session was scheduled, and based on Sean's comments, another report of abuse had to be filed, this time causing Sean's case to be trans-ferred to the Department of Social Services. During the last month, Sean had started soiling again, causing his mother to schedule another appointment for him. This time, though, the soiling appeared to be related to rage over his mis-treatment at home by his stepfather.

Sean's case is quite unfortunate, as it is the story of a boy who not only was sexually abused by individuals outside of the home, but who also had to contend with physical abuse inside the home. While the simple trauma aspect of the soiling was rapidly taken care of by EMDR, the ongoing abuse caused a recurrence of the symptom. At that point, follow-up therapy was appropriately family therapy, and was conducted by the Department of Social Services.

The next case is more typical of the kind of cases referred for soiling in an outpatient practice, Norman, age 5, was referred for encopresis and acting out anger at school. Norman's parents had just separated. He was a bright and perceptive child and seemed to be acutely aware of the conflict between his parents—in fact, he didn't want to go to school (he preferred to be at home where he could keep an eye on things). He figured that if he got enough "red slips" at school for bad behavior, he would get kicked out. In addition, his grandmother, to whom he was close, had recently died. He had also drawn a picture of his parents where he scribbled over their faces.

Initially in EMDR we targeted his sadness about his father moving out and his dislike of school, targets that were important to him. In the next session we again targeted his sadness about his dad leaving, as well as his anger in school and his grandmother's death. In the third EMDR session, we targeted his soiling, which had been occurring on a daily basis. In this session, we used drumming instead of eye movements or hand taps. We also focused on his grandmother's death, and a fight that his parents had had prior to his starting therapy where they were both pulling at him. In addition to theme development with children, it also makes sense to desensitize all possible targets. Following that session, Norman had some partial improvement in his encopresis, going several days without soiling.

In the fourth session, we again worked on the same targets: his grandmother's death, his parents' separation, doing well in school, staying clean (not soiling). He stopped soiling after that session, having 10 straight days of no encopresis. Finances were a problem for his parents, so no further appointments were made, but follow-up phone calls over the next six months indicated that although Norman had occasional mistakes (one or two a month), encopresis was no longer a serious problem.

Here is a more complex case that illustrates well the oppositional difficulties involved in working with children who are encopretic. George was 10 when he was referred to me. His mother indicated in intake materials that he had ADHD, stress from low self-esteem, poor peer relationships, and difficulty with a younger brother in special education. In addition, his parents were going through a divorce that was very angry and bitter. In reaction to all this, George had gouged his arms, expressed suicidal thoughts, and frequently soiled himself. He was also nocturnally and diurnally enuretic. He was so opposed to being in therapy that his mother had to wrestle him to the ground to get him to come to the first session. In George's fourth session, he was willing to use EMDR for a daytime wetting incident that happened at school in the second grade. Following that session, George wet and soiled himself all week on a daily basis. The next session, we again focused on the wetting and soiling, with the result that he did not wet or soil for the whole week.

The next time I saw George, he was extremely regressed in the session, crawling on the floor, physically fighting against his mother who brought him, and refusing to work in the session. Several sessions followed, which were up and down, in the sense that George would refuse to work in some, but would be cooperative and delightful in others. However, his wetting and soiling had generally improved to the point that it was not occurring every day. After he stayed with his father, he reported in a session that he now understood that visiting his father caused him stress, and that caused him to soil. He said that when he returned to his mother's home, he continued to soil because the stress didn't go away immediately. I was very pleased that EMDR had caused the enuresis and encopresis to diminish to the point that George could make this connection. However, George continued to be very emotionally volatile. He hated school because he was in special education, although he was gifted in many ways. His emotional distress and his ADHD interfered with his ability to do well. He was picked on by other students because of his incontinence. He hated going to his day care setting after school because he was the oldest there and disliked how he was treated.

By now, George had had 20 sessions, half of which were EMDR. Situational problems were almost overwhelming for him. He refused to work in EMDR at all. We had some family sessions, with both of his parents attending, to focus on reducing the animosity between them and to work out plans that would be of benefit to George. He was suicidal at times, got caught shoplifting, felt miserable. His dad remarried, which caused George further distress. Wetting and soiling continued on an intermittent basis.

Finally, a year and a half after George started therapy, he had a soiling incident at school which was so embarrassing that it brought the problem to a head. George was now 12 years old and in sixth grade. He lost control of his bowels in the classroom and had to go to the restroom to clean up. He returned to the classroom with some fecal material smeared on his shirt and was humiliated by the teasing and derision that ensued. However, he insisted that he was going to work on it on his own. I said to him that if he could have such a success on his own that would be wonderful, but since he had been working on it on his own over the past year, it might make sense to limit his efforts to the next month. If he was successful in that month he would have a real accomplishment, but if he wasn't successful, he would have to agree to use EMDR again. He consented to this course of action. After three weeks George admitted he was not successful and asked to use EMDR. Although 12, George had visual tracking problems, so we used hand taps. We targeted the humiliating episode at school and George could feel his emotions shift. He was jubilant, shouting, "Hey, it works!" We continued to target enuresis and encopresis, as well as other upsetting events, and within a month he was no longer wetting and soiling. We terminated six months later. George's life was far from idyllic at termination, but the improvement in wetting and soiling and continued focus on self-esteem targets had improved his self-esteem so that he was now able to begin developing friendships.

George's case is one where EMDR produced symptomatic improvement despite an overall situation that was almost overwhelmingly difficult. The final case that I will describe with respect to encopresis is one where the overall situation was stable, but a single debilitating symptom was destroying the young woman's life. I am including the case to illustrate the long-term effects on self-esteem if a chronic soiling problem goes unresolved.

When I first met with Joyce, she was an adolescent, but her problem had existed since elementary school. As a young child, she had a urinary reflex problem, which caused repeated vaginal infections that were treated with antibiotics. The antibiotics caused her to have constant diarrhea. Eventually, in her sleep, she began to cause herself to have bowel movements through digital stimulation and would wake up with fecal material on her hands. Over the years, Joyce made desperate attempts to stop this behavior, which had reached compulsive proportions, at times tying her hands to the bedpost when she went to bed. She had had a number of complete medical work-ups but no medical causes were found; extensive psychotherapy did not relieve her nighttime soiling.

Joyce felt the soiling was ruining her life. An attractive and intelligent young woman, she feared going to college where any roommate would be repulsed by the odors, the sheets, and her clothing, just as her family had. She avoided any intimate or romantic relationship for fear that a boyfriend would discover her literal "dirty secret," which wasn't so little. It would be easy to speculate psychodynamically about what she was doing to herself with her compulsive soiling, and how the symptom met certain needs, but the other side of the coin was that she and her parents were truly distressed by the persistence of the soiling and all of its ramifications. Her impetus to try psychotherapy one more time was that she was going to leave for college in the fall. She didn't want her soiling to ruin her college experience.

Joyce had a total of three EMDR sessions before she was symptom-free. In the first, her starting image was from an incident in the eighth grade where she was by her locker, and some boys were commenting on the foul odor and wondering where it was coming from. Her negative cognition was "I don't belong" and her positive cognition was "I can be clean" with a VOC of 3. Her emotions were "alone, hurt, sad" at a SUDS level of 6, felt in her heart. The session was incomplete, with SUDS declining to 3 and her VOC rising to 6. Her next session was three weeks later, but she had had no episodes of soiling since the last session. Prior to that first EMDR session, she had been soiling on an average of two times per week. We used the same starting image, and this time her SUDS went to 0 and her VOC to 7. At the end of the session, she said, "Now I feel like a different person." In the next session, we focused on future projections and self-efficacy installations. In our final session, three months after she started EMDR, she indicated that she had not soiled for two months and that she was now confident to attend college, felt good about herself, and would return if the soiling recurred. She didn't think it would.

## GUILT

Because of my work with EMDR and children, I have come to see guilt as a basic emotion that children have very early in life, and as a socializing force. It seems to develop before logic, and only as children become more "logical" in their thinking, do they ascribe guilt in ways that make sense to adults. Prior to that, they assume guilt for things they can't possibly be responsible for, such as parental divorce, being sexually abused, natural disasters, in fact, *anything* bad that happens. What I am suggesting here, is that guilt is innate, but logic and reasoning develop as the child matures. EMDR, more than any other therapy I have used, strips away the defensive layers so that the therapist can see (and treat) the underlying guilt.

For example, Judy (chapter 6) felt responsible for her mother's death, her grandfather's death, and how her family was falling apart. She felt like she was to blame because she had been a bad child and run away from her mother. Judy was a very intelligent girl, but in spite of this intelligence she felt guilty for all those events. Prior to EMDR, only rage was visible in her behavior. Kevin (chapter 6) also felt guilty for his mother's death, saying, "If I had been a better kid, she wouldn't have died." Ken (chapter 7) felt guilty that he couldn't protect his younger brothers from being physically abused.

From these examples, it can be seen that either the guilt, the trauma, or the event can be targeted directly in EMDR. In fact, an overall message from this chapter, is that generally speaking, any of those can be a starting point in EMDR, regardless of the symptom or the situation.

## ANGER AND TANTRUMS

In young children, anger and tantrums are often symptoms of psychological distress, and not simply an expression of temperament or deliberate defiance. In many of the cases detailed in this book, anger, tantrums, rage, and emotional volatility have been reactions to trauma. It is harder for adults to relate to these symptoms than others, such as anxiety or depression, which are more likely to engender concern and support by adults closest to the child. Angry children get disciplined by frustrated parents and the school systems, rejected by peers, admonished by strangers, and labeled by mental health professionals (hey, we make mistakes too). In fact, there currently seems to be an upsurge in books about raising children that recommend direct and even corporal punishment of angry and defiant behavior. Because so much of this behavior can relate to prior traumatization, I regard simple punishment for defiance and anger as a dangerous course of action that is not likely to benefit the child.

Much of Judy's (chapter 6) behavior was rageful after her mother's death. She jammed a pencil into her older brother's arm, driving it into the muscle. She deliberately provoked him into fights. She could even provoke her teacher into losing his temper. She raged at her friends so much that she alienated and lost them. Allen (chapter 9), upset at his parents' divorce, had tantrums that lasted hours. Two other clinical examples can provide additional information that anger in children can stem from diverse situations.

Three-year-old Ron was referred for "uncontrollable raging tantrums." These were the words his mother used on the intake forms that she filled out prior to the first appointment. The tantrums had been occurring over the last five months prior to referral. The developmental history indicated that Ron underwent heart surgery at one year of age. Ron's family had gone through three moves in the last year, and two months prior to their first appointment Ron's mother delivered a baby girl. Both of Ron's parents seemed to have a high level of parenting ability and they got along well with each other.

In the first session, we targeted Ron's anger, but without good results. In the following week, he had five lengthy tantrums and was highly aggressive in his preschool, hitting, kicking, and biting other children. With one child, he broke the skin with a bite. Interestingly, he expressed a lot of anger toward a veterinarian who had just conducted surgery on the family dog. A second EMDR session, again focusing on Ron's anger (his parents were in the room on both occasions, as Ron was reluctant to separate from them), produced no discernible changes in behavior during the next week. In both of those sessions, we used hand taps, drumming, and some eye movements. Ron's mother mentioned in that session that she had a number of photos that had been taken of Ron when he was in the hospital at one year of age when he had his heart surgery. I asked her to bring those in to the next session.

In the following session, Ron looked at the pictures while I tapped his hands and knees. He didn't say much, but seemed highly interested. There was even a picture of the surgeon, brought in deliberately because of Ron's anger at the veterinarian. When Ron first looked at the picture, he burst out with a single word, "Hey!" but didn't say more than that. He then got very wiggly and squirmy for the next few minutes. This time, there was a subsequent positive change in Ron's behavior: He had only one tantrum during the week. The night after the session, Ron woke up three times, which was unusual for him. We again had Ron look at hospital pictures during the next session, accompanying that with hand, knee, and foot taps; he had no tantrums during the next two weeks.

Ron and his family are now out of town for two months. It will be interesting to see if the additional changes will produce more tantrums or whether he will be able to handle the changes now that he has reprocessed the surgery that occurred when he was younger.

Four-year-old Arnie was another young boy who had extreme anger problems. His parents had separated when he was 2, and divorced when he was 3. By age 4, Arnie was being aggressive and disobedient at preschool and angry and uncooperative at home with his mother. At times, he would steal things from preschool, fight with other kids, argue with teachers, and scribble on the walls with crayons. He had regular visitation with his father, following a split-week schedule. His father spent a lot of time with Arnie, but undermined Arnie's relationship with his mother by telling Arnie that his mother didn't love him and that the divorce was her fault. Arnie reacted with tantrums, especially when he had to take a bath every night before bed. In the first EMDR session, we focused on his feelings of anger. Arnie was the only child I have ever worked with who was so intent on being independent that he insisted on moving his eyes back and forth on his own, without following my fingers. Nonetheless, the EMDR was immediately effective. After the first session, he had no more tantrums, not even at bathtime. In fact on several occasions in the next week, he asked his mother to get his bath ready. She was astounded.

Arnie continued to be tantrum-free for the next seven weeks, but defiant behaviors were occasionally a problem at preschool, so we scheduled a session on that.

That session resulted in positive changes, and through the four years since then, Arnie has continued to do well, getting good grades in school and maintaining good relationships with both of his parents. His mother is about to remarry and Arnie wants to be adopted by his stepfather-to-be, as they have a good relationship. Unfortunately, his mother and father continue to skirmish with each other and occasionally go back to court over issues related to Arnie. As Arnie's father continues to put Arnie in the middle (i.e., choose between conflicted parents on different issues), Arnie's behavior continues to show ups and downs. Conjoint sessions were occasionally held with his parents to minimize this kind of behavior, but with only moderate success.

In all of the above cases I shudder to think of the effects on the child if the parents had done nothing more than punish the angry, defiant behavior. Rather, these were exceptional parents who recognized that the anger was a symptom of emotional distress and sought out professional help for their child.

## DEPRESSION

In depression with children, EMDR treatment tends to be longer-term, as it does with adults. For example, Matt (chapter 9) was in EMDR treatment for a lengthy period of time before he could be taken off antidepressant medication, and then for an additional period when the medication was reinstituted. In all, he was in therapy for a year.

However, EMDR therapy with depressed children can be shorter than one year. A case in point is Jim (chapter 6), who was severely depressed after his father committed suicide. Jim was helped within three months. Also, Barry (chapter 6), whose father was killed when Barry was 4, and whose grandfather died when Barry was 11, was treated for his depression within five sessions. Barry was one of the participants in our children's research, so EMDR was the only form of treatment that he received.

Overall, a depressed child is not likely to respond to EMDR within one to three sessions, and treatment is likely to be between five sessions to a year or more, depending on whether there are ongoing situational factors maintaining the depression or whether there are hereditary factors relating to temperament. The depressive feelings themselves or the situations leading to the depression can be targeted. Symptoms are often so intensely emotional, like depression, that they make excellent starting points, in addition to the situational targets.

## HALLUCINATIONS

Hallucinations are not always a sign of psychosis in children. Often, when children become terrorized enough, they hallucinate. Art (chapter 7) hallucinated out of fear after he reported his mother and her new husband for being physically and emotionally abusive. He was so afraid of their retaliation that he hallucinated for weeks at bedtime. In EMDR, at times, we targeted the hallucinations, which helped diminish his anxiety, but did not lead to cessation of the apparitions until the overall situation improved.

Barry (chapter 6) hallucinated a black mass on the ceiling of his bedroom several times per week after his grandfather died. The hallucination stopped after successful EMDR treatment. In EMDR, we did not target the hallucinations, but rather his life situations that led to his depression and his hallucinations.

In EMDR, either the hallucinations (as in Art's case) or the situation that causes them (as in Barry's case) can be targeted directly. If there is an ongoing situation, however, that needs to be dealt with before the hallucinations remit, although some symptomatic improvement may occur.

## OPPOSITIONAL BEHAVIOR

Oppositional behavior usually has anger behind it. For example, Allen (chapter 9), in addition to having tantrums, would simply refuse to cooperate at times. He refused to go into a restaurant with his mother and stayed in the car. When younger, he refused to sleep in his own bed, repeatedly returning to his parents' room throughout the entire night. Kip (chapter 7) often became passive and oppositional when confronted, refusing to speak, answer, or move. In Kip's case, this oppositional behavior continues to be a problem and it seems to worsen around attachment issues. When he stayed with another family for two weeks in the summer, he was much more oppositional when he returned.

With oppositional behavior, it seems to work better to target the anger behind the oppositional behavior and the reasons for the anger, rather than focus on the behavior itself. In Allen's case, it was his parents' divorce and his anger about it. Kip's anger was attachment-related. Arnie's (earlier in this chapter) oppositional behavior about taking a bath every night was related to his anger at his mother, promulgated by his father, who blamed the divorce on Arnie's mother. However, with Shirley (chapter 4), I did target her oppositional behavior (refusing to have a bowel movement in the toilet) directly by using a game format. There's room for therapist discretion once again.

## DISSOCIATION

Dissociation is a symptom in children that can't be targeted directly, much as night terrors can't be, as the child has no awareness of the dissociation. Rather the situation or trauma or the emotions that the child is aware of must be targeted. A 6-year-old boy who was in our children's study began dissociating at school and soiling himself after his uncle shot and killed himself in the boy's home. The dissociation was so extreme that he was medically evaluated for seizures to make sure that was not accounting for his periods of being out of contact with his surroundings. For example, when his class would be dismissed for recess, he would sit staring straight ahead, not aware that the class had been dismissed. Such behavior is reminiscent of the "two thousand yard stare" that is referred to in dissociated combat veterans. After five sessions, he had stopped dissociating and soiling, but the focus had been on the traumatic incident, not the dissociation. Judy (chapter 6), whose mother died, dissociated in the EMDR session itself. Techniques to minimize the dissociation were employed in the session, such as helping her stay in the process, using verbal encouragement, taking her back to the target more frequently. Other methods could have been used as well if those had not been successful, such as employing hand taps instead of eye movements, making physical contact to keep her present, such as holding one of her hands, while continuing eye movements. These and other approaches for dealing with dissociation are detailed in chapters 4 (see table 4.1) and 8.

## HYPERACTIVITY

Hyperactivity is another symptom that is hard to target directly, though it is possible ("Think of that time you were so spazzed out in class"). Rather, it is more beneficial to focus on the upsetting events. Examples here would be with Davy (chapter 4), traumatized from surgery on his cleft palate, and Tom (chapter 9), who was diagnosed ADHD. As indicated in chapter 9, hyperactive behavior may stem from traumatization and not necessarily from a biological cause. If no trauma can be identified, the symptom of hyperactivity can be the focus.

## ACADEMIC DIFFICULTIES

Academic difficulties can certainly arise after a child has been traumatized. It is hard to concentrate on math facts when someone has just punched you in the nose during recess. It is difficult to pay attention when your uncle has committed suicide in your living room. It is hard to want to go to school when your parents are getting divorced and you need to stay at home to keep track of what is going on there. If the sexual abuse is going on for a year at a time, the shame, the guilt, the fear make everything else seem unimportant.

Target the events. When the events have been reprocessed, the learning gaps themselves can be targeted, if the therapist has expertise in teaching the subject (as I have not done this, I defer to Robbie Dunton, who has the child learn small segments of a subject, installing the new learning with sets of eye movements). Potentially, a therapist could work with a tutor, installing the new material each step of the way.

## CONCLUSION

As this chapter points out, symptoms (with a few exceptions) make wonderful starting points for EMDR, especially as they are so directly connected to emotions. Emotions are spurs for behavior, and emotions, more than anything else, are what change, fade, and transform in EMDR. Thus, EMDR can start with the trauma, the emotional stuck point (ESP), or the symptom. There is room for therapeutic choice and clinical intuition in the process of selection.

In *Through the Eyes of a Child*, we have looked at modifications of the adult EMDR protocol so that EMDR can be applied to children of different ages. I have proposed a diagnostic system which focuses on the characteristics of the traumas so that treatment process and outcome can be predicted. In addition, we have examined how EMDR can be applied to traditional *DSM-IV* diagnoses and how it can be applied to frequently occurring symptoms in childhood. Thus, the practicing clinician can turn to age, trauma, diagnosis, or symptom for ideas on how to apply EMDR with children. As can be seen from the many gaps in the application of EMDR to children, there is much to be learned. On the other hand, there is much in our work with children that will inform and illuminate our work with adults. It is an exciting time in the world of psychotherapy; we now have the ability to help children who could never be helped before, or who could not be helped so quickly and easily.

# References

Abel, J. L. (1993). Exposure with response prevention and serotonergic antidepressants in the treatment of obsessive compulsive disorder: A review and implications for interdisciplinary treatment. *Behavior Research and Therapy, 31,* 463–478.

Agras, W. (1987). *Eating disorders.* New York: Pergamon.

American Psychiatric Association. (1994) . *Diagnostic and statistical manual for mental disorders* (4th ed.) . Washington DC: Author.

Anastopoulos, A. D., DuPaul, G. J., & Barkley, R. A. (1991). Stimulant medication and parent training therapies for attention-deficit/hyperactivity disorder. *Journal of Learning Disabilities, 24,* 210–217.

Barkley, R. A. (1990). *Attention-deficit/hyperactivity disorder: Diagnosis and treatment.* New York: Guilford.

Barkley, R. A. (1995). *Taking charge of ADHD: The complete, authoritative guide for parents.* New York: Guilford.

Beck, A. T. (1976). Cognitive therapy and the emotional disorders. New York: International Universities.

Bellman, M. M. (1966). Studies on encopresis. *Acta Paediatrica Scandinavia, 56*(Suppl. 170), 1–151.

Bisiach, E., Rusconi, M. L., & Vallar, G. (1992) . Remission of somatophrenic delusion through vestibular stimulation. *Neuropsychologica, 29,* 1029–1031.

Blanchard, E. B., & Hickling, E. J. (1997). *After the crash: Assessment and treatment of motor vehicle accident survivors.* Washington, DC: American Psychological Association.

Bowlby, J. (1982). *Attachment and loss: Vol. 1. Attachment* (2nd ed.). New York: Basic.

Bowlby, J. (1988). *A secure base: Parent-child attachment and healthy human attachment.* New York: Basic.

Bremner, J. D., Randall, P., Scott, T. M., Bronen, R. A., Seibyl, J. P., Southwick, S. M., Delaney, R. C., McCarthy, G., Charney, D. S., & Innis, R. B. (1995). MRI-based measures of hippocampal volume in patients with PTSD. *American Journal of Psychiatry, 152,* 973–981.

Breslau, N., Davis, G. C., Andreski, P., & Peterson, E. (1991). Traumatic events and posttraumatic stress disorder in an urban population of young adults. *Archives of General Psychiatry, 48,* 216–222.

Briere, J. (1992). *Child abuse trauma: Theory and treatment of the lasting effects.* New York: Sage.

Briere, J., Woo, R., McRae, B., Foltz, J., & Sitzman, R. (1997). Lifetime victimization history, demographics, and clinical status in female psychiatric emergency room patients. *Journal of Nervous and Mental Disease, 185,* 95–101.

Bruch, H., Czyzewski, D., & Suhr, M. (1988). *Conversations with anorexics.* New York: Basic.

Carmen, E., Rieker, P. P., & Mills, T. (1984). Victims of violence and psychiatric illness. *American Journal of Psychiatry, 141,* 378–383.

Cerrelli, E. C. (1997). *1997 traffic crashes, injuries and fatalities—preliminary report* [Online]. Available: http://www.nhtsa.dot.gov/people/ncsa/prelim.html

Chemtob, C., & Nakashima, J. (1996, November). Brief psychosocial intervention for elementary school children with disaster-related posttraumatic stress disorder: A field study. In P. Resick (Chair), *Cognitive-behavioral treatments for PTSD: New findings.* Symposium conducted at the meeting of the International Society for Trauma Stress Studies, San Francisco, CA.

Cohn, L. (1993). Art psychotherapy and the new eye treatment desensitization and reprocessing (EMDR) method, an integrated approach. In Evelyne Dishup (Ed.), *California art therapy trends.* Chicago: Magnolia Street.

De Jongh, A., Ten Broeke, M. S., & Renssen, M. S. (in press). Treatment of specific phobias with eye movement desensitization and reprocessing (EMDR): Protocol, empirical status and conceptual issues. *Journal of Anxiety Disorders.*

Doleys, D. M. (1977). Behavioral treatments for nocturnal enuresis in children: A review of the recent literature. *Psychological Bulletin, 84,* 30–54.

Donovan, D. M., & McIntyre, D. (1990) . *Healing the hurt child.* New York: W. W. Norton.

Elliot, D. M. (1997). Traumatic events: Prevalence and delayed recall in the general population. *Journal of Consulting and Clinical Psychology, 65,* 811–820.

Emmelkamp, P. M. G., Kloek, J., & Blaauw, E. (1992). Obsessive-compulsive disorders. In P. H. Wilson (Ed.), *Principles and practice of relapse prevention* (pp. 213–234). New York: Guilford.

Fischer, G., & Riedesser, P. (1998). *Lehrbuch der psychotraumatologie.* Munich: Ernst Reinhardt, GmbH & Co.

Fletcher, K. E. (1994). *What we know about children's posttraumatic stress responses: A meta-analysis of the empirical literature.* Unpublished manuscript, University of Massachusetts Medical Center, Worcester, MA.

Fletcher, K. E. (1996). Childhood posttraumatic stress disorder. In E. J. Mash & R. A. Barkley (Eds.), *Child psychopathology* (pp. 242–276). New York: Guilford.

Foa, E. B., Rothbaum, B. O., Riggs, D. S., Murdock, T. B., & Walsh, W. (1991) . Treatment of posttraumatic stress disorder in rape victims: A comparison between cognitive-behavioral procedures and counseling. *Journal of Consulting and Clinical Psychology, 59,* 715–723.

Freud, S. (1909). Analysis of a phobia in a five-year-old boy. *Standard edition, 10,* (pp. 5–149). London: Hogarth.

Gardner, R. A. (1986). *The psychotherapeutic techniques of Richard A. Gardner*. Cresskill, NJ: Creative Therapeutics.

Giaconia, R. M., Reinherz, H. Z., Silverman, A. B., Pakis, B., Frost, A. K., & Cohen, E. (1995). Traumas and posttraumatic stress disorder in a community population of older adolescents. *Journal of the Academy of Child and Adolescent Psyciatry, 34,* 1369–1380.

Goldstein, A., & Feske, U. (1994) . Eye movement desensitization and reprocessing for panic disorder: A case series. *Journal of Anxiety disorders, 8,* 351–362.

Greenfield, S. F., Strakowski, S. M., Tohen, M., Batson, S. C., & Kolbrener, M. L. (1994). Childhood abuse in first-episode psychosis. *British Journal of Psychiatry, 164,* 831–834.

Greenhill, L. L. (1992). Treatment issues in children with attention-deficit/hyperactivity disorder. *Psychiatric Annals, 19,* 604–613.

Harlow, H. F. (1959). Love in infant monkeys. In S. Coopersmith (Ed.), *Readings from Scientific American: Frontiers of psychological research* (pp. 92–98). San Francisco: W. H. Freeman.

Herman, J. L. (1992) . *Trauma and recovery: The aftermath of violence—from domestic abuse to political terror.* New York: Basic.

Husain, S. A., & Kashani, J. H. (1992). *Anxiety disorders in children and adolescents.* Washington, DC: American Psychiatric Press.

Hyer, L., & Brandsma, J. M. (1997). EMDR minus eye movements equals good psychotherapy. *Journal of Traumatic Stress, 10,* 515–522.

James, B. (1989). *Treating traumatized children.* Lexington MA: D. C. Heath.

Johnson, K. (1998) . *Trauma in the lives of children: Crisis and stress management techniques for counselors, teachers, and other professionals.* Alameda, CA: Hunter House.

Kazdin, A. E. (1989). Childhood depression. In E. J. Mash & R. A. Barkley (Eds.), *Treatment of childhood disorders* (pp. 135–166). New York: Guilford.

Kendall, P. C. (1994). Treating anxiety disorders in children: Results of a randomized clinical trial. *Journal of Consulting and Clinical Psychology, 62,* 100–110.

Kendall, P. C., Flannery-Schroeder, E., Panichelli-Mindel, S. M., Southam-Gerow, M., Henin, A., & Warman, M. (1997). Therapy for youths with anxiety disorders: A second randomized clinical trial. *Journal of Consulting and Clinical Psychology, 65,* 366–380.

Kendall, P. C., & Southam-Gerow, M. A. (1996). Long-term follow-up of a cognitive-behavioral therapy for anxiety-disordered youth. *Journal of Consulting and Clinical Psychology, 64,* 724–730.

Klaff, F. (1998, July). EMDR with children: New approaches. In R. Nurse (Chair) *A symposium on EMDR and family therapy.* Symposium conducted at the EMDR International Association Conference, Baltimore, MD.

Kronenberger, W. G., & Meyer, R. G. (1996). *The child clinician's handbook.* Boston: Allyn & Bacon.

Lazarus, A. A. (1981). *The practice of multimodal therapy.* New York: McGraw-Hill.

LeDoux, J. E. (1992). Emotion as memory: Anatomical systems underlying indelible neural traces. In S. A. Christianson (Ed.), *Handbook of emotion and memory* (pp. 269–288). Hillsdale, NJ: Lawrence Erlbaum.

LeDoux, J. E. (1996). *The emotional brain.* New York: Simon & Schuster.

LeDoux, J. E., Romanski, L., & Xagoraris, A. (1991). Indelibility of subcortical emotional memories. *Journal of Cognitive Neuroscience, 1,* 238–243.

Leonard, H. L., Swedo, S. E., & Rapoport, J. L. (1991). Diagnosis and treatment of obsessive-compulsive disorder in children and adolescents. In M. T. Pato & J. Zohar (Eds.), *Current treatments of obsessive-compulsive disorder* (pp. 87–102). Washington, DC: American Psychiatric Press.

Levis, D. L. (1990, November). The role of encoded traumatic conditioning memories involving severe physical and sexual abuse in the etiology and treatment of psychopathology. Paper presented at the 24th Annual AABT Convention, San Francisco, CA.

Lipke, H. (1996) A four activity model of psychotherapy and its relationship to eye movement desensitization and reprocessing (EMDR) and other methods of psychotherapy. *The International Electronic Journal of Innovations in the Study of the Traumatization Process and Methods for Reducing or Eliminating Related Human Suffering.*

Lohr, J. M., Tolin, D. F., & Lilienfeld, S. O. (1998) . Efficacy of eye movement desensitization and reprocessing: Implications for behavior therapy. *Behavior Therapy, 29,* 123–156.

Lovett, J. (1997, July). *EMDR with children: Treating "cascades of trauma" in a young child.* Paper presented at the EMDR International Association Conference, Denver, CO.

Lunnen, K. M., & Ogles, B. M. (1998). A multiperspective, multivariable evaluation of reliable change. *Journal of Consulting and Clinical Psychology, 66,* 400–410.

Marks, I., Lovell, K., Noshirvani, H., Livanou, M., & Thrasher, S. (1998). Treatment of posttraumatic stress disorder by exposure and/or cognitive restructuring. *Archives of General Psychiatry, 55,* 317–325.

Mash, E. J., & Dozois, D. J. A. (1996). Child Psychopathology: A Developmental-Systems Perspective. In E. J. Mash & R. A. Barkley (Eds.), *Child Psychopathology* (pp. 3–60). New York: Guilford.

Maslow, A. H. (1968). *Toward a psychology of being* (2nd ed.). Princeton, New Jersey: Van Nostrand.

Masson, J. M. (1992) . *The assault on truth: Freud's suppression of the seduction theory.* New York: HarperCollins.

McCarthy, P. R., & Foa, E. B. (1988). Obsessive-compulsive disorder. In M. Hersen & C. G. Last (Eds.), *Child behavior therapy casebook* (pp. 55–69). New York: Plenum.

Meuser, K. T., Goodman, L. B., Trumbetta, S. L., Rosenberg, S. D., Osher, F. C., Auciello, P., & Foy, D. W. (1998). Trauma and posttraumatic stress disorder in severe mental illness. *Journal of Consulting and Clinical Psychology, 66,* 493–499.

Monahon, C. (1993) . *Children and trauma: A parent's guide to helping children heal.* New York: Lexington.

Muris, P., Merckelbach, H., Holdrinet, I., & Sijsenaar, M. (1998). Treating phobic children: Effects of EMDR versus exposure. *Journal of Consulting and Clinical Psychology, 66,* 193–198.

National Highway Transportation & Safety Administration. (1996). People. In *1996 motor vehicle crash data from FARS and GES* [On-line}. Available: http://www.nhtsa.dot.gov

Nijenhuis, E. R. S., Vanderlinden, J., & Spinhoven, P. (1998). Animal defensive reactions as a model for trauma-induced dissociative reactions. *Journal of Traumatic Stress, 11*, 243–260.

Paige, S., Reid, G., Allen, M., & Newton, J. (1990). Psychophysiological correlates of PTSD. *Biological Psychiatry, 58*, 329–355.

Pennington, B. F. (1991). *Diagnosing learning disorders: A neuropsychological framework.* New York: Guilford.

Perry, B. D. (1998). *Diagnosis and treatment of childhood trauma: New developments.* Conference conducted by the Menninger Clinic, Topeka, KS.

Perry, B. (in press) . Memories of fear: How the brain stores and retrieves physiologic states, feelings, behaviors and thoughts from traumatic events. In J. Goodwin & R. Attias (Eds.), *Images of the body in trauma.* New York: Basic.

Pert, C. B. (1997). *Molecules of emotion: Why you feel the way you feel.* New York: Scribner.

Pitman, R. K., Orr, S. P., Forgue, D. F., de Jong, J., & Clairborn, J. M. (1987). Psychophysiologic assessment of posttraumatic stress disorder imagery in Vietnam combat veterans. *Archives of General Psychiatry, 17*, 970–975.

Pitman, R. K., Orr, S. P., Altman, B., Longpre, R. E., Poire, R. E., & Macklin, M. L. (1996) . Emotional processing during eye-movement desensitization and reprocessing therapy of Vietnam veterans with chronic post-traumatic stress disorder. *Comprehensive Psychiatry, 37*, 419–429.

Putnam, F. W. (1997). *Dissociation in children and adolescents.* New York: The Guilford.

Ramachandran, V. (1995). Anosognosia in parietal lobe syndrome. *Consciousness and Cognition, 4*, 22–51.

Rauch, S., van der Kolk, B. A., Fisler, R., Alpert, N., Orr, S., Savage, C., Jenike, M., & Pitman, R. (1996). A symptom provocation study using positron emission tomography and script driven imagery. *Archives of General Psychiatry, 53*, 380–387.

Renfrey, G., & Spates, C. R. (1994). Eye movement desensitization and reprocessing: A partial dismantling procedure. *Journal of Behavior Therapy and Experimental Psychiatry, 25*, 231–239.

Risse, G. L., & Gazzaniga, M. S. (1979). Well-kept secrets of the right hemisphere. *Neurology, 28*, 950–953.

Robinson, D. P., Greene, J. W., & Walker, L. S. (1988). Functional somatic complaints in adolescents: Relationship to negative life events, self-concept, and family characteristics. *Journal of Pediatrics, 113*, 588–593.

Scharf, M. B., Pravada, M. F., Jennings, W. W., Kauffman, R., & Ringel, J. (1987). Childhood enuresis: A comprehensive treatment program. *Psychiatric Clinics of North America, 10*, 655–667.

Scheck, M. M., Schaeffer, J. A., & Gillette, C. (1998). Brief psychological intervention with traumatized young women: The efficacy of eye movement desensitization and reprocessing. *Journal of Traumatic Stress, 11*, 25–44.

Scheflin, A. W., & Brown, D. (1966). Repressed memory of dissociative amnesia: What the science says. *Journal of Psychiatry and Law, 24*, 143–188.

Schwarz, E. D., & Kowalski, J. M. (1991a). Malignant memories: PTSD in children and adults after a school shooting. *Journal of the American Academy of Child and Adolescent Psychiatry, 30,* 936–944.

Schwarz, E. D., & Kowalski, J. M. (1991b). Posttraumatic stress disorder after a school shooting: Effects of symptom threshold selection and diagnosis by DSM-III, DSM-III-R, or proposed DSM-IV. *American Journal of Psychiatry, 148,* 592–597.

Schwarz, E. D., & Perry, B. D (1994). The post-traumatic response in children and adolescents. *Psychiatric Clinics of North America, 17,* 311–326.

Sedlack, A., & Broadhurst, D. (1996). *Executive summary of the third National Incidence Study of Child Abuse and Neglect.* Washington, DC: National Center on Child Abuse and Neglect, US Department of Health and Human Services.

Seligman, M. E. P., & Peterson, C. (1986). A learned helplessness perspective on childhood depression: Theory and research. In M. Rutter, C. E. Izard, & P. B. Read (Eds.), *Depression in young people: Developmental and clinical perspectives* (pp. 223–249). New York: Guilford.

Shafii, M., & Shafii, S. L. (1992). Clinical manifestations and developmental psychopathology of depression. In M. Shafii & S. L. Shafii (Eds.), *Clinical guide to depression in children and adolescents* (pp. 3–42). Washington, DC: American Psychiatric Press.

Shapiro, F. (1989a). Efficacy of the eye movement desensitization procedure in the treatment of traumatic memories. *Journal of Traumatic Stress, 2,* 199–223.

Shapiro, F. (1989b). Eye movement desensitization: A new treatment for post-traumatic stress disorder. *Journal of Behavior Therapy and Experimental Psychiatry, 20,* 211–217.

Shapiro, F. (1995). *Eye movement desensitization and reprocessing: Basic principles, protocols, and procedures.* New York: Guilford.

Shapiro, F., & Forrest, M. S. (1997). *EMDR: The breakthrough therapy for overcoming anxiety, stress, and trauma.* New York: Basic.

Sherman, R. A. (1997). *Phantom pain.* New York: Plenum.

Shirar, L. (1996). *Dissociative children: Bridging the inner and outer worlds.* New York: W. W. Norton.

Stampfl, T. G., & Levis, D. J. (1967). Essentials of implosive therapy: A learning theory based on psychodynamic behavioral therapy. *Journal of Abnormal Psychology, 72,* 496–503.

Stark, L. J., Spirito, A., Lewis, A. V., & Hart, K. J. (1990). Encopresis: Behavioral parameters associated with children who fail medical management. *Child Psychiatry and Human Development, 20,* 169–179.

Teicher, M. H. (1997, March). Neurodevelopmental abnormalities in abused children. *Psychological Trauma.* Conference conducted by Harvard Medical School Department of Continuing Education and Massachusetts Mental Health Center, Boston, MA.

Terr, L. (1990). *Too scared to cry.* New York: Basic.

van der Kolk, B. A. (1994) . The body keeps the score: Memory and the evolving psychobiology of PTSD. *Harvard Review of Psychiatry, 1,* 253–265.

van der Kolk, B. A. (1997, March) . The psychobiology of traumatic memories: Clinical implications of neuroimaging studies. *Psychological Trauma*. Conference conducted by Harvard Medical School Department of Continuing Education and Massachusetts Mental Health Center, Boston, MA.

van der Kolk, B. A. (1998, July). Understanding the psychobiology of trauma. Conference conducted by the EMDR International Association, Baltimore, Maryland.

van der Kolk, B. A., Burbridge, J. A., & Suzuki, J. (1997). The psychobiology of traumatic memory: Clinical implications of neuroimaging studies. In R. Yehuda & A. C. McFarlane (Eds.), *Annals of the New York Academy of Sciences (Vol. 821): Psychobiology of Posttraumatic Stress Disorder*. New York: New York Academy of Sciences.

van der Kolk, B. A., & McFarlane, A. C. (1996) . *Traumatic stress: The effects of overwhelming experience on mind, body, and society.* New York: Guilford.

Van Etten, M. L., & Taylor, S. (in press) . Comparative efficacy of treatments of posttraumatic stress disorder: A meta-analysis. *Clinical Psychology & Psychotherapy.*

Wald, A., & Handen, B. L. (1987). Behavioral aspects of disorders of defecation and fecal continence. *Annals of Behavioral Medicine, 9,* 19–23.

Walker, L. S., McLaughlin, F. J., & Greene, J. W. (1988). Functional illness and family functioning: A comparison of healthy and somaticizing adolescents. *Family Process, 27,* 317–320.

Wekerle, C., & Wolfe, D. A. (1996). Child maltreatment. In E. J. Mash & R. A. Barkley (Eds.), *Child Psychopathology* (pp. 492–537). New York: Guilford.

Weisz, J. R., Weiss, B., & Donenberg, G. R. (1992). Effects of child and adolescent psychotherapy. *American Psychologist, 47,* 1578–1585.

Williams, L. M. (1994). Recall of childhood trauma: A prospective study of women's memories of child sexual abuse. *Journal of Consulting and Clinical Psychology, 62,* 1167–1176.

Williams, L. M., & Banyard, V. L. (1997). Gender and recall of child sexual abuse: A prospective study. In J. D. Read & D. S. Lindsay (Eds.), *Recollections of trauma: Scientific evidence and clinical practice,* (pp. 371–377). New York: Plenum.

Wilson, S. A., Becker, L. A., & Tinker, R. H. (1995). Eye movement desensitization and reprocessing (EMDR) treatment for psychologically traumatized individuals. *Journal of Consulting and Clinical Psychology, 63,* 928–937.

Wilson, S. A., Becker, L. A., & Tinker, R. H. (1997) . Fifteenth-month follow-up of eye movement desensitization and reprocessing (EMDR) treatment for posttraumatic stress disorder and psychological trauma. *Journal of Consulting and Clinical Psychology, 65,* 1047–1056.

Wilson, D., Silver, S. M., Covi, W., & Foster, S. (1996). Eye movement desensitization and reprocessing: Effectiveness and ANS correlates. *Journal of Behavior Therapy and Experimental Psychiatry, 27,* 219–229.

Wilson, S. A., Tinker, R. H., & Becker, l. A. (1997, July). *Phantom limb pain treatment with EMDR.* Paper presented at the EMDR International Assocation Conference, San Francisco, California.

Zaslow, R. W. (1975). *The psychology of the z-process: Attachment and activation* (2nd ed.). San Jose, CA: San Jose State University.

# Index